# Lost
## on Planet
### China

Also by
J. MAARTEN TROOST

The Sex Lives of Cannibals

Getting Stoned with Savages

The Strange and True Story of One Man's Attempt

## J. Maarten Troost

Broadway Books • *New York*

# Lost
## on Planet
### China

*to Understand the World's Most Mystifying Nation,*

OR

How He

Became Comfortable

Eating Live Squid

PUBLISHED BY BROADWAY BOOKS

Published in the United States by Broadway Books, an imprint of The Doubleday Publishing Group, a division of Random House, Inc., New York.
www.broadwaybooks.com

BROADWAY BOOKS and its logo, a letter B bisected on the diagonal, are trademarks of Random House, Inc.

*Book design by Maria Carella*
*Map designed by Kevin Sprouls*
*Dragon illustration is adapted from an image by New Vision Technologies, Inc.,*
*Digital Vision/Getty Images*

Library of Congress Cataloging-in-Publication Data

Troost, J. Maarten.
  Lost on planet China : the strange and true story of one man's attempt to understand the world's most mystifying nation, or how he became comfortable eating live squid /
J. Maarten Troost.
  p. cm.
1. China—Social life and customs—2002– 2. China—Description and travel. 3. China—Humor. 4. Troost, J. Maarten—Travel—China. I. Title. II. Title: Strange and true story of one man's attempt to understand the world's most mystifying nation, or how he became comfortable eating live squid.

DS779.43.T76 2008
915.104'6—dc22
2008011281

ISBN 978-0-7679-2200-5

PRINTED IN THE UNITED STATES OF AMERICA

10 9 8 7 6 5 4 3 2 1

First Edition

*For my parents*

# Author's Note

One day, inside a coffeehouse, the author turned on his laptop and confidently typed the words *Chapter One*. Now what, he thought. He was supposed to write a book about China. This, after all, is what he had told people. *So what are you working on now?* they'd ask, and he'd casually mention that he was working on a book about China. *Really?* they'd say, and stagger back in admiration. Surely, it requires fluency in Mandarin to write a book about China. But the author is not fluent in Mandarin. He can say hello in Mandarin Chinese, but not in Cantonese Chinese. He can, however, count to ten in Chinese, albeit with his hands. Well then, surely the author was at the very least in possession of vast amounts of scholarly knowledge about China—perhaps he had a Ph.D. in Chinese History from the Oriental Studies Program at Oxford, for example. After all, Chinese civilization is more than 5,000 years old. Only an expert could write a book about China, right?

.

.

.

The author wishes to acknowledge that he is not an expert on China. His academic expertise, such as it is, lies more toward Mitteleuropa than the Middle Kingdom. He does, however, know the difference between the Ming and the Qing dynasties and of this he is quite proud. But should you meet him, please do not ask him anything about the Song Dynasty. Or the Tang Dynasty. Or the Wu Dynasty. Please.

How then can this author, who neither speaks Chinese nor has any particular expertise regarding their history or culture, write a book, a biggish book, about China? This is the question that the author mulled inside the coffeehouse that day. He pondered the matter, turned it over, approached it from every angle. And finally he decided that there was only one way to do it. He would write honestly about China. He would write from the perspective of a guy who neither speaks Chinese nor has all that much knowledge pertaining to things Chinese, a guy who spent month after month just kind of wandering around this massive and rapidly changing country, without a plan, learning and experiencing life there.

The author does not read many travel books. True, he has sometimes been accused of being a travel writer. He has written about faraway places. But he was living in these faraway places, so technically, it wasn't travel writing; it was domestic writing. From his perspective, he has never done much travel writing—at least not the kind you find in glossy magazines. In his experience, these magazines prefer to hear about the sunsets on some distant tropical isle, or how said island is an antidote to all the stresses of the continental world, rather than about how the author contracted typhoid while he was there (true), or how the island's young men are all signing up for the war in Iraq because their job prospects are so poor. The author doesn't like this kind of travel writing. He'd rather call it like it is. And so, since this is his book and he can do as he wishes, he has tried to write honestly about China. And he hopes that by writing honestly, that by sharing his experiences, readers might, in fact, get a sense of this vast and complex country. Because it's important. We need to understand China. Really. You'll see. So there will be no fucking sunsets in the pages that follow.

# Lost
## on Planet
## China

# 1

There are two kinds of people roaming the far fringes of the world: Mormon missionaries and Chinese businessmen. I know this because for a long while I lived off the map, flitting from island to island in the South Pacific, and invariably, just as I arrived at what surely was the ends of the earth, I would soon find myself in the company of Elder Ryan and Elder Leviticus, twenty-year-old kids from suburban Provo, who faced the challenging task of convincing islanders that they were not native islanders at all but lost Israelites. Not just lost Israelites, mind you, but lost and wicked Israelites. One would think that this would be a hard thing to convince people of, but the Mormons are persistent and today they can be found on even the most remote of islands. On Onotoa, an atoll of trifling size in the southern Gilbert group, and about as far as one can be on this planet without quite leaving it, I was startled to discover two Mormon missionaries, wearing their customary black pants and white short-sleeved dress shirts, complete with name tags, biking up and down the island's lonesome dirt path, searching for wayward souls to rescue. I also found them in Tonga, on the arresting islets of Vava'u, and even in the rugged hills of Vanuatu. Whenever I encountered them, I immediately reached for a dose of caffeine, nicotine, or alcohol, something to demonstrate that conversion was a hopeless cause with me, and soon they were on their way, hustling errant Israelites.

Eventually, I grew accustomed to their presence. Missionaries, after all, have long been found in the world's most distant corners. Where else would one find a tribe of lost and forgotten Hebrews? But as one year on the far side of the world passed into another, and then another, and another, until it seemed likely that my time on the islands would outlast Robinson Crusoe's, I began to notice a different visitor—the Chinese businessman.

This, frankly, surprised me to no end, possibly because news travels slowly on the coconut wireless. No doubt in other parts of the world the presence of Chinese businessmen—capitalists!—would elicit nary a reaction. Mao Zedong had been dead for thirty years. China had moved on, changed, adapted, and eventually become the world's factory. But if you live on an island where prices are still quoted in pigs, and where the news of the day is likely to involve two chiefs disputing each other's lineage, you might not know this. You might, in fact, still believe that the Chinese pedal ancient black bicycles to their designated work unit, which is part of a cadre, though you're not quite sure what a cadre is. When you envision China, you might imagine factory workers, each waving a Little Red Book, marching in sync past enormous portraits of the Heroes of the

Revolution. You can almost hear the loudspeakers, the voices exhorting the proletariat to strive ever further, so that the goals of the Five-Year Plan are attained. You can imagine little children, all wearing red handkerchiefs around their necks, learning to despise imperialist dogs and debauched class enemies. This is what happens when you live in a place far, far away, thousands of miles from a continent. Nothing ever changes on an island, and you assume that the continental world, too, has resolved to cease spinning. But it hasn't, of course, and one day you discover that you're sharing an odd, faraway island with a businessman from China.

Consider Onotoa, an atoll in the southern Gilbert Islands. Go on. Take out the atlas. You can't find it, can you? This is because it is a mere speck of an island, not more than a hundred yards across. If you were a tribe of ancient, wicked Israelites with a pressing need to disappear, you could not do better than to set forth for Onotoa. It wasn't until a whaling ship alighted upon the island in 1826 that the outside world was made to learn of its existence, a fact that was quickly and thoroughly forgotten by all. The island exists as it always has, suspended in time, a world unto its own. It is devoid of electricity and running water. It is plagued by drought. There is nothing to eat except fish; thus the islanders have a well-deserved reputation for frugality. Periodically, a wheezing prop plane lands on a strip of coral and drops off a wandering missionary or government official. Rarer still, the plane returns to pick them up, often months later. On Onotoa, you could not be farther from the world of commerce, and yet here was where I found Mr. Wu and Mr. Yang, two entrepreneurs from Guangdong Province in southeastern China. They had come all this way to establish a live reef fish trade operation. Every few months a Chinese vessel called upon Onotoa to gather a tank of live lagoon fish, which were then sent to upmarket restaurants in Hong Kong, where diners could peer into an aquarium, select their meal, and promptly experience the first spasms of ciguatera poisoning, a disagreeable and periodically fatal condition. Apparently, Mr. Wu and Mr. Yang had failed to notice that for the good people of Onotoa, the lagoon was also the toilet, an omission of observation that I found baffling.

Nevertheless, I was more flabbergasted by their very presence on the island. Elder Ryan and Elder Leviticus I had come to expect. Not so Mr. Wu and Mr. Yang. At the time, I was living on Tarawa, a sliver of an island in the Republic of Kiribati notable for straddling that very wide chasm between cesspool and paradise. I had followed my girlfriend Sylvia to Tarawa because that is what I did—followed Sylvia around as she pursued a career in international development. In the peripatetic years that followed, we moved on from Kiribati to Vanuatu and onward to Fiji, and on every island we touched upon we were invariably struck by the presence of the Chinese. On Kosrae, in the Federated States of Micronesia, on a lonely windswept beach where herons plunged after crabs, I stumbled across Mr. Lu, an engineer from Beijing who had arrived on the island to bid on a building contract. In Vanuatu, where politics and graft are tightly coiled, entrepreneurs from China discovered that the country made for an excellent conduit to smuggle heroin. True, technically heroin smuggling is illegal, but it is most certainly a business. Even blighted Port Moresby, the capital of Papua New Guinea, and officially the Worst Place in the World, according to *The Economist*, was experiencing a boom in Chinese investors lured to the country by its natural resources.

More confounding—for me, in any case—was the scale of Chinese emigration to the islands. When I first alighted upon Suva, the capital of Fiji, in the mid-1990s, Victoria Parade was a venerable, though dilapidated, boulevard of colonial-era buildings. Nothing much happened in Suva except for the occasional coup. A few years later, Victoria Parade had become a veritable Chinatown, an avenue of Chinese shops, restaurants, and nightclubs catering to mainland fishermen and garment workers. Other islands, too, experienced a surge of Chinese immigrants, lured to a region where market competition is nonexistent. Sadly for them, they weren't particularly welcome. Rampaging mobs in Nuku'alofa, the balmy capital of the Kingdom of Tonga, burned down thirty Chinese-owned shops. In Honiara, the blighted capital of the Solomon Islands, the Chinese navy had to rescue 300 of their citizens after locals set the predominantly Chinese business district ablaze.

Nevertheless, within a short decade, the South Pacific was well on its way to becoming a Chinese lake. The better hotels were often full of official delegations. Some were there to forge commercial links. Others had come with their checkbooks ready, doling out "foreign aid" to receptive governments, who in turn needed to do nothing more than acknowledge that despite appearances otherwise, Taiwan was not a country. By conceding that Taiwan was merely a quarrelsome province within the People's Republic of China, governments in the South Pacific soon found themselves in the possession of fleets of high-end SUVs, which they drove to their new and considerably more lavish offices, where they could ponder the work being done on their brand-new stadiums. This was foreign aid, Chinese-style, and governments in the South Pacific discovered that they liked it very much.

It was the appearance of Chinese tourists in Fiji, however, that really got me thinking that something was afoot in China. *Chinese tourists? In Fiji?* I first came across some at low tide on a beach on the Coral Coast on the island of Viti Levu, where a group of mainland tourists was happily emptying the reef of its population of luminous starfish. Gently reminded by their tour guide that they could not in fact wander off with forty-some starfish, they deposited them in stacks atop the boulders that jutted above the reef.

"Did you notice that?" I said to my wife, Sylvia, as we set about returning the displaced starfish to the shallow water.

"You mean the interesting approach to wildlife?"

"Yes, that too. But that they were tourists from China. When exactly did tourists from China start coming to the South Pacific?"

I, frankly, had stopped paying attention to China sometime in 1989, that magical year when Communism dissolved elsewhere in the world. Then, in an historical blink of an eye, dissident shipyard workers and philosophers suddenly found themselves transformed into elected presidents. Democracy flourished and the Czechs, bless them, stumbled over themselves to join the Beer Drinkers Party. Borders were opened, and soon Hungarian tourists could be found camping in the shadow of the Eiffel Tower, while Westerners, myself included, settled in cities like Prague, where the women were beautiful, the beer cheap, and the times significant. For two generations,

Eastern Europe had existed under the gray shroud of totalitarian rule, and suddenly they, too, were free to compete with campy bands from Liechtenstein and punk-monster groups from Finland for the awesome privilege of winning the Eurovision Song of the Year Competition. This was freedom.

Nineteen eighty-nine played out a little differently in China, of course. When thousands of students converged upon Tiananmen Square in Beijing to demand a little democracy— *Hey hey, hey ho, Maosim has got to go*—they were greeted with a decidedly old-school response. Deng Xiaoping, the chain-smoking gnome with the twinkling eyes who then ruled China, simply reached for his totalitarian rulebook, flipped toward the index—*Democracy protesters, suitable response*— and followed directions. He shot them. And that was that.

Except, of course, it wasn't, and therein lay the dissonance I was feeling about China. Something was clearly happening there. The presence of Chinese tourists blithely frolicking on the beaches of Fiji suggested that China was no longer solely a nation of peasants, factory workers, and clipboard-toting political officers. And yet, as far as I could tell, China remained ruled by the very same clipboard-toting political officers who had brought forth the excitement of the Cultural Revolution, those last years of the Mao era when China went stark raving mad. In the early seventies, one pushed boundaries in the U.S. by lighting up a joint and engaging in a sit-in at Berkeley. For the Red Guards of the Cultural Revolution, a good day might be spent destroying a Ming-era temple and torturing the teachers and intellectuals accused of possessing revanchist tendencies. When it came to pushing boundaries, the hippies had nothing on the Red Guards. Maybe Charles Manson did. But Charles Manson is in prison. The Red Guards simply faded away.

Once Sylvia and I returned to the United States, this sense of incongruity only deepened. Wading through the thunder and bombast of what passes for news programming today—*Motto: All terror, all the time*—I'd come across little nuggets of information such as the startling fact that IBM Computers is now owned by the Chinese company Lenovo. Clearly, the creators of *2001: A Space Odyssey* miscalled that one; HAL should have been speaking Mandarin. And then, sometime later, as the television news paused for a commercial—*Coming up next: Are we all going to die tomorrow?*—I'd pick up the newspaper and learn that to combat a few cases of rabies, Chinese authorities had decided to club or electrocute, or even bury alive, hundreds of thousands of pet dogs. Even for someone like me, who had long lived in a region where dogs are regarded as either a menacing nuisance or a good choice for lunch, the response seemed a tad barbaric. IBM had long represented the future—the American future—and now that particular future was in the hands of barbarous dog-killers.

Mostly, however, as I refreshed myself in the events of the day, I was struck by the gnawing sense that despite the best efforts of the freedom-hating Islamofascists, the bigger news seemed to be elsewhere. "Let China sleep, for when she wakes, she will shake the world," Napoleon had famously remarked. China, clearly, had awoken. For some, this had been evident for some time. For others—say, like those who had spent a good part of the past decade living on remote islands in the South Pacific—it was something of a surprise to learn just how big China had become. Officially, there were 1.3 billion people in

China. Unofficially, there were 1.5 billion. It had become the industrial capital of the world. The 200 million migrants who had left the fields for the cities reflected the largest human migration in history. China had managed to achieve an annual economic growth rate of 9.5 percent or more for twenty-eight years straight. It is presently the world's third-largest economy after the U.S. and Japan and it is expected to become the second in the foreseeable future. China currently exports more than a trillion dollars' worth of goods annually and will soon account for nearly 50 percent of world trade. There are more than ninety cities within its borders with populations over one million, most of which, to be perfectly honest, I had never heard of.

And yet, despite China's having become one of the economic engines of the world, I had no sense of what China actually was. Not since Deng Xiaoping has China had a leader that reflected a personality, a sense of *Chineseness* that foreigners could latch on to. Say what you will about Bill Clinton and George W. Bush, but they are, in their own ways, America writ large. Watching those two, the charmer who exuded empathy and insatiable appetites, and the smirking bully whose very strut is enough to send otherwise reasonable people into an inchoate, apoplectic quiver of rage, it is clear that Bill and George could only be American. Hu Jintao, on the other hand, simply comes across as the guy in the office that you really need to watch out for.

Instead, all I could discern were contrasts. Beijing had been awarded the 2008 Summer Olympics and you'd think, okay, we're a long way now from the events of June 4, 1989. In preparation, the authorities had decided to finally release the student who had hurled a paint bomb at the giant portrait of

Chairman Mao that looms over Tiananmen Square. Well, good, you think. And then it emerges that after eighteen years of what we now soothingly call enhanced interrogation techniques, the student had been shattered, and today is free only to roam through his insanity. Yet many of our most esteemed commentators—and how, exactly, does one become an esteemed commenter?—speak reassuringly about the newfound freedom in China. Maybe, but who wants to unfurl a Falun Gong banner in Tiananmen Square? You first, Mr. Commentator.

Clearly, a quick look at China from the outside invariably turns into a thorough investigation of the *yin* and the *yang*. China had launched men into space, and yet in some western parts of the country people still lived in caves. China produces some of the most lavish and poignant movies of our time, yet its literature remains stunted. China is quickly becoming a manufacturer not only of the cheap, plastic goods that stock the shelves of Wal-Mart, but also of high-tech goods like computers, and yet they haven't quite managed to ensure that the toothpaste they export doesn't kill people in Panama. It was all very perplexing to me. What exactly was China?

"China is today's Wild West," said my friend Greg. I had first met Greg in graduate school in Washington, D.C. This was in the early 1990s, and as I pursued my studies on Eastern Europe, I always felt a little sorry for those who focused on China. The poor, misguided fools, I thought. Didn't they know that Moldova was the future? In the years that followed, Greg, a fluent speaker of Chinese and Japanese, eventually left the world of finance and became a high school history teacher in San Jose. I was on the road one summer, and after a reading in San Francisco, I caught up with Greg at a bar near Union

Square. He had just returned from a yearlong sabbatical in Shanghai, where he had taught English, and he spoke effusively about the country.

"It's where it's all happening now," he said with his California drawl. "I've spent most of my life chasing the next new thing. And now the next new thing is China. The center of gravity has moved east—business, finance, manufacturing, everything revolves around China. For the first time in their history, the average Chinese has an opportunity to get rich. They know that opportunity might close at any time. So they're going after it with everything they have. It's just crazy over there."

The China he spoke of seemed so vastly at odds with the China I had grown up with. Where were the May Day parades, the ominous displays of military might, the calls to revolution? Where were the workers in the jaunty Mao jackets?

"That China is gone," Greg said. "You need to go and see for yourself. And you definitely need to teach your kids Mandarin. When they grow up, they'll be working for Chinese companies. If I were you, I'd move to China for a few years, because you're not going to understand this world if you don't understand China."

This seemed like an excellent idea. Of course, lots of ideas look good after a few beers. Nevertheless, I had been looking to make a change anyway. Once again, Sylvia had led me to one of the more exotic corners of the world—Sacramento. Every morning, I'd wake up and think, What events in space and time have brought me to this strange place? Don't get me wrong. Sacramento is a lovely place, particularly for those with a fondness for methamphetamines. For the meth-addled, Sacramento had conveniently placed a Greyhound bus station just yards from the statehouse where Austria's finest was sworn in as governor of the great state of California. Around the corner, the budget-conscious speed freak can find a half-dozen $5-a-night flophouses that will happily overlook their need to bounce off walls. And should a meth addict have a disagreeable experience with law enforcement, downtown Sacramento offered a plethora of bail bondsmen only too happy to assist.

We even had meth addicts for neighbors, which made for some very lively evenings. Our neighborhood, a standard California burb of stucco and tile, had been overtaken by America's latest, greatest search for free money—the housing bubble. Working on my laptop in cafés, I listened to the yammering of mortgage brokers, all pushing the zero-down, introductory teaser rate, interest-only, optional payment, adjustable rate, here's-a-half-million-if-you-can-fog-a-mirror kind of mortgages that fueled the exhilaration of collective financial madness. Within three years, houses had doubled in value. Within six, they had tripled. Speculators were buying houses a dozen at a time. Homebuilders reacted by building thousands of new homes and people bought them as investments because, of course, real estate only goes up in California. Everyone wants to live here, even in Sacramento, a little corner of Oklahoma that got lost and found itself on the other side of the Sierra Nevada. Our neighbor's house was one such "investment," and while the owner applauded herself for her financial acumen, her renters happily used her property to conduct a brisk business in stolen cars and crystal meth. The couple who lived there had three children. For simplicity's sake, each was apparently named Motherfucker, as in *Motherfucker, turn the fucking TV down,* followed by *Motherfucker, you woke motherfucker up, motherfucker.*

We could see where this was going, and the last thing my wife and I wanted was to endure the inevitable housing bust as our kids clamored to go next door because they wanted to play pharmacist with their good friend Motherfucker. We sold our house, briefly contemplated buying a new one, and then decided that buying a hyperinflated house with a time bomb of a mortgage was one of the more uninteresting ways to commit financial ruin. And so, for the foreseeable future, we would become renters, a state of affairs that we soon regarded as liberating. Leaking faucets and busted air conditioners would no longer be my problem. The burden of keeping grass alive would fall to someone else. Then, once our second son was born and Sylvia quit her job in favor of consulting, we suddenly found ourselves with no good reason to remain in Sacramento. And without a reason to be in Sacramento, we were ready to fly.

"I'm thinking China," I said to Sylvia one evening. Why not, I thought. True, we had small kids. Normally, one would buy another house, settle down, do normal-type family things, give the kids stability. We had tried that. And we had found it wanting. Perhaps it was the meth dealers next door. That wasn't part of the American dream. Perhaps it was the Sisyphean task of trying to keep a lawn green in 105-degree heat. It is the unwritten rule of suburban life: The grass must be green, even if you live in a desert. Perhaps it was all the massive SUVs driving to Target and Wal-Mart with the little yellow ribbon decal. I don't know. Whatever it was, I did not want to raise a family like this. And so I was amenable to some out-of-the-box thinking. China was the future. That's what everyone said. It would be a few years until the mess in the housing market sorted itself out, allowing us to prudently plant the flag in some other town far removed from the box-store burbs. So why not take the kids to China and live there for a while? It could be done. It would undoubtedly be interesting. It would be good for the kids. Probably.

"I'm thinking Monterey," Sylvia replied. This was her out-of-the-box retort. We were unable to afford to buy a home in coastal California, so we would rent there. We couldn't buy anywhere, but we could rent everywhere. And Sylvia was from the central coast of California. So it would be a homecoming of sorts.

"I don't know," I said. "I'm thinking big cities, a country in transition, history in the making."

"I'm thinking beaches, clean air, perfect weather. Besides, you don't speak Chinese," she noted.

"Not yet."

Sylvia gave me a dubious look. "I'm all for making some changes," she said, "but *China*?"

Why not China? One out of every five people on this planet lived there. We should get to know them better, I argued. And we'd spent years living on the far peripheries of the world—Kiribati, Vanuatu, Sacramento. It seemed reasonable to want to spend some time in the very center. And from what I'd read and heard, that center was moving to China. It seemed important to try to understand this place. Besides, I like a little dissonance in my life. And the prospect of shifting one's gaze from the smallest countries in the world to its largest was supremely discordant.

But there were little people in our lives now. On the one hand, it would be good for them to learn Mandarin and to experience another culture. That would be good parenting. On the other hand, impulsively moving to the other side of the planet and setting the children down in a city that was reportedly swirling with clouds of pollution would not be good. That would be bad parenting. It's complex, this parenting thing. And so we decided that I would set forth on a scouting mission to China. While Sylvia perused the rental listings in Monterey, I was off to the bookstore. It was time to learn Chinese.

# 2

I want to be very clear about this. I am not blaming anyone. No one is at fault. I am even willing to consider the possibility that it wasn't done on purpose. But, as I delved into *Chinese for Dummies,* I couldn't help but conclude that the Chinese language is the Great Wall of languages, a clever linguistic barrier erected to keep outsiders out. What, frankly, is wrong with Esperanto? Or alphabets? What is so deficient about an alphabet that uses a judicious twenty-six letters? We can make lots of words with those twenty-six letters, big words even. Don't get me wrong. I'm a big fan of linguistic diversity. In fact, I take no small amount of pride in the fact that I can order a pint in eight languages. I am even, dare I say it, fairly good at languages. Typically, it takes me no more than a few weeks of study until I can more or less function: I can get myself from point A to point B, I can discern the general drift of a conversation, I can sit in a restaurant and feel reasonably confident that the dish

I just ordered wasn't the Monkey Penis Special. But, as soon became coldly apparent to me, there was not a chance that I was going to even manage that in Chinese. And that worried me.

Take the issue of Chinese characters. There are 20,000 of them. Fortunately, you don't need to learn all 20,000, just 7,000 should you wish to understand what an educated Chinese person is talking about. Three thousand might get you through a newspaper. But as I delved into this black and yellow Reference Book For The Rest Of Us, I soon realized that if it was indeed sufficient to teach Chinese to a dummy, then clearly I must be a feeble-minded moron. I was not going to learn 3,000 characters. In truth, I was rather taken aback by how complex a Chinese character is. I had always assumed that a character was essentially a pictograph and that to discern its meaning one simply had to understand Chinese drawing. *Happy* would be a happy face with Chinese characteristics. Like nearly everything else I assumed about China, I was wrong. The vast majority of Chinese characters are singular mixtures of the phonetic and the semantic. They are unique composites that offer both meaning and sound. But then, remembering that human beings cannot produce 20,000 unique sounds, even if you were to include belching and hawking great globs of phlegm (which I think counts in Chinese), the linguistic powers that be—whoever they are—threw in tones, possibly to ensure that no foreigner over the age of thirty would have any chance whatsoever of understanding the Chinese language. There are four primary tones, which means that if I were to pronounce the exact same sound in four different tones, I would be conveying four distinct meanings. You see how difficult this gets.

To further muddy the waters, there was the question of which Chinese language in particular should I be studying.

There is, of course, Mandarin Chinese, which is spoken in Beijing, but take a train south to Shanghai, and you will find yourself surrounded by people—many, many people, this being China—who speak the Shanghainese dialect of Wu Chinese, and who will look at you a little quizzically as you try to order dim sum (they'll look at you quizzically anyway). Travel even farther south to Guangdong Province and Hong Kong and you will enter the world of the Cantonese, who speak a language also said to be Chinese, but which is utterly unintelligible to the speakers of Wu and Mandarin. There are seven other major linguistic groups within the Chinese language, and within each there are a plethora of dialects, which are called *fangyan,* or "speech of a place." And then there are sub-*fangyan,* of course. For a traveler, this is not good.

And so, as I arrived at the airport to begin the long flight to Beijing, I practiced the few phrases of Mandarin I had memorized. Yes, the Chinese language, every variant of it, would be unfathomable to me, but that didn't mean I had to arrive completely unprepared. "*Qingwen. Wo buhui dun zhege cesuo. Youmeiyou biede cesuo keyi yong?*"

"What does that mean, Daddy?" asked my four-year-old son, Lukas.

"It's Chinese for *Excuse me. I am not proficient at squatting. Is there another toilet option?*"

Lukas reflected. "So do people in China use different potties?"

"Apparently, from what I've read. I'll call to let you know."

Four-year-olds are inquisitive, and I do nothing to crush it. "*Zhege zhende shi jirou ma?*" I offered.

"What does that mean?" Lukas asked again. My one-year-old son, Samuel, repeated what I'd said with a baby accent. *Zhe ge zhe ge.*

"It means *Are you sure that's chicken?*"

I said a difficult good-bye to the boys, kissed my wife, pledged my eternal ardor and devotion, and set forth to enter the departure terminal, where a few moments later I was pleasantly startled to once again encounter Sylvia.

"You might need this," she said, holding a small backpack.

"Right," I said, considering it contained my passport, plane tickets, and traveler's checks.

"I'm trying to envision you in China," Sylvia said, "and I can't decide whether to laugh or weep."

I empathized. It's a thin line that separates tragedy from farce.

It was an awfully long flight. From San Francisco, we flew parallel to the Inside Passage along the western coast of Canada, up and over the Aleutian Islands in the northern Pacific, following the curve of the Arctic over sheets of glistening ice not yet melted by spring. I endured three movies of sufficient banality that I can now recall nothing more than the passage of time. I read. I dozed fitfully. Now and then, I chatted with the man next to me, a manager with Boeing who was relocating to central China. I asked him what, precisely, Boeing was planning on doing in central China.

"We'll be building wings."

Wings? The one part of an airplane that cannot be made redundant?

Super.

It was somewhere in the vicinity of Siberia, just off the Kamchatka Peninsula, that I began to ponder the implications of this. It was, of course, informative to learn that even the manufacturing of Boeing airplanes was now being outsourced to China. Apparently, America has a surplus of well-paying manufacturing jobs and is now helpfully sprinkling them elsewhere. But this wasn't what I was musing about as we hit a brick wall of an air pocket. As the aircraft shuddered and swooned, and the wings fluttered like a bird's, I hoped, really hoped, that I would like China, that I would be reassured by it, that one day I would feel secure and confident flying upon a Chinese wing.

Finally, below, there was land, a hard land, brown but not quite dead, studded with lonesome villages, surrounded by barren fields. And then we descended, hurtling through a gray-brown swirl of what? Clouds? Pollution? I had never before seen air like this. It was otherworldly in its strangeness. We landed and I felt that quiet elation I always feel when arriving someplace utterly foreign to my experience. I was in China.

I didn't know what to expect, and without expectations, I followed the other passengers through the terminal in a state of absorption. I handed my passport to the immigration officer, half expecting to be denied entry. I had, of course, lied on my visa application. I had known enough about China to realize that one profession that must never be listed on a visa application is *Writer*. Instead, I had professed to be a real estate investor, an answer that made me chuckle, which I acknowledge is a little sad. Moreover, I was concerned because I had once written about Chinese spies in Kiribati, and I suspected that my name may have been entered into some secret government database used to identify Undesirable Elements. I tried to look bored as the immigration officer pondered my passport. Since I had written about the spies in Kiribati, the Chinese had been kicked out of the country. Their satellite-tracking station had been dismantled and, even more disturbing for the Chinese, the government of Kiribati now affirmed that Taiwan is the true China, while the People's Republic was merely an usurper. Did they think I had anything to do with that? Were Chinese intelligence agents now being alerted to my presence? *Mr. Troost. We have been waiting for you. Come with us.* And I'd be taken to a cell room aglow in the faint glare of a single lightbulb.

Fortunately, my skills at parrying an interrogation remained untested, and I emerged into the arrivals hall, which had an interesting odor, like a thousand people who had all just stepped in from a smoke break. Through the tumult, I could see the familiar storefronts of a Starbucks and a KFC Express, which left me befuddled, since I was in the turbid throes of jet lag and I had assumed that after traveling such a vast distance, I would have made it somewhere farther than the food court at a shopping mall in Sacramento, an impression that was swiftly and thoroughly upended once I stepped outside.

The haze that hung over our surroundings was unearthly. It swirled in gray and brown and yellow plumes. It suggested that not far away, something catastrophic had occurred—a volcanic eruption, a meteor strike, a thermonuclear bomb—and now life had been reduced to a state of grim survival. But this was China, not the slopes of Mount Saint Helens. This was Beijing, not Hiroshima. Under a grim, eternal twilight of a sky,

I followed the unarguable dictates of a skinny teenage boy in an olive uniform and slowly shuffled forth toward the taxi line.

Lining up in China, I soon discovered, was played as a contact sport. Men and women, young and old, cigarettes dangling from their lips, used their elbows and shoulders to muscle their way to the cabs. With knobby elbows in my ribs, strange hands on my arms, and my back feeling the amassing weight of the hundreds who had not yet slinked ahead of me, I began to ponder the idea of personal space, and whether the Chinese have a character for personal space, and after being shimmied aside by a grandmother who could not have been more than three and a half feet tall, concluded that no, such a concept is evidently alien to the Chinese. And so I, too, began to dig in against the line hoppers, flinging my shoulders to contest the passage of three businessmen behind me. A shoulder here, a foot there, soon I was moving like a heaving linebacker. Some fifty people had managed to bypass me in the scrum, but now that I knew that lining up and getting bruised were intertwined, I was determined not to let this troika of businessmen pass me by. If I hadn't begun to regard the queue as a forum for physical sport, it is quite likely that I would still be there today, for lining up in China is not for the meek.

Finally, I was directed toward a small green taxi. I had printed out the name and address of my hotel in Chinese characters before I left and now I handed it to the driver. Inside, he offered me a cigarette.

"No, thank you," I said. "I'm reformed." Though why bother not smoking in China, I wondered, as I again noted the dull gray haze stained with soot and sand from the encroaching Gobi Desert, which was a mere fifty miles away. I indicated that

I didn't mind if he smoked, and soon, as the driver approached what I was pleased to learn from a passing sign was called a carriageway, I relaxed. Carriageway suggested an idyllic ramble through a thicket of woods. And while I was reasonably certain that the drive from the airport to the center of the city would not be an idyllic ramble, my addled brain was nevertheless wholly unprepared for the mayhem that is highway driving in Beijing.

Elsewhere in the world, a four-lane highway suggests that no more than four vehicles can move forth side by side. Yet somehow, in China, seven cars manage to share a space designed for four. There was an unforgiving frenzy to get ahead. We leapt forth, swerved, smited competitors for position, and in leaps and fits made our way into the city. The taxi driver drove without consulting his mirrors, and often, far too often, we'd swerve into another lane, sending cars screeching and swaying in every direction, and as my heart palpitations threatened to turn into a full-on cardiac event, the driver calmly sipped tea from his thermos, smoked his cigarettes, and unleashed the clamor of his horn. Chinese drivers, I was discovering, speak with their horns. They blast it when they're about to pass someone. They blast it while they're passing. And they blast it when they're done passing. Then they blast it some more, just because. Then there are the other horn blasts, the short ones that convey mild irritation, and the long Munchian screams that reflect a troubled soul. Together, the blasting horns converge into one endless sonic wail. We tolerated no other car, until a black Audi A6 with tinted windows rocketed behind us, flashing ominous blue lights and a panic-inducing siren. Swiftly, we changed lanes, and as the Audi sped ahead, we returned to its lane and allowed ourselves to be pulled in its wake.

"Police?" I asked.

The driver indicated otherwise as he again offered me a cigarette. Around us, the scene had turned into something familiar. There were thousands of squat apartment buildings constructed in the flimsy Communist-bloc style I remembered from my time in Eastern Europe. They are called *panelaky* in Czech, soulless and austere apartments designed to crush the soul. Most were in advanced stages of dereliction. But throughout the city, everywhere and in immense numbers, there were also cranes. It was a city of cranes. It was the invasion of the cranes. They stood atop hundreds of buildings as if they were nesting. There were big cranes and little cranes, yellow cranes and green cranes. They ruled the city from their perches in the sky as a toxic haze swirled around their steel facades. They were the tools of Beijing's transformation. They were destroying buildings and they were creating buildings. Above all, it is the cranes that dominate Beijing.

Darkness descended and there was a long moment of gloom. What? I thought. Did they not have electricity in Beijing? Did Chinese cars not come with lights? And then, as if some unseen deity had flipped the proverbial switch, Beijing emerged in a sea of light. We passed restaurants bathed in a harsh fluorescent glare. This pleased me. It was familiar. Chinese restaurants with bad lighting. It was just like home. But this wasn't home. I had, of course, seen Chinese characters aglow in neon. I had been to dozens of Chinatowns. But this was the mother of all Chinatowns, and these thousands of signs, all presumably offering information, directions, imploring you to buy this and do that, were utterly alien to me. I understood nothing, a sensation that disturbed my psyche. I felt profoundly out of my element.

We careened around a corner, scattering pedestrians and cyclists. Why did he do that? I wondered. They had the right of way. Was my driver an asshole? He did not seem like an asshole. This was perplexing. He drove as if to kill. Why was this so? Finally, I was deposited at my hotel, and I was left with my head throbbing with jet lag and sensory overload.

I entered the modest lobby and waited for the woman at the check-in counter to notice me.

"WHAT?" she barked.

"Er . . . I have a reservation," I said.

"PASSPORT!" she wailed.

I gave it to her.

"ROOM 587! KEYS! GO THERE!"

I thanked her for her kindness and made my way to my room. Off the lobby, there was a restaurant full of Chinese patrons. That's always a good sign with Chinese restaurants. As I stood waiting for the elevator, a woman rushed out of the restaurant carrying her toddler son. She stopped beside me, opened the flap of his pants, and directed a stream of urine into the ashtray to my right. When the boy was done, they returned to their table. Right, I thought. There's pee in the ashtrays. In the taxi, I had briefly toyed with the idea of relaxing my no-smoking rule to "No smoking in North America." But the prospect of stubbing out a smoke in a pond of pee encouraged fortitude.

I made my way upstairs. I had an overwhelming urge to simply collapse upon the bed, but I wanted to adjust to the time difference as quickly as possible, and so I forced myself to go out for a walk and possibly find something to eat. I emerged into the din outside, consulted my map, and soon found myself wandering upon Wangfujing DaJie, a pedestrian arcade that runs north to south in Central Beijing. The evening was warm. Up on the billboards, I spotted the familiar visages of Tiger, LeBron, and Ronaldinho, and in the square in front of the gothic facade of St. Joseph's Church, a gathering of scruffy-haired migrant workers with hard, shell-shocked faces. Three mistrals played their instruments, singing a song in a language I could not place. Everything felt strange and I wondered whether it was the jet lag. Or was it the presence of a Gothic cathedral in Beijing? I had not expected to see a cathedral before which brides were having their photos taken, inline skaters loitered, and men with tousled hair and dirty faces stared at the world around them with an expression of despair. As I absorbed the scene, a woman approached me. "Night lady?" she whispered.

*Night lady.*

I had begun my day in Sacramento, and now I found myself in front of a church in Beijing, surrounded by shoppers and migrant workers, being propositioned by a lady of the night. It had been a long and strange day. I walked on. Ahead, blinking brightly, I could see a sign that announced itself as the "Moslem Restaurant." Encouraged by the English words, and the implication that there might even be English menus, I entered. It was busy, and as I settled into a seat, I was gratified to receive a menu I could comprehend. And as I perused the restaurant's offerings, I was more than a little thankful.

> *Cattle Penis with Garlic*
> *Chicken and Sheep's Placenta in Soup*
> *Ox's Penis and Sheep Whip in the Soup*
> *Processed Ox Stomach*

*Sheep's Heart*
*Sheep's Testicle*
*Sheep Brain*
*Ox Larynx*

When the waiter returned, I pointed to the Grilled Chicken. I am amenable to eating anything, but not after a long airplane journey, which for me results in a strange and inexplicable knotting of the stomach. Some time later, he returned with a dish that was manifestly not what I thought I had ordered. It was vaguely gelatinous. It quivered. I called the waiter over.

"*Zhege zhende shi jirou ma?*" I asked.

He looked at me blankly.

"*Zhege zhende shi jirou ma?*" I repeated, indicating the food. Surely this wasn't the chicken I had ordered.

He fetched the menu. I pointed to the dish I thought I had requested. The waiter nodded his head effusively. I looked at the menu a little more closely. And then I recognized the enormity of my mistake. Cultural hegemonist that I was, I had assumed that the menu items were displayed in English first, followed by their Chinese translation. The reverse, of course, was true. And now I learned that the grisly mass that lay before me was not a chicken but the brain of an unfortunate sheep. As I sat there, chopsticks in hand, it occurred to me that it was time to start paying attention in China, because there are consequences for not paying attention in China. Big consequences.

3

Let's begin with Chairman Mao. So much in modern China begins and ends with the colorful tyrant from Hunan. When the China of yore, that long twilight presided over by the doddering Qing Dynasty, finally collapsed with the abdication of the boy emperor, sad little Puyi, it was Mao who emerged in 1949 as the last man standing after decades of civil war. There are still some, apparently, who regard this as a fundamentally good thing, arguing that a fractious, backward country like China could only have entered the modern age under the steely guidance of a megalomaniac like Mao Zedong. Indeed, this view is often expressed empirically as 70:30—70 percent of what Mao did was pretty darn good, while 30 percent of his actions were a trifle excessive. This is, in fact, the official view in China.

Of course, the government acknowledges, here and there mistakes were made. In retrospect, the Great Leap Forward was probably not such a good idea after all. In the spring of 1958,

Mao had decided that China should be a superpower. Not just any superpower, mind you; Mao was nothing if not ambitious. As he unleashed his Great Leap Forward, Mao idly drew plans for what he called the Earth Control Committee. At the time, China was a land of peasants still reeling from years of war and centuries of impoverishment. And yet Mao believed China should rule the world. He just needed a year or two to boost the country up and prepare it for global domination. And thus the Great Leap Forward, a headlong rush to transform a country of farms into a nation of factories. Gazing at a vista of temples and pagodas from his perch in the Forbidden City, Mao declared: "In the future, I want to look around and see chimneys everywhere!"

And so it would be. Throughout China, city walls that had withstood the Mongols were destroyed and replaced with steel factories. The ancient cores of cities were flattened and from the ashes new power plants were built. Some people, of course, objected to this willful destruction of China's cultural heritage. In response, Mao put them on the wrecking crews. Meanwhile, in the countryside, a half-billion peasants suddenly found their lives in turmoil. Massive waterworks projects were inflicted on the country, including a dam in Henan Province that would subsequently collapse in 1975, killing 250,000 people. Villages were abandoned for communes, where soon the villagers lost their names and gained a number. Numbers, after all, were more efficient than names. Tools and cooking utensils were melted into steel in millions of backyard furnaces so that Mao could claim to have doubled China's steel production within a year. The steel, of course, was useless, and any pilot flying a plane made with the steel produced in a backyard furnace would soon be dead. But the steel quotas were met, and this is what mattered to Mao.

So too did the grain quotas. Superpowers exported grain. Ergo, China must export grain. To achieve this, Mao ordered the death of every sparrow in China. Sparrows ate grain seeds; thus they had to die. This probably looked like a good idea on paper. Who would have thought that the sudden demise of the lowly sparrow would contribute to one of the worst catastrophes to ever befall humanity? Over the next three years, China would starve like no other nation had starved before. There were, of course, scientists and economists and steelmakers and farmers who could have told Mao that these were not particularly good ideas. But no one dared raise their concerns to the Chairman, who had nothing but disdain for experts, those irksome people who possessed something so irritating as knowledge.

Indeed, in 1956, during what came to be known as the Hundred Flowers Campaign, Mao encouraged dissenting voices to speak up, which they did. So identified, Mao unleashed one of his periodic purges. He ultimately praised the province of Hunan, which had "denounced 100,000, arrested 10,000, and killed 1,000," and concluded, "the other provinces did the same. So our problems were solved." In the 1950s alone, as Mao consolidated his power, his purges took the lives of more than 800,000 people. Subsequently, no one dared point out that the steel the peasants were ordered to produce in backyard furnaces was worthless, that the elimination of every sparrow would lead to a plague of locusts, and that the revolutionary changes he had applied to farming were based on nothing more than nonsensical musings. In the ensuing famine, more than

30 million people died. It became the single most devastating famine in human history. Mao, however, remained nonplussed. "Deaths have benefits," he said. "They can fertilize the ground." And here's the real stunner: While China starved, Mao continued to *export* grain.

There were other ideas, of course, that didn't turn out so well. Mao's cult of personality found its most intense expression during the Cultural Revolution, a calculated madness in the late sixties and early seventies designed by Mao's most ferocious supporters to consolidate power and cripple his rivals. Even Deng Xiaoping, who would one day rule China, was sent into exile in distant Jiangxi Province, where he toiled in a tractor factory. But this was no mere power struggle, and the phrase *cultural revolution* doesn't quite do justice to the terror of that time. It was a war against the "Four Olds"—Old Customs, Old Ideas, Old Habits, and Old Culture—carried out by brainwashed, rampaging teenagers, the so-called Red Guards, bands of youths suddenly given free rein to release their inner sadists. "Be Violent," Mao had instructed them, and they did their best to comply. The police and soldiers were told to not interfere as the youths set about beating and torturing their teachers and anyone else suspected of having "rightist" tendencies.

"Peking is not violent enough," Mao said of Beijing, using the name by which the capital was then known, during what came to be known as Red August. "Peking is too civilized." Nearly 2,000 people would die in Beijing alone that month. Mao abolished school and instructed that his Red Guards be given free travel, and soon all of China trembled at the sight of psychopathic gangs of teenagers in homemade olive uniforms and red armbands. And it is no wonder. In Guangxi Province, not only did the Red Guards torture and kill their teachers, they ate them too. In the lunchroom, no less. "Smash old culture," Mao commanded. Paintings were destroyed, books set ablaze. Anyone caught with a musical instrument was likely to be tortured and even killed. Thousands of historical monuments were destroyed. China was seized in a paroxysm of terror as Mao sought to obliterate Chinese history.

In the end, the horror of that age only really came to a close with Mao's death in 1976. Roughly 70 million people are believed to have perished under his reign, a feat that allows him to seriously compete with Adolf Hitler and Joseph Stalin for the title Baddest Person Ever. But what makes contemporary China just a little odd is that even today one can't escape his porcine face. I think it is fair to say that on the day Hitler killed himself in his bunker, surrounded by a shattered country and a million Soviet troops, most Germans were probably quite ready to move on, to take their leave of Adolf, and indeed that is what they did. Of course, they really didn't have any say in the matter, but thirty years after his death, there couldn't have been more than a handful of cretinous skinheads who could muster a *Heil Hitler* with any enthusiasm. When Joseph Stalin, born Joseph Vissarionovich Dzhugashvili (say it fast), died on a gloomy night in 1953, it wasn't long before he was denounced by Nikita Khrushchev, who proceeded to undertake an intense program of de-Stalinization. Communism lingered on for nearly another forty years, but one would have been hard-pressed to find a statue or portrait of Uncle Joe.

Contrast this with China. Whenever I opened my wallet, I was greeted by Mao Zedong, looking serene and confident as his visage graced every paper yuan. Nearly every city of consequence has a Renmin Guangchang, or People's Square, and the vast majority are still dominated by a colossal statue of Mao, looking proud and heroic. An enormous portrait of the Great Helmsman dominates Tiananmen Square, and more creepy still, his gaze is directed toward his mausoleum, where even today he accepts visitors. This pleased me, because it's not every day that one gets to meet one of history's greatest villains. And so early one morning, I set off to have a look.

But first I had to get there. My hotel, which appeared to be very popular with package tourists from Eastern Europe, was located within walking distance of Tiananmen Square and the Forbidden City. I stepped out and watched the doorman do his morning ritual, which consisted of purging an immense, glutinous loogie from somewhere deep within his innards, followed by the expulsion of a dribble of snot from first one nostril and then the other, and then, apparently satisfied with this ousting of liquids, lighting up a cigarette. And good morning to you, I thought, as I made my way through the acrid smoke, delicately stepping around a millpond of phlegm and mucus that had gathered at the hotel's entrance. I couldn't decide what was more disturbing—the splattering loogie or the dribbling snot—but as I wandered through the early-morning haze toward the mausoleum, it soon became apparent that somehow I'd have to come to terms with the interesting methods the Chinese use for expelling the contents of their noses and lungs. The Chinese have invented many things, but the handkerchief is not among them. I walked on and watched the residents of Beijing, young and old, male and even a few elderly women, greet the new day with an immense hawk and a resonant splatter, and then, just as I thought the streets of Beijing could not be further befouled, I came across a man who squatted beside the curb. He was holding a toddler in split pants over the gutter so that the boy could take a shit here in downtown Beijing, inches from passing bicycles and sputtering mopeds. Interesting, I thought as I pondered the diseases that might be lurking in China this year—SARS, Avian Flu, dysentery. They have a happy home in China.

It was after crossing a street that I came to my second observation about life in Beijing: Do not play chicken with Chinese drivers. Even if they see you, they will not slow down. Even if the pedestrian light is green, they will not slow down. So do not play chicken with Chinese drivers. Or you will die.

A moment later, I made my third observation about life in Beijing: *Do not play chicken with Chinese cyclists. See observation 2. Same applies. You will die.*

And most of Beijing hadn't even woken up yet.

Never before had I felt so fearful as a pedestrian as I did on that early morning. After dodging the loogies that came whistling past, I'd find myself at an intersection. I would dutifully wait for the pedestrian light, the flashing man, to turn green, and then, assured that I had the right of way, I would confidently take my foot off the curb, only to nearly lose it a moment later as a car hurtled past, sending me sputtering back toward the sidewalk. A moment later, while the little man still flashed green, I'd spy an opening in the traffic and again set forth, only to find myself dangerously entangled amid a dozen cyclists, who may or may not have been cursing at me. I couldn't say for sure. *Chinese for Dummies* didn't cover colloquial cussing.

How, I wondered, was one expected to cross a four-lane

road in China, a road shared by cars lined six abreast, with another two lanes carved by a sea of bicycles and mopeds? How does one navigate through the mayhem that is a Chinese city? Very, very carefully, I deduced. Crossing a street was no straightforward wander from curb to curb. It was a problem to be broken down into six parts. First, I'd dart through the mass of bicycles and mopeds that hugged the road near the curb. From there, I'd cross the street one lane at a time as cars whished by just inches from my being, and I'd try very hard to not linger on the noteworthy fact that China has the world's highest per capita rate of vehicular fatalities. And so I moved, a quick leap at a time, as fleets of cars zoomed around me, driven by people who, it occurred to me, probably hadn't been driving for all that long.

It was with some surprise, then, that I suddenly found myself on the vast expanse that is Tiananmen Square. I was excited to be there, not merely because I had crossed a dozen intersections to get there and managed to live, but because Tiananmen Square is one of those iconic places that I had always wanted to see. It was gratifyingly familiar in that Communist theme park sort of way. Here was Red China—the lustrous portrait of Mao hanging in its place of honor above the Gate of Heavenly Peace, the fluttering red flags, the immense Great Hall of the People, the towering Monument to the People's Heroes, and of course, the Workers Cultural Palace, because no celebration of all things red is complete without a Workers Palace. Vehicles are forbidden on the square, though exceptions are made for tanks, and in the early, hazy morning, only a scattering of Chinese tour groups were beginning to assemble there. With so few people, its massiveness was laid bare. More than a million people could fit comfortably within its dimensions. Now and then, Mao had enjoyed rallying his Red Guards, and as I strolled about my spine tingled at the thought of Mao's call and response with a million homicidal teenagers. *Be violent! Destroy old culture!*

But today there were Chinese tourists. They were easy to identify. Each group was given a distinctive baseball cap. There was the red group and the green group and the baby blue group, and each was tightly gathered around a guide holding an umbrella. As I wandered around, happily gawking, I played an exciting game of spot the secret policeman, and by the time I reached the Chairman Mao Mausoleum, I figured I'd counted more than twenty, though I may have been mistaken. It is entirely possible that the tough-looking men wandering about in their Members Only jackets were conventioneers and not government goons. Still, it seemed imprudent to let out a lusty *"Free Tibet Now"*—Tiananmen Square, of course, being one of the better places in the world to get beat up for protesting.

I absorbed this celebration of Socialist Realism, the architectural style that glorifies the proletariat by making a mere individual seem very, very small. As I neared the entrance to the mausoleum, I was approached by a young man in a honey-colored Members Only jacket.

"You cannot take a bag here," he said in English, pointing to my daypack.

"Can I leave it someplace?" I asked.

"I will take you," he offered.

I had no idea whether he was a policeman, an employee of the mausoleum, a hustler, or just a helpful fellow looking to assist a befuddled foreigner. I followed him, and suppressing the dread I felt as he directed me through six lanes of traffic, I became his shadow, which was okay because, as I'd already discovered, the Chinese are very accommodating when it comes to infringing their personal space. He led me toward a building where I could drop off my bag.

"*Xie xie,*" I said, mangling the word for "thank you."

"You have money?" he said after we had darted back across the road.

"Yes, I kept my wallet. Thanks for asking."

"Twenty yuan," he said with a hopeful smile.

I gave him ten, which was far more than his service required, but I was new to China and hadn't yet acquired the flinty-eyed determination to haggle for the Chinese price. I took my place in line; it was still early, before 9 A.M., and by Chinese standards the line remained relatively short. Perhaps 500 of us waited for a chance to gaze upon the Chairman. Meanwhile, over a loudspeaker we listened to a recounting of the life and times of Mao Zedong while waiting for the grim-faced guards in crisp blue uniforms and white gloves to let us in. Actually, I had no idea what they were talking about over the loudspeaker. Perhaps the voice was informing us that there was a blue-tag special on Mao watches in aisle three of the gift shop. Who could say? Certainly not me.

A flower vendor sold fake roses, and a fair portion of the waiting crowd purchased them. I guessed that most of the visitors were from somewhere in the far hinterlands of China. Having lived in Sacramento, I can recognize a fellow yokel anywhere.

Finally, we surged up the steps and entered. Inside, we were greeted by a white statue of the Great Helmsman, and it was here that visitors deposited their roses, bowing deeply as they did so. Mao as Buddha. I wondered what happened to the daily pile of plastic flowers. I guessed they were probably swept up and sold to the next group. Dillydallying wasn't encouraged, and the crowd shuffled forward, carried by its own momentum. In the adjoining room lay Mao himself, tucked under a cozy red flag featuring the hammer and sickle.

Typically, I find the presence of dead people a little unsettling, but there was nothing ghoulish or macabre about Mao. This is because he is orange—a festive playful orange, toylike, as if he were nothing more than a waxen action figure in repose. And that is probably all that he is after thirty years of death. I almost felt sorry for him, a diabolical tyrant reduced to a morbid curio. But then I noticed the reaction of my Chinese companions. I had expected some good-natured joshing— *Look how orange he is. Do you think he's a fake? It's so hard to tell in China.* Mao had been quite dead now for thirty years. Surely, one could poke a little fun at the fat despot. But I couldn't have been more wrong. People bowed before him. Some of the older ones even wept. They couldn't have been more reverent if they were viewing their own grandfathers, a spell broken only by our emergence into the next room, the souvenir emporium, where we were encouraged to buy authentic, straight-from-the-source, Mao watches and Mao cuff links and Mao portraits and, of course, *Quotations from Chairman Mao Zedong*, otherwise known as The Little Red Book. More than 900 million copies have been sold since it was first published in 1964. And it is no wonder. During the Cultural Revolution, to leave home without one was to risk a thumping by a deranged youth or even exile to a labor camp. To stand before Mao Zedong, dead though he may be, must be an interesting experience for those whose formative years were spent learning that there is no god but Mao.

I reclaimed my bag and returned to the square, which was now, only an hour later, seething with crowds. There were more vendors selling The Little Red Book. I walked past legless peasants on carts. A man offered to sell me his charcoal portraits of Mao, Vladimir Putin, and George W. Bush. How to choose a favorite? In the distance, near the imposing walls of the Forbidden City, soldiers marched past the looming portrait of the former Chairman. I walked back to my hotel, noting the plethora of black Audis with tinted windows, the vehicle of choice for Communist Party officials. Chinese drivers yield to this car, and from what I'd observed, they yield for no other.

A strange place, I thought. Wandering around Tiananmen Square had felt like a walk into the rapidly receding past. Perhaps it was also the smell of burning coal that prevailed in Beijing, an odor I associate to this day with the Communism I remembered from my childhood visits to Czechoslovakia. I am half-Czech, and when Soviet tanks invaded Czechoslovakia in 1968, most of my family had thought it was an excellent time to leave the country. My grandfather, however, had remained, and my mother, who had legally emigrated when she married my Dutch father, often took my sister and me to visit during the gloomy years that followed as Czechoslovakia discovered that it wasn't quite done with Marxist Leninism just yet. Tiananmen Square, with its red stars and Stalinist architecture, reminded me of those years, except that at no point in Czech history would people there have regarded a man such as Mao as anything other than a villainous despot. But perhaps the

Czechs had had better information. Indeed, even today in China one can still be tossed in jail for "incitement to over-throw the government" simply by publishing articles about the Cultural Revolution that deviate from the official line, which holds that the excesses of the time demonstrate the perils of allowing the public to participate in politics. At least the gov-ernment acknowledges that Mao was capable of excess. Never-theless, that to this day there are people in China—the vast majority, in fact, who regard Mao Zedong with adoration, while his heirs commute to work in luxurious black sedans—suggested to me that this new China people were speaking of wasn't quite here just yet.

And then, back at my hotel, I turned on the television.

Of all the things I never expected to see in China, Tweety Bird speaking in Mandarin was certainly one of them. I watched as once again Tweety Bird confounded a sputtering Sylvester the Cat. How odd, I thought, to hear a cartoon cat speaking Mandarin Chinese with a lisp. Then I turned the channel. It was a commercial for Stay Fit Health Powder, a powerful new cream that enlarges breasts. It showed a woman being mercilessly mocked by her big-breasted friends. She had tried breast-growth lotion after breast-growth lotion without results. Until she tried Stay Fit Health Powder. The advertise-ment tastefully demonstrated its enhancement power by show-ing anime-type breasts ballooning upon application of the cream. It finished with happy testimonials of other customers, who were shown carelessly reclining on the couch, reading a magazine, bending over to water the plants—and all this could be yours for 99 yuan.

Okay, I thought. In a single morning I had gone from

Mao Zedong to Stay Fit Health Powder. Perhaps China isn't so simple after all.

Fortunately, I had a friend in Beijing. And a friend is a very good thing to have in Beijing, a city of 17 million people, give or take a million, inhabiting a municipality that is roughly the size of Slovenia. For many years, I had lived in another capital, Washington, D.C., a city that many think has been transformed over the past twenty years. Not so long ago, Washington was a sleepy hamlet in the South notable for its swampy weather and dissolute politicians. The weather has remained the same, of course, and so too the dissolution of the politicians, but what's changed in Washington is the exponential growth of lobbyists. It is really quite amazing that the government of the United States was able to function without them for quite so long, but now that everything from education to war is regarded as a commercial enterprise, the private sector has moved in. Whereas once you could be reasonably confident that the neighbor next door was an employee of the federal government, today should you have a pressing need for a cup of sugar, it is just as likely that you'll be knocking on the door of Blackwater's friendly representative in Washington. Money permeates the city. Untidy neighborhoods have been transformed by Whole Foods. The mom-and-pop delis have made way for Pottery Barn, and today Washingtonians speak smugly of their rivalry with New York, a self-proclaimed rivalry about which New Yorkers can barely muster a snort of derision. Nevertheless, it remains true that the Washington of the mid-aughts looks and feels like a vastly different place than the Washington of the mid-1980s, that colorful era when the city was ruled by a mayor with a fondness for crack and whose most celebrated zinger was "The bitch set me up."

But nothing can compare with the transformation of Beijing. It is an immense, seething city. Washington still has but one ring road, the notorious Beltway, and you are either inside where you matter or outside where you don't. Beijing is constructing its sixth ring road, and within those six rings, an entire city is being razed and reborn. Tiananmen Square will always remain an ode to Stalinism, but just past the Great Hall Of The People lies an ode to the odd—the new and otherworldly National Theater, otherwise known as the Alien Egg. Throughout Beijing, the superstars of international architecture have been given license to realize their inner whimsy, with the result that today no city can claim to have embraced the avant-garde with greater enthusiasm than the capital of the People's Republic of China. From the Bird's Nest, or Olympic Stadium, to the Twisted Donut, the new home of CCTV, Beijing has said good-bye to the bland uniformity of Mao's day. Whether it succeeds in creating a cutting-edge capital for the twenty-first century—China's century, they hope—or whether they're merely constructing tomorrow's Brasília remains to be seen, but there is no denying that today's Beijing is buzzing.

To help me navigate the wonder that is contemporary Beijing, I called my friend Dan. Once upon a time, Dan had been an unassuming temp in Washington, D.C. Like me, he had received a graduate degree in international relations, and while our fellow graduates were finding jobs with the State Department, the United Nations, and Citibank, Dan spent his days filing and rearranging supply closets—also like me. But, unlike me, Dan had real-world skills. He spoke Chinese. He had studied in Nanjing. He had even been the quality-control manager at a shoe factory in China. And so one day he stuffed his last binder, organized his last supply closet, typed his last invoice order, and left the world of temping for the new land of opportunity to become the man he is today.

Dan the Man, titan of the Orient.

Dan and his business partner had arrived in Beijing several years earlier to help fill the yawning gap between foreign investors and Chinese businesses. "There's the Western way of doing things," he explained, "and there's the Chinese way of doing things. We try to bridge the two."

And make some money. I felt so proud. I remembered when he was a mere pup, just another temp at the National Association for the Advancement of Proctology, and now here he was, fixer extraordinaire in China. Dan knew Beijing, and as he showed me around, he was very helpful in pointing out the best market for pirated software and in explaining that the migrant women standing on the corner with their babies were not merely migrant women standing on corners with their babies, but also purveyors of pornography, a fact that flummoxed me just a little until he explained that policemen don't want to deal with babies, ergo the baby accessory for dealers of pornography. Very thoughtfully, he then turned my attention to the Dongba Hospital for Anus and Intestine Disease.

At night, once I could safely stay up past 8 P.M. without nodding off into a jet-lag-induced, drool-producing slumber, Dan introduced me to the trippy mayhem that is Beijing nightlife. It was breathtaking. Of course, as a parent of two kids under the age of five living in Sacramento, it didn't take much to impress me. Indeed, I couldn't recall the last time I had been inside anything fancying itself a club, though I'm fairly certain it must have been back when INXS was king. Twenty years ago, Beijing had been about as sexless a city as humanity is capable of creating, and now here I was, somewhere in the slinky depths of Club Banana, listening to a throbbing techno-funk-house-electronica-groove. Dan, helpful as always, translated as the stunningly beautiful young woman who stood before me inquired whether I'd like to dance with her, and just as I was beginning to feel particularly good-looking, I was informed that the privilege would cost me 300 yuan.

Now and then at night, I'd feel as if I were anywhere—London, Tokyo, New York, feeling as groovy in a nightclub in Beijing as I did in a lounge in London. The China of the Mao era seemed far removed. In the darkness of night, beneath the glimmering neon, this Beijing, with its thumping nightclubs and plethora of elegant restaurants, felt familiar—provided, of course, one ignored the loogies landing at your feet. But, of course, things in China are not always as they seem. One evening, while I was enjoying a delectable duck cooked in the Peking manner at a restaurant in the Embassy District, I asked the Australian businessman who had joined Dan and me for dinner what it was like to do business here.

"China is a dictatorship, and if you cross the government, or someone connected to it, then your life is literally in danger. It's all done very quietly. So you don't cross the government."

"Really?"

"Doing business in China is like doing business with the mafia," he added. "You have to be careful. And you don't cross the wrong person."

And then the conversation turned to factory workers on roller skates.

"I'm sorry," I said. "Did you just say factory workers on roller skates?"

"Yes," said the businessman. "They work faster on roller skates. It's more efficient."

"But don't people get hurt?"

"Welcome to China," he said. "It's different here."

Interesting as this was, I had hopes of actually talking to a Chinese person about the changes in Beijing. And so one afternoon I asked Dan if he could help me find a translator, someone to wander around with as I explored the tumultuous capital.

"Sure," he said. "We can do that right now if you want."

Puzzled, I followed him inside the Oriental Plaza, a luxurious shopping arcade near Tiananmen Square. The Oriental Plaza is an emporium for the wealthy and the nearly wealthy, a glittering mall full of high-end Chinese boutiques, as well as more familiar stores such as Coach and Burberry. There was even a store selling what it claimed was the BMW Lifestyle, and on the lowest level, tucked into a corner, was the Coca-Cola shop, which seemed like a vestige of the eighties, when the Communist world got its first taste of the West.

"This wasn't exactly what I was expecting to see in China," I noted as we walked past the Hugo Boss store. "I feel poor here. I shouldn't feel poor in China, should I?"

"There are about 300 million people in China who could be called middle class or even wealthy. But if you'd really like to feel poor, I'll take you to the Ferrari dealership."

"The Ferrari dealership?"

"There are eleven Ferrari dealerships in China now."

I wondered if the owners of these Ferraris drove them with the same manic gusto as Beijing's cabdrivers. Would one have to be truly insane to drive a Ferrari on the streets of China? Would people here even know how to operate a Ferrari? From what I'd discerned on the streets of Beijing, the Chinese, while in possession of cars, didn't actually know how to drive them.

Having cut through the Oriental Plaza, we stopped in front of the entrance to the Grand Hyatt, one of the most luxurious hotels in Beijing, whereupon Dan approached two attractive young women who were loitering near the doorway. They wore makeup and tight, form-fitting clothes that suggested that they were either unusually curvaceous for Chinese women or dedicated customers of Stay Fit Health Powder.

*Dude. What are you doing?*

"She says she speaks English," Dan said, gesturing to one of the women.

"Yes, I speak English," she confirmed.

"My friend here would like to hire you for the afternoon," Dan explained.

*Dude!*

Around us, shoppers turned to stare. There were children. *Jesus.*

"As a translator," I stammered.

"What's your name?" Dan inquired.

"Meow Meow."

*Meow Meow.*

"Meow Meow, meet Maarten."

Who was this Meow Meow? And why was this woman with the Bond-girl name lingering at the entrance of an upscale hotel?

"You need translator," she said. "I can be translator. How much money? Money very important in China."

Dan took charge of the negotiations. He had long ago absorbed the rules of China, and while I still instinctually paid the first asking price, bargaining had become second nature to him and he now haggled down everything from a restaurant meal to a cab ride to a bottle of water. It still seemed presumptuous to me to quibble over a restaurant bill, but in China no one ever took offense. One bargains for everything in China, including, apparently, the services of an attractive translator hanging around the Grand Hyatt in Beijing.

"Let's get a coffee," Dan said, having come to an arrangement that was satisfactory for all parties. We walked back toward the Starbucks in the Oriental Plaza, which was just like any other Starbucks, except that small isn't Tall. It's just small. "China is Starbucks' second-largest market," Dan blithely noted, as I stood wondering what, precisely, Meow Meow did for a living.

As she waited for her frappuccino, I approached Dan. "Just an observation here," I said, "but in other countries the young women lingering outside swanky hotels aren't usually translators."

"Do you think she's a take-out girl?"

"A take-out girl?"

"That's what the prostitutes in the karaoke bars are

called. But I don't think she's a take-out girl. But if she is, just think of her as a full-service translator."

"Thanks, Dan."

"You're welcome."

We settled at a table and sipped our coffees. "So, Meow Meow," I began, searching for a way to ascertain her profession. I could, of course, have simply asked her what she did for a living, but I'd spent enough years in Washington, where *What do you do?* is the template for tedious conversation, that I hesitated. "Your English is excellent," I offered.

"No," she said. "But it is better than your Chinese."

Very true.

"I am a student," she continued. "I study English."

What luck. Suddenly, I felt like I could be helpful.

"You are American?" she asked.

It's a complicated question for a half-Dutch, half-Czech, Holland-born Canadian citizen with a Dutch passport and a green card presently living in California.

"I live there," I offered. "Have you ever been to America?" I asked her. She hadn't. "Well, it's kind of like this," I said, waving my hand around the mall. Except this was far nicer. I watched the shoppers mosey about, and reflected that surely this kind of economic transformation had been matched by some sort of social and political transformation. I asked Meow Meow if she discussed politics with her friends.

"See, in my country," I said, "we talk about politics a lot. There are two groups—or factions, as I think you call them in China. There is one faction that believes George Bush is a simpleton with the brain capacity of plankton, and that is why we are in the mess we're in. Then there's another faction that believes George Bush is not only smarter than plankton, but that he is a diabolical mastermind, possibly even the spawn of Satan himself, and that is why we are in the mess we're in. Do you have similar conversations about President Hu Jintao?"

"No," Meow Meow finally replied. "Politics are more the concern of poor people."

Of course, there are 900 million or so of those in China, give or take. The Communist Party has nothing to worry about. Still, I found Meow Meow's answer revealing. In 1989, it was the students, the children of the elite, who gathered in Tiananmen Square and nearly toppled the regime. Today, students like Meow Meow are sipping vente frappuccinos inside upscale shopping malls. I asked her about what she had heard about the massacre in 1989.

She looked befuddled. Dan translated. "He's asking about the events of 6/4," he said, using the Chinese expression for the bloodshed that had occurred on June 4.

Meow Meow shook her head. "I don't know about this. Was it something that occurred during the Cultural Revolution?"

This, frankly, was a remarkable answer. A little more than fifteen years earlier, the People's Liberation Army had slaughtered hundreds, possibly more than a thousand, of unarmed kids just yards from where we sat, and yet that recent tragedy had already been obliterated from memory.

Dan smiled. "There's reality, and there's Chinese reality. They're different."

We started to talk about traveling in China. I had a loose plan to slowly make my way south, but nothing firm. I wondered about crime. I had noticed that many of Beijing's taxi drivers sat encased within a protective cage. Was crime a problem?

"Yes," Meow Meow said.

"Well," Dan interjected. "It's nothing like the U.S. I feel a lot safer here than I do in D.C. But it's probably a little worse here now than it was ten years ago. My business partner's girl-friend—she's English—had her backpack stolen at the Beijing train station. She reported it to the police. Twenty-four hours later, they tracked her down at her hotel in Shanghai and told her that they had found her backpack and not to worry—they had already executed the thief."

"Do you believe that?" I asked Meow Meow.

"Yes," she said matter-of-factly.

It was odd having this conversation. Here we were, embraced by the familiar and unchanging confines of a Star-bucks, deep inside a shopping mall that would not be out of place in suburban Chicago, and yet we inhabited an alternate world where massacres didn't happen and thieves were dis-posed of for good. My cognitive dissonance was throbbing mightily.

And so, too, was my head. I had, of course, read that China is a little polluted. It's just one of those things you know about China, along with the fact that it has more than a billion people. You know they use chopsticks. They have an expansive view of what constitutes food. And the country is a little pol-luted. I had no expectations that my wanderings through China's cities would be accompanied by crisp, clean air. I knew it would be a trifle smoggy. But in no way was I ready for the swirling filth that constitutes air in Beijing. It was, frankly, apocalyptic.

Living in Sacramento, I had grown familiar with air pollution. Now and then, on a cool winter day, I'd catch a glimpse of the High Sierras and I'd be reminded that we lived awfully close to the mountains. Indeed, the Sierra foothills roll into the suburbs of Sacramento. Mostly, however, this mountain range remained hidden behind the nasty haze that blights life in the Central Valley of California. For a while, I blamed the people of San Francisco, blithely gallivanting about their fine city while sending us their air pollution, which became trapped behind the Sierras and above us. But, as studies on the Sierra snowpack confirmed, more than *a third* of the air pollution affecting California originates in China. When one considers that China is more than 4,000 miles from California, one would be forgiven for concluding that they have an awful lot of pollution. And they do. In their race to be number one, the Chinese have already eclipsed the United States in one significant area. Today, China leads the world in carbon emissions.

Dan had left us to tend to his duties as a Titan of the Orient, leaving me to walk around Beijing with Meow Meow. As we walked, clouds of filth swirled through the city's canyons, obscuring the massive new high-rises. Cranes peeked through the smog, appearing to levitate. I suddenly had an inkling of what a post-strike nuclear winter might look like. Some people had taken to wearing surgeon's masks. This seemed completely inadequate to me; I yearned for scuba gear. Meanwhile, my head hurt. My eyes itched. I coughed, and while I hadn't picked up the locals' colorful habit of hawking and spitting phlegm, I wouldn't have been at all surprised if the contents of my lungs had blackened to the color of coal.

I couldn't begin to guess at the number of pollutants swishing through the air. But among all the colorfully named toxins, many are what really smart people call particulate matter. In the United States, anything more than 50 micrograms of particulates per cubic meter of air is considered unsafe, leading authorities to issue red alerts advising children and elderly people to remain inside. In Beijing, the average particulate matter swirling through the air on any given day is 141. For a foreigner, even for someone accustomed to the haze of Sacramento, this is unimaginably foul.

"It's very interesting air you have here in Beijing," I noted to Meow Meow. "I don't think I've ever seen anything like it before."

"Yes. It is very dirty. More bad today because of dust storms last week."

"Dust storms?" This only seemed to heighten the End Times atmosphere.

"Yes, every spring we get dust storms. You can still see the sand."

It was true. Beijing remained coated in a fine layer of sand. This, too, was unexpected for me. When I had envisioned Beijing, I didn't think it would be particularly green, but I certainly didn't expect it to be quite so brown. Then again, this too is a new problem for China. More than a quarter of China is a desert, and sadly for the people of Beijing, the Gobi Desert is coming for them. Not more than fifty miles from the center of Beijing, great sand dunes are moving inexorably toward the city. Forty years ago, sandstorms were rarely seen here, but today, they are a seasonal event. Every year, the *shachenbo,* or dust-cloud tempest, deposits more than a million tons of sand on Beijing, and some scientists believe that within the next couple of decades Beijing will be swallowed by the Gobi Desert.

"So you've got hideous pollution compounded by dust storms," I observed.

"Los Angeles is polluted too," noted Meow Meow.

I nearly blurted out, *Thanks to China,* but, of course, that wasn't entirely true. We're pretty good at pollution too. We didn't just hand over the title of world's greatest polluter, we made China earn it. Indeed, somehow, inexplicably, we've even made owning an SUV seem like a patriotic thing to do. Nevertheless, the refrain *Los Angeles is polluted too* is something I would come to hear often in China, as if the swirling clouds of toxins that churn through Beijing are merely the unavoidable cost of development. But I've seen polluted cities before. I've been to Mexico City. I've trampled through the soot-stained streets of Katowice, a grim city in industrial Poland. And I've spent more time than I cared to in Los Angeles. And I can state with some confidence that none of these places have air quite so vile as Beijing's.

"Do you want to walk or catch taxi?" Meow Meow asked.

I wanted to walk. I figured that the quicker I became accustomed to the pollution of Beijing, the quicker my headache would recede. Perhaps my eyes would stop itching too. And possibly my lungs might stop wheezing as if I'd just chain-smoked three packs of Marlboro Reds. So I wanted to walk through Beijing. For health reasons.

Once upon a time, the capital was regarded as a fussy,

imperial sort of town full of officious bureaucrats who disdained provincials. This suggested an orderly place. Clearly, this must have been a long time ago. What I saw now as we walked along was mayhem. In the dismal haze, people screamed into their cell phones. Beggars pleaded for money. And everywhere there were crowds, seething masses of people, striding up sidewalks, filling underpasses, crossing roads as speeding cars cleaved them apart. And there was noise, an earthshaking wail of jackhammers and buzz saws and, of course, the ever-present howl of car horns. In China, I'd discovered, when getting into a car, the first thing a driver is expected to do is blast the horn. This is to be repeated in ten-second intervals, and because, by my count, there are now a bazillion cars in Beijing the result is an endless honk, a ceaseless clamor amplified by the ear-rattling grind of construction. Half the city seemed to be going up, while the other half seemed to be coming down. And it was only when I found myself in the presence of a bucket of live scorpions that I was able to tune out the havoc of Beijing. There's nothing like coming face-to-face with a black scorpion to concentrate the mind.

"You want to try?" Meow Meow asked. "Good for heart."

We wandered into a crowded alleyway market. There were snakes, grasshoppers, crickets, starfish, and seahorses in buckets and cases strewn about our feet. And the black scorpions. A vendor approached me waving a stick upon which a half-dozen of the live scorpions had been impaled.

"He says it is very tasty," Meow Meow translated.

But it didn't look tasty. It looked like a stick squirming with scorpions.

"Do you eat this?" I asked, gesturing at these alleged delicacies.

"No," she said. "But my grandfather eat one scorpion every year. He eat it for medicine. Sometimes, he eat snake too."

Perhaps the ingestion of these critters had medicinal value, but as I watched these scorpions meet their end on a hot grill, I concluded that it would take more than that for me to eat one. Some kind of sauce at least. Or seasoning. Perhaps a dry rub. If I was going to swallow a strong dose of venom, it better taste good. And this didn't look like it tasted too good at all.

We returned to the main streets of Beijing, where I noted the billboards featuring celebrities pimping for Dunhill (Jude Law) and Adidas (David Beckham) and, strangely, PETA (Pamela Anderson), and just as I thought my senses would be overwhelmed, we found ourselves in a blissful park just east of the Forbidden City hidden behind high, red ocher walls. Trees were in bloom. Ornate bridges crossed a babbling brook. The ponds were filled with glimmering goldfish. Decorative buildings graced the pathway. It was a genteel retreat from the havoc raging beyond the walls.

"This nice park," Meow Meow observed.

In the midst of the serenity, I noticed a large group of middle-aged people lingering. They didn't seem to know each other, but now and then one couple would approach another to engage in conversation.

"What are they doing?" I asked.

"They are here to find husband or wife for their children," Meow Meow said.

"Pardon?" I thought I had misheard.

"If they have daughter, they come to park to find a husband. Same with son. Come to park to find a wife for him."

"Really?"

"Yes."

"And is this something that only occurs in this park?" I asked.

"No," Meow Meow said. "This occurs in all parks now. It is very new, only since last winter, but now it is very common.

"Getting married today is very complicated," she went on. "Because of One Child policy, older people now have only one child. Before, there were more children who could take care of them in old age. Now who their one child marries decides how well they are taken care of when they are older. So there is a lot of pressure. And this," she said, gesturing toward the middle-aged couples, "is the result."

I would come to hear about this as the 1-2-4 problem. When one person marries, the couple assumes responsibility for the welfare of four parents, should they all be living. And the generation that is now approaching retirement is the generation least likely to have prospered from the changes that have taken place in China recently. Indeed, their formative years were spent being whipsawed by Mao in an era not particularly encouraging of 401(k) plans. So even with nearly a billion and a half people, China finds itself short of young people to take care of the elderly. As we left the park, a sign informed us that if we wanted to reenter the park, we would have to return to the East Gate. It was a one-way park. I thought about all the parents milling among the trees. Enter a father, and if you get lucky, leave as a father-in-law.

"So what you say? You want to go to karaoke now?" Meow Meow asked.

Karaoke? I didn't want to go to karaoke. I would rather have major dental work done than engage in karaoke. Among the top ten bad things the Japanese have inflicted upon the rest of the world, karaoke ranks very high in my opinion. Possibly, my feelings about karaoke arise from the sad fact that I was born without the music gene. I listen to it. I like it. But I cannot produce it. I have tinkered with guitars and harmonicas and can manage to play nothing more than discordant noise. Nor can I sing. When I do, dogs cower, children cry, and everyone else looks upon me aghast as if I've just unleashed a deep, throaty, malodorous belch. I cannot even hum a tune. I can, however, whistle, and when I do my children plead for me to stop. A karaoke bar is, therefore, not my natural milieu.

"I can't sing, Meow Meow. People whimper when they hear me sing."

"I don't believe you. I think you can sing. And you said you wanted to see how people in Beijing live. Karaoke very popular in China. Many businessmen relax with karaoke."

I wasn't entirely certain what Meow Meow meant by "relax." There still remained an air of ambiguity about her. Perhaps she was a student. Perhaps she was a take-out girl. Perhaps she was both or neither. I wasn't particularly concerned anymore. If my translator enjoyed getting dolled up and loitering outside hotel lobbies, who was I to question it? She was an agreeable companion. She spoke English. She was informative. And she was undoubtedly correct in pointing out the popularity of karaoke in Beijing. Every block seemed to have a building with a flashing, neon KTV sign. And so, despite my misgivings,

I decided to engage in some pith-helmeted anthropological exploration of the karaoke phenomenon in Beijing.

I followed Meow Meow up a broken escalator to a landing where we were greeted by an attendant in a white shirt and a black vest.

"Give him 50 *kuai*," Meow Meow instructed me, using the local vernacular for yuan. "Better service." We followed him as he led us through a hallway, past a warren of rooms that contained the warbling customers of this karaoke emporium, until he led us to a room with a long cushioned coach facing a television screen. "What do you drink in America?" Meow Meow asked. "Whiskey? Cognac?"

"Usually just beer or wine," I said.

"You want to try Chinese wine?"

"Sure," I said.

I had expected a glass, but the attendant returned with a full bottle of what the label informed me was Great Wall Wine, which he proceeded to pour into a decanter full of ice.

"What you think?" Meow Meow asked.

"I've never had red wine that's quite so . . . icy."

"Wine is very new in China. People are not sure how to drink it."

"I kind of got that impression."

Meow Meow turned to the karaoke machine. "I will sing for you," she said, choosing a love ballad. She picked up the microphone, and as the words appeared upon the screen, she proceeded to sing . . . very well, as it turned out.

"That was very nice, Meow Meow," I told her. "But is this really what people do in Beijing for entertainment, sing to each other?"

"They make relationships at karaoke."

Again with the ambiguity.

"You have wife?" Meow Meow suddenly asked me.

"Yes, I'm married. Very happily married. Excellent marriage. Great marriage," I told her.

"You have picture?"

I showed her a picture of my wife.

"You lucky man. Very beautiful. She very skinny. American women very fat. So you lucky man. You have children?"

I showed her photos of my sons.

"Two boys. So handsome. Lucky man. Do you have car?"

"I do. It's very difficult to live in America without a car."

"What kind of car?"

"A Volkswagen station wagon."

"You rich man too. Pretty wife, two sons, Volkswagen. You lucky man."

Yes, I thought wryly. That's what rich folks in the U.S. drive—VW station wagons full of strollers, diaper bags, and discarded sippy cups. But in China, VW was actually a luxury brand.

"Now it's your turn to sing," Meow Meow continued, handing me the microphone. Naturally, I demurred. I shunned the microphone. I explained in great detail to her my deficiencies as a singer. When I sing, I explained, people are sometimes scarred for life. They did not know that there could be such terrible sounds in the world, and their psyches suffer irreparable damage. Often they end up in counseling. But really, little can be done for them.

She was having none of it.

She pored over a small list of English-language songs,

which included that well-known song by the Beatles, "Hey Judy," as well as, mysteriously, "Starfuckers Inc." by Nine Inch Nails, a song not often found on a karaoke machine.

"You live in California?" Meow Meow asked.

I nodded. *Please, no. Please, please no. Anything but . . .*

"'Hotel California.' You will sing 'Hotel California,'" she informed me, handing me the microphone.

And there on the screen appeared the words *On a dark desert highway, cool wind in my hair,* and soon throughout Beijing, windows shattered, small children wailed, dogs howled, and a short distance away, inside the mausoleum in Tiananmen Square, even Chairman Mao was said to turn.

# 1

The Forbidden City was the longtime home of the Son of Heaven, and the Son of Heaven, of course, couldn't live just anywhere. At least not this Son. What he (He?) needed was a home that would make mere mortals quiver in awe. And thus the Forbidden City came to be. It is immense, sprawling over nearly 200 acres and imposing to the degree that even today, when a mortal can enter with some confidence that he will leave with his head intact, it still leaves one shaking in awe. It intimidates. It overwhelms. It is also the most wickedly cool palace I have ever been to.

I had joined Dan one morning to have a gander at this home of the Son of Heaven. It was a warm and, invariably, hazy day as we marched with the crowds toward the red-ocher walls of the Forbidden City.

"So was Meow Meow helpful?" Dan asked as we

approached the Gate of Heavenly Peace, the imposing archway that marks the entrance to the palace grounds.

"Yes, she was. She took me to karaoke."

"Interesting. And did she turn out to be a take-out girl?"

"I have no idea. She did, however, refuse to be paid for translating for me."

"She's probably paid a commission by the karaoke bar for bringing people in."

If so, Meow Meow had certainly earned her commission. I studied the cracks in the looming walls of the Forbidden City. I'd probably caused those cracks, I thought, with my rendition of "Hotel California."

We joined a dense crowd of Chinese tourists and entered through the Gate of Heavenly Peace, walking shoulder to shoulder with the mass of visitors as we passed below Mao's portrait.

"It's a little crowded," I noted, stating the obvious.

"Well," Dan said. "If you don't like crowds, the Forbidden City is probably not for you. Now that I think of it, if you don't like crowds, China is probably not for you."

This was undeniably true. From the outside, 1.3 billion people is simply a statistic. Inside China, the enormity of the country's population colors everything.

"Also, it's particularly crowded because of the Golden Week holiday," Dan added.

I had, apparently, managed to be in Beijing during one of China's busiest travel weeks. There are three Golden Weeks a year in China, officially mandated weeklong holidays when urban workers and students return to their home provinces, and domestic tourists descend upon the country's most famous sights, including, of course, the Forbidden City. Up to 150 million people were expected to jam the bus and train stations during this time.

"Imagine traveling in the U.S. during Thanksgiving," Dan said. "Now multiply the scale by a factor of five, and you get an idea of what Golden Week is like in China."

Despite the crush of sightseers, once we were through the first gate, the Forbidden City revealed its magnificence. Before us stood the imposing Meridian Gate, an enormous red wall of brick upon which stood a palace with a golden roof. It was here, upon its ramparts, that the emperors of the Ming and Qing Dynasties had ordered the decapitations of prisoners of war.

"It's easy to imagine, isn't it?" Dan observed. *"Off with their heads!"*

It was, in fact, easy to imagine. Perhaps it was the towering walls. They are the color of blood. There were three central arches and we passed through the middle one, where once only emperors could walk. Beyond was an enormous courtyard, which was known as the Outer Court, where the Emperor had conducted his ceremonial functions. The purpose of the Outer Court was to intimidate, to banish any doubts that the emperor was indeed the Son of Heaven. Surely, back in the day, one could but conclude that only the divine could live in a place so vast and magnificent. Inside the walls, there were dozens of palaces and hallways, and the names alone of each towering edifice left me captivated. There to our left was the Hall of Military Prowess, which stood directly across from the Literary Glory Hall. Before us stood the spectacular Hall of Supreme Harmony, beyond which lay the riveting Hall of Preserving Harmony, which could be reached by passing through the Hall of Middle Harmony, which makes sense when you think about it. But it doesn't just stop there. There is a hall devoted to Mental Cultivation, something every home should have. There is an Earthly Tranquility Palace and a Palace of Heavenly Purity, which should not be confused with the Eternal Spring Palace or the Western Palace. Should you need to step out, you'll pass through the Divine Military Genius Gate.

There are some 9,000 rooms in the Forbidden City, which makes you wonder who could possibly need 9,000 rooms in a place where, technically speaking, most people were forbidden from entering. And who would build such a palace in the first place?

I had read the book *1421—The Year China Discovered the World* by Gavin Menzies and become intrigued by his perspective on the era. Menzies, of course, had made the provocative claim that in all likelihood it was the Chinese who were the first foreigners to stumble upon the New World. Most scholars dispute this, but there's no arguing that, at the time, China was a power to be reckoned with.

In the early fifteenth century, when Imperial China was near its apex, the country was ruled by one of the more extraordinary emperors to ever put his derriere on the throne inside the Hall of Preserving Harmony. Indeed, Emperor Zhu Di was the very Son of Heaven who originally built the Forbidden City. The fourth son of the first Ming emperor, Zhu Yuanzhang, Zhu Di was not chosen for succession upon the death of his father. This was not good for Zhu Di. As was the custom, the new emperor, Zhu Di's nephew, set about killing possible rivals to his succession. Zhu Di promptly gave up the good life of being part of the imperial household in Nanjing (then the imperial capital) and escaped to Beijing, where he became a homeless vagrant. Apparently, he must have been a very charismatic drifter, for he was soon able to raise an army that he marched down to Nanjing, where he was enthusiastically greeted by the city's eunuchs.

Eunuchs! And you wonder where Chinese cinema comes from. Within the Imperial Court, it was typically the eunuchs who controlled the levers of power. This is because, severed from their manhood, they could be trusted to wander among the hundreds of comely concubines that resided with the emperor. The new emperor, however, had fallen under the sway of the mandarins, the well-educated bureaucrats who managed the empire's day-to-day affairs. This did not please the eunuchs. They'd been castrated, after all, and while being able to hit the high notes in the imperial karaoke bar had its benefits, it did little to alleviate this sudden fall from favor. And so when Zhu Di arrived in Nanjing with his army, the eunuchs flung open the gates. *We welcome Zhu Di!* they squeaked.

Zhu Di claimed the Dragon Throne for himself, changed his name to Yongle, and set about killing any possible rivals to his reign. The old emperor, Zhu Di's nephew, Zhu Yunwen, was never found. Some suggest that he may have died in the fire that consumed his palace. Others that he escaped by disguising himself as a monk. In any event, Zhu Di issued a decree ordering the extermination of the ten agnates. Traditionally in China, when killing political opponents, it was acceptable to exterminate the three agnates—the father, son, and grandson of the doomed opponent. Zhu Di extended this to the tenth degree to include pretty much anyone remotely related to the former emperor, excepting of course himself. Some 8,000 family and friends of Zhu Yunwen were killed, often in a gruesome, highly creative manner.

Zhu Di then moved the capital to Beijing, which had once been the imperial capital of the Yuan Dynasty, which is the polite term for describing the Mongol hordes who ruled China in the thirteenth and fourteenth centuries. The dynastic capital was an itinerant place, having been located as far west as Xian during much of the first millennium, and emperors saw it as their privilege as Sons of Heaven to move the capital according to their whims and needs. The Mongol leader Kublai Khan had made his capital in present-day Beijing, then called Dadu. It was Zhu Di's father, the peasant Zhu Yuanzhang, who had led an uprising that dislodged the Mongols from Beijing, a feat that enabled him to call himself the Son of Heaven, founder of the Ming Dynasty, without anybody calling him out on it.

When Zhu Di came to power, trouble still lurked on the northern border. Tamerlane, a Mongol leader who had a notable penchant for stacking the skulls of his slain enemies in enormous pyramids, was threatening to invade China, returning the country to Mongol rule. Zhu Di didn't much like the sound of that; thus he moved his capital and his million-man army north to Beijing, where he could counter the threat. Fortunately, Tamerlane soon died, and as his descendants began the squabbling that would eventually doom the Mongol Empire, Zhu Di found himself with some idle time on his hands. And so he began to build.

The scale of building can only be described as epic. Hundreds of thousands of people were forcibly uprooted from towns and villages around the country and sent to Beijing, where they were guarded by the army, since without Mongols to fight they didn't have anything else to do. The challenge, of course, was feeding such a multitude of people in a region where winters were long and bleak and the growing season was short. Zhu Di's solution was to enlarge the Grand Canal, which had first been constructed during the Wu Dynasty, way back in the late fifth century. At that point, Europe had descended into the Dark Ages and men like Conan the Barbarian roamed the earth, smiting enemies while reveling in the lamentations of their women, whereas China was already building a canal that would eventually link Beijing with Hangzhou, more than a thousand miles away.

With the canal enlarged, Zhu Di ordered thousands of barges to deliver the enormous amount of grain needed to feed this city of soldiers and workers. Elsewhere in China people starved, but Zhu Di pushed relentlessly on. He had aspirations. Forests were denuded of wood to build not only the Forbidden City, but the vast number of barges plying up and down the Grand Canal. And then, once the scope of his ambition was realized, he began emptying forests as far away as Vietnam. This was because Zhu Di wanted a navy.

Not just any navy, but the most powerful and immense navy the world had ever seen. Enormous treasure ships were constructed, each requiring the wood of roughly 300 acres of hardwood forest. Said to be more than 400 feet long, a treasure ship was capable of carrying upward of 500 people. Zhu Di built a fleet around his sixty-two treasure ships, and by the time this armada was put to water there were more than 300 ships capable of carrying 28,000 people.

This mass of ships was led by Admiral Zheng He, one of the more intriguing men to take to sea at the dawn of the age of exploration. To begin with, he carried his penis in a box. And not just his penis, but his *cojones* too. His dismemberment had been particularly thorough. A Muslim, Zheng He had been captured as a boy of eleven by the Ming Army in distant Yunnan Province. Deprived of water, Zheng He was then castrated, and once the threat of infection subsided, he was given gallons of water to drink, until finally his urethra burst and a tube was inserted. (The author is wincing; he can barely go on.) Few people survived the procedure, and yet an imperial decree was needed to prevent men from self-castration (the author doesn't know what to say), but such, apparently, was the lure of the power held by the imperial eunuchs that men were willing to take the knife to their own manhood (completely inexplicable).

Zheng He went on to become a servant of the Ming emperor, and soon he had acquired a nickname, San Bao, which—unsurprising, really—means the Three Jewels. With his special box beside him, Zheng He moved on to become possibly the best-traveled man of his era. Eighty years before Columbus set forth in the *Santa Maria,* a pitifully small boat compared to one of Zhu Di's treasure ships, Zheng He roamed the seas during the seven grand expeditions he undertook between 1405 and 1433. He crossed the Indian Ocean, alighted upon India and Sri Lanka, visited the Arabian Peninsula, moseyed down the coast of Africa, picked up a few giraffes to stock the zoo in Beijing, and brought back local envoys and ambassadors so they could kowtow before the emperor. Some, like Menzies, even speculate that Zheng He was the first foreigner to discover North America. In any event, China stood on the cusp of ruling the world. No nation had a fleet that could match that of the eunuch from Yunnan.

And then China disappeared behind its walls. Its fleet of treasure ships was left to rot. The Middle Kingdom would become peripheral as Europe arose from its long slumber. How can this be, you wonder? China was at the very edge of global domination, something every nation wants, no? And yet they turned back.

Apparently, Heaven had become unhappy with the Son of Heaven. Heaven went so far as to hurl a lightning bolt at the Forbidden City, burning most of it to the barest embers. Crushed by this display of celestial approbation, Zhu Di was no longer a match for the imperial mandarins, who had become appalled at the expense of money and resources that Zhu Di's ambitions cost. Conscious that the dynasty was at stake, Zhu Di began the retreat inward that culminated with his successor. And the eunuch admiral died at sea on the last great voyage of the treasure ships.

The Forbidden City would be rebuilt. But global dominance would have to wait. As I wandered through the resplendent halls of the Forbidden City—noting, as I watched a group of small boys, that while smoking was clearly advertised as forbidden, peeing on walls was apparently okay—I couldn't help but wonder about what a fickle thing fate can be.

"Imagine," I said to Dan, "if lightning hadn't struck that day. The Chinese Empire could have swallowed the world."

"Oh," said Dan cheerily. "There's still time for that."

# 5

It is remarkable how quickly a country like China can reduce a foreigner—this foreigner, in any case—to a state of childlike powerlessness. True, I had traveled to places where people could still recall what a human being tastes like (it tastes like pork). I had visited islands where the inhabitants had not seen more than a dozen foreigners in their lives. I had wandered in Russia when the country seemed on the cusp of civil war, and, for one particularly memorable week, I had found myself in the midst of an actual civil war in Bosnia after making my way to a Muslim enclave that was presently being obliterated by Serbian shelling. Perhaps more important, I had made my way out of that war zone. And yet in Beijing, as a traveler, I felt like a quivering cupcake.

No doubt this was partly the result of my incomprehension of the language. In China, if you don't speak Chinese, and even more important, if you can't read Chinese, you are essentially helpless. When an elderly man began to speak with me as I wandered through one of Beijing's *hutongs,* the rapidly dwindling labyrinths of traditional neighborhoods in Beijing, I had absolutely no idea what he was saying. Perhaps he was encouraging me to have a savory dumpling. It would make me feel harmonious inside. Or perhaps he was expressing some indelicate thought about the barbarian wandering around his neighborhood. You just don't know, and all you can muster is a shrug and a big dopey grin, causing your counterpart to offer a contemptuous wave because, clearly, you are an imbecile.

It was the same when trying to get myself from point A to point B with a minimum of drama. While Beijing has gone to some lengths to make things easier for the Chinese-impaired, including offering some signs with the street names translated into Roman letters (or pinyin, as the Chinese call the Romanized version of their language), the fact remains that the vast majority of signs offer nothing more than Chinese characters, which makes things just a trifle problematic for those with a predilection for getting lost. I might set forth for what my map confidently informed me was the broad avenue known as Dongzhimenwai Daijie. Invariably, I'd soon find myself wandering around, hopelessly lost, staring at a sign in Chinese that did nothing to alleviate the complete and total befuddlement I felt.

Even Dan, who had lived in China for years now, periodically had difficulty getting himself from one place to another. Aware of how utterly incapable I was, he had taken to escorting me back to my hotel whenever we parted ways. One evening, after he had given directions to the cabdriver, the driver apologized and explained that he was new to the job, had just arrived in Beijing from his village, and could he please repeat the street name.

"Dengshikou Xijie," Dan repeated.

"Dengshikou Xijie?" said the driver.

"Dui, Dengshikou Xijie."

They spent a minute going back and forth, repeating the street name, which was apparently the name of a well-known avenue in central Beijing that every cabdriver surely knows.

"Just explain that it's near the Crowne Plaza," I offered helpfully.

"I can't," Dan said. "I don't know the character for Crowne Plaza."

"Do you mean to tell me that you can't just say Crowne Plaza or Holiday Inn and have the taxi driver take you there?"

"No. You need to say it in Chinese."

Jesus, I thought. I had no intention of staying in Western hotels during my travels, but I'd hoped to be able to use their brand names as landmarks in the major cities. For the next couple of minutes, Dan sought to explain precisely where it was that we hoped to go, until finally the driver had his ah-ha moment.

Ahhh . . . *Dengshikou Xijie!*

"But that's what you've been saying all along," I pointed out.

"He said that I used the wrong tone and that's why he didn't understand."

This did not bode well for me. Dan had studied Chinese for fifteen years and still tripped over tones. I had studied *Chinese for Dummies* for a matter of weeks and hadn't even reached the tone section.

But it was written Chinese that truly had me stymied, and with my level of ignorance menus had become my nemesis. I carried a pocket dictionary, of course, but it was useless as a tool for navigating a menu. Dictionaries are written in pinyin, which is helpful when you're trying to say something but not when you're trying to read something. And the Chinese don't read pinyin. They read Chinese. No method of translation will allow a traveler to look at a Chinese character on a menu, flip open the dictionary, and learn that this amalgamation of lines and squiggles is the character for Basted Elephant Testicles. Perhaps you want Basted Elephant Testicles. Perhaps you don't. But what you do really want to know in China is what, precisely, you're ordering. Or maybe not.

And so one day, I found myself on an English-speaking tour bus heading for the Great Wall of China. I was in the general vicinity and felt compelled to at least see it, this wall. I had asked Dan what he, as a titan of the Orient, would recommend for a superior Wall-viewing experience.

"You should hike the Wall from Jinshanling to Simatai," he told me. "It's a very evocative part of the Wall away from all the tourists, and you can really get a feel for Imperial China."

"Excellent. And how would one get to this place, Jin-shin-shin?"

"From the northern Beijing bus station, you can get on a minibus to Miyun. From there, you need to find another minibus to Bakeshiyang. And make sure you take a daypack with food and water. You probably won't encounter anyone there, and it's a pretty rugged hike."

I considered.

"Or I could take a tour."

"Or you could take a tour."

Given that I still didn't have a clue what I was doing, the cocoon of a tour bus seemed, at the time, like a good option. And so one morning I was greeted by a young Chinese man who called himself Tony, which, I suspected, was not his birth name.

"How much you pay for your ticket?" Tony asked.

"Two hundred and fifty yuan."

"Okay. Don't tell anyone. Other people paid 300."

Or 200, and I was the sucker. Nevertheless, the trip to see the Great Wall at Badaling, fifty miles north of Beijing, would soon offer plenty more opportunities for me to divest myself of yuan. As we finally escaped through the ever-sprawling, traffic-congested, filthy haze of Beijing, I listened to the conversations among my fellow tourists.

"I think there's too much of an entitlement mentality in Europe," David, a middle-aged denizen of Kansas, was saying. "I am very much in favor of free trade, but there's too much government involvement over there." He wagged his finger at the Frenchman beside him. "And Jacques Chirac," he snorted, "was a disaster for France."

Behind David, an Australian Muslim of Lebanese descent was chatting with the Venezuelan Jew sitting beside him.

"Halal and Kosher? It's the same thing, mate. Arab and Jew? We're the same people. We're Semites with big noses."

Other than David of Kansas, his apparently mute wife, and myself, all the other passengers on this love bus had come to China for business reasons. The Venezuelan had arrived with his equally fashion-conscious brother to buy motorcycles for the dealership they owned in Caracas. The two Australians had come for the Spring China Import and Export Fair in Guangzhou, otherwise known as the Canton Fair, a biannual event that attracts upward of 25,000 booths and nearly 200,000 attendees. A German had just finished a six-month stint on the island of Hainan, where he was involved with a factory making car-engine parts. The Bolivian man was in China to obtain training from a Chinese cell phone company. And the Frenchman stoically absorbing the opining of one David of Kansas had spent his time in China hiring programmers for his software company.

I turned my attention away from David of Kansas and his thoughts about the evils of socialized medicine, and paid heed to the landscape unraveling outside the window. We sped past villages and wound our way around cragged hills speckled with farms. How anyone managed to grow anything here was a mystery I could not resolve. The land was profoundly parched. Once, not so long ago, a farmer in the region wouldn't have had to dig more than a few feet to establish a well. Now he'd have to dig a half-mile or so until he reached an aquifer. That's a lot of shoveling. As I watched the barren landscape roll by, Tony pointed out the obvious.

"You see, it is very dry here. We are experiencing a very long drought. So I ask you, on behalf of the people of Beijing, not to use too much water. Don't take long showers. There's only five years of water supply left for Beijing."

Well, I thought. No wonder the Chinese government was doing everything possible short of a rain dance to seed the clouds for rain. Every few months, authorities would announce that scientists had succeeded in discovering a method for triggering rain showers. Meanwhile, the drought continued. In response, the Chinese government drew up a plan to bring water north. Naturally, this being China, it would be a big plan, a $60 billion network of rivers and canals that would transport water from the drenched south to the bone-dry northern provinces.

One would think, after all the fussing Zhu Di had had to endure with his canals, that perhaps the Chinese might want to reconsider having their capital in a subarctic desert. But, of course, in China it's not really possible to move tens of millions of people anymore except, apparently, from the countryside into the cities, which doesn't quite alleviate a water problem. There is no vast empty hinterland in China capable of sustaining a huge population that isn't already presently sustaining— barely—a huge population. There is no great emptiness in the middle of the country like there is in the United States. (I know. Technically speaking, there are people in Nebraska. I've been there. I met both of them.)

And so the Chinese have turned to engineering. Even if they should succeed in pumping the floods of the south to the dry north, it's not entirely clear whether northerners would be grateful, considering the quality of the water. One-third of all the freshwater in China—that is, all the rivers and lakes in this enormous country—is considered unsafe for *industrial* use. When the water is so vile that you can't even use it in a lead paint factory because it's too dirty, I'd say you have a water problem.

"So we are approaching the tomb of Zhu Di," Tony said as our bus clambered toward a parking lot.

Oh good, I thought. I hadn't realized it would be my buddy Zhu Di's tomb that we would be visiting. All I had heard about the Ming Tombs was that they were awfully boring, a sideshow really from the Great Wall, and just another way for tour operators to extract money from tourists not yet brave enough to ride a local bus on their own.

"Do you see where the tombs are located, on the hillside overlooking the river? It's located there for good feng shui."

"But, Tony," I noted. "There is no river."

"This is true. But in former times there was a river."

"So does the absence of a river change the feng shui?" I asked. "Are we now in a place with bad feng shui?"

"This is a good question to which I do not have a good answer."

In any event, there was very little to see, simply a small hole in a hillside surrounded by a few pagodas and gardens. Though, very helpfully, there was a sign informing us that *Zhu Di was an outstanding and remarkable emperor of the Ming Dynasty. Sporting a well-groomed beard, he was pleasant and good-looking.*

I had always suspected that Zhu Di was pleasant and good-looking. But the aforementioned rumors were correct. The Ming Tombs were not among the more scintillating sights in China.

"We cannot excavate anymore," Tony informed us. "Because as soon as we take old things out of the ground, the pollution destroys it. So we are waiting for new technology before we dig further."

Reducing pollution, apparently, wasn't the obvious go-to solution. We returned to the bus according to our cultural heritage—Anglo-Saxons first, Latins dawdling in the distance—and drove onward to join a thousand other buses parked in front of the Traditional Jade Factory. I spent possibly twenty-five seconds lingering inside the cavernous showroom before realizing that there are far more interesting ways to get ripped off in China. Indeed, I would soon discover one as we pulled into the parking lot in front of our next stop: the Traditional Chinese Medicine Center.

We were led into a classroom, where we were greeted by a nurse—or at least a woman dressed up like a nurse—who proceeded to inform us of the wonders of traditional Chinese medicine, and that here, right now, were world-class specialists who could help us, today, now, diagnose our ailments and provide the treatment garnered from a 3,000-year tradition of medical knowledge. In came the doctors, looking very doctor-like, and soon my fellow tourists were lining up for this once-in-a-lifetime opportunity to be seen by the World's Very Greatest specialists in this area. Strangely, I did not see any Chinese people lining up for a consultation with the superstars of traditional Chinese medicine. As it turned out, the young among us were all suspiciously healthy. But if you happened to be a middle-aged man with an inner tube of a gut and a florid expression, oh dear. There were gallbladder problems. Kidney issues. And the liver? Best not to ask. Fortunately, there were cures. And there was a traditional pharmacy right here on the premises, available now to fill orders for powdered gingerroot and the crumbled leaves of a birch tree.

David of Kansas, I was pleased to see, did indeed have an open mind when it came to other cultures, and he returned to the bus with five bags of powder and an ashen expression. I could not bring myself to see the doctor, since I'm highly susceptible to the power of suggestion, and I feared precisely what had befallen him—he who now knew that the welfare of his colon depended entirely on the consumption of eggshells from the red-bellied swiftlet, found only in the high mountains of Sichuan.

At last we moved on to Badaling, one of the most well-preserved sections of the wall. It is indeed a very great wall, this Great Wall of China. Richard Nixon said so himself. "I think that you would have to conclude that this is a great wall," he said when he visited Badaling in 1972. Unsurprisingly, one doesn't find Nixon's ringing endorsement of the wall in the Chinese government's marketing literature. Instead, what you find is this:

*The Great Wall is not only the magnum opus of human being but also the soul of China!*

The soul of China! The magnum opus of human being!

They sure do know how to bring in a crowd, I thought as I joined, I don't know, perhaps a million, possibly 2 million, visitors jostling among stalls and carts selling trinkets and postcards on the edge of the parking lot. There were camel rides and donkey rides and immense lines for the cable cars bringing people up to the Great Wall itself. Badaling is the place where the wall becomes a spectacle, a place where daredevils leap over the wall on skateboards and motorcycles. Upon its stone ramparts were vast crowds and innumerable beggars; the restored guardhouses smelled like urine, and it wasn't long before I began to wonder what, exactly, I was doing there.

*If you come to China without climbing the Great Wall, just as well you come to Paris without visiting the Iron Tower!*

So true. And so I climbed farther. As I made my way through the swarming crowds, I resolved to stop being such a cupcake, that it was time to forgo the tour buses, because I could see nothing of China through the teeming masses of tourists. I followed the worn stones past the refreshment stands, up and over the steep inclines, until at last the crowd had dribbled to the last outliers, and finally I could see, really see, this Great Wall of China.

It cascaded over rugged mountains—indifferent to cliffs, unimpressed by summits, impervious to obstacles—as it spilled into the distance, a jagged stone snake uncoiling across China. No one seems to know quite how long the Great Wall really is. Some say it's 4,500 miles long; others that it's a more modest 1,500 miles. The true scope is unknown, because they are still finding parts of it; in 2001 and 2002, another 360 miles of the Great Wall revealed itself. But surely, you think, measuring the length of the Great Wall must be a straightforward thing to do. Simply start at one end—say, its eastern terminus near North Korea—and keep walking until you reach the other end. But the Great Wall of China, it turns out, is not one long continuous wall of bricks. It is, in fact, several walls. The oldest were built during the Qin Dynasty in the third century B.C. Designed to keep the Mongols out, the original walls were built with pressed earth, stones, and, when available, the bodies of the workers who died during the construction. Over the centuries, as successive emperors added to the walls, more than two million peasants would die building what would come to be known as the 10,000 Li Wall, a *li* being a unit of measurement that is roughly 500 yards long.

Much of the wall we see today, however, was built in the sixteenth century during the Ming Dynasty. Scholars still speculate as to why, exactly, the Ming emperors went to such great lengths to build a wall that Mongol invaders could, very simply, go around. Some have posited that the Great Wall was reflective of imperial paralysis—*Should I attack the Mongols? Should I trade with them? I dunno. Maybe I'll just build a really big wall.*

And, of course, the Chinese are very fond of walls. All the farms we passed had walled compounds. In restaurants, patrons prefer to be seated among the walls within the private dining rooms. Karaoke is conducted not out in the open, but behind walls. It is a nation of walls. Walls are celebrated; they are insisted upon. There must always be walls. And so it's unsurprising that the greatest wall ever built is in China.

But this wall, unlike most in China, was not ultimately effective. Subsequently, over the centuries that followed its construction, it was allowed to fall into ruin, becoming nothing more than a brick repository for nearby villages. Why buy new bricks when there's a really big wall nearby, just sitting there doing nothing? It was simply a huge, pointless wall that went on and on and on. So they took the bricks, built homes, shops, and wells until some enterprising official discovered that there was good money to be made with the Great Wall, that tourists would flock there wanting camel rides and bird whistles, and they could combine a trip to the Wall with a visit to the Traditional Medicine Center. And a jade factory too. Build it and they will come, he thought, and so he took pen to paper.

*The Great Wall which be created by the human being will be your nice mind forever!*

And so it is.

# 6

I had, during my time in Beijing, already managed to find myself yearning for a place far, far away from the pounding of jackhammers and the wailing of buzz saws and the unrelenting honkyness of urban life in China. This, I recognized, was not a good sign when confronted by a journey through coastal China, a region proudly called home by hundreds of millions of people. But really, you could say that about any region of China. Beyond the deserts of Xinjiang and the cold steppes of Inner Mongolia and the lofty summits of Tibet, every region in China calls itself home to hundreds of millions of people. It is indeed a very crowded country. And so, for what I hoped might be a brief respite from the urban whirl, I'd decided to climb mighty Tai Shan, the most revered mountain in China. It is said that those who climb Tai Shan live to be a hundred. I wasn't at all certain I wanted to live to be a hundred, but I did know that I'd like to have the option.

I had often been cautioned that in China I should put my regular glasses aside and replace them with special lenses that allow me to see things in the Chinese context. It was always the same words: *Chinese context*. And so that is what I did. Somehow, I had managed to navigate the tumult of the Beijing train station and boarded the train to Tai'an, 250 miles to the south. And so, rolling out of Beijing and into Shandong Province, I took my glasses off and put my magic spectacles on and looked out the window and viewed the world within the Chinese context. There, I observed. The hundreds of people scavenging in the dump. It's fine. Fifty years ago, they would have been dead from hunger. Look. A bird's nest, the first evidence I had yet encountered that there are, in fact, birds in China. True, I hadn't actually seen the bird, but a nest suggested bird life. And, of course, forty years ago during Mao's great bird purge, that wasn't the case. That village of crumbling red bricks nestled against a pond of luminous colors. A kaleidoscope of colors because the water was profoundly toxic. But it's okay, it was evidence of progress. Opportunities. There was pollution thirty years ago, but no opportunities. Now anyone can make money in China. And what's a little pollution? It's a sign of development. The dry, barren riverbeds . . . No worries. Chinese engineering will always triumph over nature.

And then I put my reading glasses back on and read the newspaper. I was sitting on a small foldout chair in the hallway of a sleeping car. I had no need for a sleeping berth as it was a midday train, a six-hour journey through green farmland under a gray, soot-stained sky. But since I was traveling the rails of China during Golden Week along with 150 million other people, every seat had been sold out except for the higher-priced sleepers. Train tickets are divided into four classes—hard seat, soft seat, hard sleeper, and soft sleeper. The Chinese, of course, are among the most frugal people on the planet. Few people spend their hard-earned *kuai* on a daytime soft-sleeper.

I shared my cabin with two cheerful kids, along with their mother and grandmother, who were happily sprawled on the two lower births contentedly munching on fish heads. In the next cabin, a quartet of Party officials was busy spewing a fog of blue smoke that hung in the train car like a carcinogenic mist. There were, I was surprised to note, prominent No Smoking signs throughout the train. As I sat reading, a young train attendant approached the cabin of smokers and bowing, deeply and often, kindly reminded them that smoking was forbidden on the train. Moments later, she returned with ashtrays.

I returned to my reading, an engrossing article in the government-run English language newspaper *China Daily* about all the shoddy Western goods that had to be recalled in China. It's terrible, the article suggested. You just can't trust what comes out of the West these days. I took a sip from my bottle of water, idly recalling that 50 percent of all bottled water in China is contaminated. The label said Nestlé, but it could just as well be Beijing tap. I put my magic spectacles back on and tried to view the bottle of water in the Chinese context. But they made my head spin and I took them off again.

Outside, beyond the gritty sprawl of Jinan, in a landscape of stony hills and farm fields in spring bloom, we rumbled past power plant after power plant. What are those, I'd wondered, a few miles back, those perfect conical mountains pointing to the sky? They were dusty slag heaps, it turned out, the enormous stacks of coal that power China. And they were everywhere, stack after stack. One, two, three, the power plants stretched on to the horizon. It's an astonishing sight, rolling past farms in the shadows of chimneys with billowing plumes of smoke. I had, of course, lost hope that I'd know what, precisely, I was eating in China, and it was enlightening to see that my vegetables came braised in the unfiltered emissions of hundreds of coal-fired plants.

And there are so very many of them. In 2005 alone, China built enough power plants to power the United Kingdom. In 2006, China built enough power plants to power France. It is, frankly, nearly impossible to comprehend the scale of China's energy demands. The United Kingdom is no Togo. France is no Fiji. These are two of the most industrialized nations in the world. And yet every year, China added another France or United Kingdom in energy production.

Most of the power plants are relatively small. And nearly all of them burn coal. This is because China has an awful lot of coal, mountains of it really, and to obtain it thousands of miners die each year, as many as six thousand a year by some estimates. In a single twelve-month period, China burns more coal than the United States, Japan, and Europe *combined*.

I'd had no intention of dwelling upon air pollution when I boarded the train. My brain was on a stirring hike in the cragged mountains of Shandong Province, far removed, I'd hoped, from the cough-inducing, eye-watering haze of the capital. Only one percent of urban residents in China—and there are 400 million of them—breathe air that might, kindly, be regarded as safe by Western standards. What block did they live on? I had wondered in Beijing, pleased at the prospect of departing the city for some fresh mountain air. But, as the train chugged through the countryside, I began to wonder. Where's the blue sky? It's got to be around here somewhere. The weather map in *China Daily* had promised sun.

And then, as we passed the umpteenth power plant, came the slow-to-dawn realization that there would be no blue sky. There would be no crisp-yet-warm, winter-has-been-con-quered, let's-celebrate-the-spring air. Instead, there would be smog. There would always be smog. Enough to drift across the vastness of the Pacific and settle like snow upon the mountains of the Sierra Nevada and even the waters of the Great Lakes.

How could people live in this? I wondered. How could they put it up with it? The air was so rank and dense with pollutants that even a Republican would be hollering for clean air. Really, it's that bad. And then, as I perused my newspaper, it occurred to me that it's very possible that the Chinese are not aware, exactly, of how appalling their air truly is.

The World Bank estimates that 700,000 people die each year in China simply from breathing air. The city of San Francisco has roughly 700,000 people. So, too, Indianapolis. And Austin. Lose these cities and people are bound to notice. One would think that the Chinese would be upset by this appalling state of affairs. And the Chinese government does, too, which is why it refuses to publish information confirming just how devastatingly foul China's air is. And thus we hear *Los Angeles is polluted too*.

Meanwhile, as I finished an article on the government's efforts to teach migrant workers good manners, the train pulled into Tai'an, the small industrial city near the base of lofty Tai Shan. I hopped off, walked briskly through a train station that smelled like piss, and found the taxi stand, where I soon understood what it is like to be regarded as prey. The taxi drivers couldn't believe their good fortune. A *laowai*! Foreigner! I felt a sudden bond with sheep. I settled on a taxi, and as the other drivers congratulated him on his good fortune, we sped past an enormous bust of Lei Feng, Hero of the Revolution. I took note of what I could understand—*Supermarket for Beverages, Tai'an Power Supply Business Hall, Silicon Valley Grand Hotel*—and tried hard to ignore the heart-thumping fact that we were racing, horn blasting, up the wrong side of the road. Microseconds before crashing into a truck, we veered away and I emerged, heart palpitating, at a garish hotel on the edge of town. This had been the only hotel I could find that still had rooms available, and now standing before it, I could see why. It was inconveniently located, and gaudy as a hotel in Reno, but one that didn't have to comply with anything so burdensome as building codes.

"Passport, please," said the young woman at the front desk. She showed it to her colleague and they spent a moment giggling. "Where you from? I have not heard of this country Netherlands. I think it is maybe in Europe."

"Excellent guess."

I made my way to my room, opened the flimsy door, and noted that among the grooming products lined up along the bathroom shelf were packets of his and her Erotic Sex Lotion and packages of his and her polyester shorts provocatively labeled "Sexywear." A moment later, the telephone rang.

*"Nihao,"* I said, and then followed a moment later with "I'm sorry. I don't speak Chinese."

There was a momentary pause. "Massagee?" said the woman on the line.

"Er . . ." What is this, *messagee*? "Thank you, but no."

I hung up, puzzled, and opened the curtains to a vista dominated by the sputtering power plant next door. Well, I thought. At least I had a view.

The next morning, I found myself in a misty drizzle pondering the cragged head of Pan Gu, the Taoist deity who, very thoughtfully, took it upon himself to separate the earth from the sky. This was no snap-of-the fingers event. Indeed, in comparison to Pan Gu's travails, creating the world in a mere seven days seems slothful in the extreme. It took Pan Gu 18,000 years to sufficiently separate the earth from the sky so that life could commence, and since he was awfully tired when at last he finished—you can hardly blame him—he settled down for a rest. His eyes became the sun and the moon, and his limbs became four of China's most sacred mountains—Hua Shan in Shanxi, Song Shan in Henan, Heng Shan in Hunan, and because this is China and everything is just a little more complicated than it needs to be, another mountain called Heng Shan in Shanxi. Tai Shan, as the head of Pan Gu, is the most revered mountain of them all.

The Buddhists, too, have a soft spot for Tai Shan, and ever since the second century B.C., people have bedecked the mountain with temples and calligraphy. There is even a staircase that winds up to the very summit of Tai Shan, nearly 6,000 feet up in the clouds. Altogether, there are 6,660 steps of stone leading up the old Imperial route. Confucius, who lived in nearby Qufu, had climbed Tai Shan and famously declared *The world is small*. Mao, too, had somehow managed to waddle up to the peak, and after viewing the first rays of dawn, he proclaimed, *The East is red*. So deep!

Over the centuries, seventy-two emperors had stood upon Tai Shan. Indeed, the mountain was so important in Chinese cosmology that a new emperor was expected to hightail it pronto to Tai Shan to receive a special heavenly blessing. Intriguingly, only five of them went on to climb to the summit. A failed attempt was regarded as a divine rebuke. So why risk it?

And, as I was very pleased to learn, Neil Peart, the drummer and lyricist for the Canadian rock band Rush, had also apparently climbed Tai Shan. In the early 1980s, Rush was the pride of the Canadian rock world. Admittedly, this was a very small world, composed, really, of Rush and the twiddly-winks from Vancouver, the band Loverboy. Nevertheless, for a certain thirteen-year-old boy in Toronto, Rush was the be-all-and-end-all of his rock world, leading, in time, to his joining the Official Rush Fan Club, which sent him buttons that he proudly wore on his parka, while he tried to conceal the intense jealousy he felt for the boy in his class who claimed to have singer Geddy Lee's mother on his paper route. Oh yes, this thirteen-year-old was a *serious* fan. He had all their records and he played them every day on his record player, a record player that was never sullied by the likes of Journey, the fakers.

And then, in 1983, Rush released the atrocity of an album that was *Signals*. What is this? cried the thirteen-year-old boy, who had stood in line for hours at the record store with money he had earned delivering newspapers *by sled* so that he could be among the very first in the whole of Canada to have the new, oh-so-eagerly awaited Rush record. He listened to this album on his record player. And he felt betrayed. He could not believe his ears. But it was true. It was unmistakable. Undeniable. There were *synthesizers*. *Et tu,* Rush, the boy said, swelling with bitterness. Have you, too, gone to the dark side? And he felt so lost that he drifted, aimlessly and alone, for two whole months, eight bleak and cruel weeks, until, from somewhere in the darkness, he was found by Bono, who raised him up and made him whole.

But eventually, this thirteen-year-old boy grew up to be a man, a man who one day found himself in a chintzy hotel in Tai'an, sitting in a smoky Business Center, idly wondering what a censored Google search would reveal about the mountain known as Tai Shan, when he discovered that in 1987—and by 1987, the year of Big Audio Dynamite, he was so over Rush—Rush had recorded a song called Tai Shan, and suddenly the memories flooded back and he was lost in a bittersweet reverie.

> *I stood at the top of the mountain*
> *And China sang to me*
> *In the peaceful haze of harvest time*
> *A song of eternity*

You're smoking crack, Neil, if you think the haze that permeates China is the peaceful haze of harvesttime. I mean, come on. Clearly, the bitterness had never lifted. Nevertheless, as I stood in line at the base of the mountain to pay the entrance fee, I hoped that China would sing to me too. Actually, as I watched a nearby vendor do a brisk business selling bird whistles, I wished that China would just quiet down for a while.

At the gate, a sign informed us that old people (sixty to seventy years old), students, and maimed persons would have to pay only 50 yuan to climb Tai Shan. Not too many mountains offer a discount to the maimed, but Tai Shan does. The sign went on to inform us that teachers, provincial model workers, and combat model heroes also received a discount. Should one be tempted to proclaim oneself a Combat Model Hero— and I certainly was—you will be asked to provide a certificate confirming your status.

I passed the First Gate of Heaven, a square arch emblazoned with calligraphy, and started to clamber up the stairs, which wound ever upward through a forest of pine and cypress trees. Huge boulders and rock formations were emblazoned with ancient calligraphy, but since for this hiker they were about as inscrutable as, well, Chinese calligraphy, I turned my attention to the signs I could read. *Please fling the rubbish into the dustbin.* And I started to look for rubbish to fling.

I continued upward through a damp, muggy drizzle and it wasn't long before I began to sweat. Tai Shan, I was discovering, was no stroll through the park. True, I was climbing stairs, but these were narrow stairs, suitable perhaps for tiny little bound feet but treacherous for others, particularly when they were as rain-slicked as they were that day. And, while I do want to commend the hard work that must have gone into building a stone staircase up a mountain, I did begin to wish that perhaps a little more effort could have been expended so that each step was similar to the others. But, of course, each step was different—a stutter step here, a two-foot chasm there—making it impossible to establish a rhythm.

I paused to take a breather. *Keep distance from the precipitous cliff,* a sign read. What cliff? I wondered. I couldn't see more than ten feet through the drizzly haze. Instead, all I could see were people. Thousands of people. Tens of thousands of people. I had, of course, known that Tai Shan was the most climbed mountain on Earth. I had envisioned a Matterhorn-type crowd, a few streams of hikers, but in no way was I prepared for the seething masses scampering up Tai Shan. Good call, I muttered to myself. Wanted to get away from it all for a couple of days, did you? A little nature. Serenity. And so you choose to climb the most climbed mountain in the world in a country of one and a half billion people, give or take a hundred million.

While I stood there ruminating, I noticed people pointing at me. *Laowai,* I heard. Very often, it's not meant kindly, either. And then "Picture," said a man waving a camera. A moment later, I was surrounded by the Zhang family from Hunan, or whoever the heck they were, smiling for the camera. *Xie xie.* Thank you. Well, good, I thought, at least my presence here as an odd curiosity to be gawked at and photographed was bringing joy and mirth to many.

I trudged upward, momentarily pleased to have summited, until I noticed a sign informing me that I was presently at the Midway Gate to Heaven, and that I had roughly another 2,000 feet in elevation yet to conquer. Well, shoot, I thought, noticing a man who had just managed to hawk an enormous amount of phlegm out of his mouth while still keeping a cigarette dangling from his lips. If he could do it, I certainly could. And with a deep breath I resumed my climb into the clouds.

Fortunately, the mountain offers plenty of diversionary temples and pagodas along the way. I entered one, a dimly lit temple dominated by a large golden Buddha. Or perhaps it was a bodhisattva. Or maybe Pan Gu. Really, it's so hard to tell. In front of the Buddha-esque statue lay plates of food. I made a mental note—snacks? why?—and as I stood pondering this curiosity I was approached by an affable young monk.

"Would you like to make an offering to the goddess?"

"Absolutely," I said, pleased to learn that the statue was a goddess.

"Sign your name here," the monk indicated, pointing to a ledger. "One hundred *kuai*."

Fifteen dollars. That's no small sum in China. I wondered what I would get in return for this largesse.

"You take the joss sticks and bow three times in front of the goddess and say a prayer," informed the monk.

"And what should I be praying for?"

"Wealth."

"Wealth?"

"Yes. You make an offering and bow and pray, and the goddess will make sure you become a wealthy man."

I pondered this for a moment. The cost of health insurance was becoming onerous. And the price of food certainly wasn't going down. And we'd probably need a new car in the next few years. I decided that I was amenable to wealth. I paid the monk. He took his chop, a carved seal that the Chinese use much as we use signatures and notary publics to legitimize a document, and stamped it next to my name. And then he placed a small red bag over my head.

"Inside," he said, "is a Taoist medallion. It is very holy."

Indeed, there was a round golden medallion inside. "A gift bag too. Thank you very much."

I did my devotions, and as I prayed for loot, I could hear from somewhere in the depths of my brain the stern voice of Sister Mary Anthony reciting the Ten Commandments—*Thou shalt have no other gods before me*—and I felt a sudden chill. But then I reflected: I was killing a lot of birds by climbing Tai Shan. I'd live to be a hundred and I'd be a wealthy man.

The last 1,000 feet or so was particularly grueling. I could feel the burn in my legs. You don't quite comprehend how many steps 6,660 steps are until you've climbed them. As I clambered up, I paused to consider the postcards available for sale. They offered a far better view of the mountain than what I could see through the damp, gray gloom. Indeed, they made it seem rather idyllic. But Tai Shan, when viewed ten, possibly twelve feet at a time, depending on the swirling mist, and all the while surrounded by thousands of breathless people, didn't leave me feeling soft and fuzzy inside. It left me feeling really knackered.

I passed through the last archway, did a desultory raising of the hands together with the others who had staggered up, and then, with my Taoist medallion dangling around my neck, found a mountaintop vendor and celebrated my ascent through the ancient Chinese custom of eating beef-flavored Ramen noodles. And it was good. And then I began to freeze. Powerful gusts of cold, cold wind buffeted the summit. I spent a half hour shivering, poking my head into temples, and then decided, That's it, I'm done. Mission accomplished. I could now confidently expect to become a rich old man.

I pondered the descent. I could man-up and climb down. Or I could take a cable car. I would take the cable car. Thousands of others were of similar thinking, and as I joined them in the now-familiar hell that is lining up in China, I thought of Neil Peart. *And China sang to me / in the peaceful haze of harvest time.* What drivel, I thought. Did you think of that while putzing about on your synthesizer, Neil? Clearly, I was in a grumpy state of mind. Indeed, I had only one thought while I was being shoved and squeezed in the line for the cable car. *The next person that cuts in front of me I am flinging off the precipitous cliff.* And yes—I glared at the elderly four-foot woman who was attempting to push me aside—that means you, Grandma.

# 7

*I*n China, it doesn't take long for a first time visitor to realize just how very delusional he has been in terms of his assumptions about the country. If nothing else, traveling through China is a profoundly humbling experience, no more so than when you realize that nearly everything you thought about the country, all your presumptions and book learning, your opinions, turn out to be utterly, completely wrong. Take, for instance, the issue of public order. I had taken as a given that in a country under one-party rule, a party that has periodically felt the need to kill a million here and a million there and to now and then run over its citizens with tanks, and that even today jails its citizens for even the slightest suggestion of dissent, public order just wouldn't be an issue. But this turns out not to be the case. Indeed, I couldn't imagine a people more disinclined to obey rules than the Chinese. And nowhere is this more evident than in a train station.

The next day, I found myself idly waiting in what a sign informed was the Communist Youth League Waiting Room inside the Tai'an train station. I was bone weary. My legs still smarted from the climb up Tai Shan. And I'd been awoken so often the night before by telephone calls from courteous young women kindly offering to provide me with a *messagee* that I finally felt compelled to take the phone off the hook. Somehow, I had managed to successfully convey my desire for a train ticket to Qingdao, a coastal city on the Yellow Sea, and after responding to the clerk's inquiries with the big dopey grin I used to answer all questions put to me in Chinese, I found a seat on a bench in the waiting room, quietly pleased that at least the Chinese were thoughtful enough to display numbers in the Western manner. I matched the numbers on my ticket with the numbers on the board, found the correct waiting area, and settled in together with hundreds of other travelers. Then the announcement came. It was time to board. And then there was pandemonium. Why? I thought, watching the melee as 500 people scrambled to squeeze through a single turnstile. Are there door prizes for the first fifty people to squeeze through? Free DVD players? Coupons offering 20 percent off the pig knuckle special at the Golden Dragon? Wearily, I looked at my ticket. It's assigned seating, right? Please?

I concluded that the seat number on my ticket was a mere ruse and that trains in China, particularly hard-seat-only trains like the one I was about to board, operate on a first-come basis. Nothing else could explain such a lunging, shove-the-kids-aside, leap-over-grandpa stampede. Grimly, I joined the horde and was sucked through, only to find that the train hadn't yet arrived. On the platform, guards checked our tickets and pointed to where each of us were to line up. Other guards were holding signs with numbers—1, 2, 3, 4, and so on—and I deduced that each number was meant to match the number of the individual train cars. I studied my ticket—seat 17 in car 4—and found the appropriate line. The train approached. The crowd tensed. The woman next to me began to vomit, extravagantly and copiously. Poor thing, I thought as I made a mental note to never, ever dine on the gloppy offerings of a train station lunch cart. Things can always be worse, however, and then, as the train pulled into the station, they grew so at an alarming pace.

As the train rolled by, conductors stood in the open doorways holding numbered signs, and as I watched them pass, I came to the startling realization that each train car was randomly numbered. 1 was not followed by 2 and then 3. There went train car 7 followed by train car 2, and was that train car 4 rolling ever farther down the platform? Again, pandemonium ensued. Hundreds of people were now running like headless chickens, chaotically dragging their bags up and down the platform, desperately seeking their car before the train departed. I leapt over the pool of vomit and raced down the platform. When at last I tumbled toward car 4, I was dismayed to discover a hundred or so others urgently trying to clamber aboard, the preferred method being to shove and toss aside anyone who might be in front. For someone coming from a culture where people are taught to wait their turn at an early age, to never push, to magnanimously insist that ladies go first, the spectacle of watching people board a train in China is a jarring, breathtaking sight to behold.

I clutched my ticket before me and noticed with some curiosity that the woman squeezed beside me carried a ticket with the same seat number. "I guess I'll be sitting on your lap," I noted with as much cheeriness as I could muster, given that my rib cage was being pummeled by a dozen elbows. I hadn't really expected to be understood, of course. I was in a provincial town in Shandong Province, and to escape the conversational dead zone caused by my linguistic limitations, I'd developed the admittedly peculiar habit of sharing my random musings with strangers, just to keep the old vocal cords humming. Typically, this was met with stony silence, and then their eyes began to flicker with the realization that they have a deranged *laowai* on their hands.

But, apparently, she had understood, and she leaned over to look at my ticket. "Is same," she agreed, and then she was swept onward into the train. By the time I boarded, all hope of obtaining a seat had long ago been lost. I wedged myself in the fetid, airless space between two cars, and as the train began the six-hour journey to Qingdao, I had a brief glimpse of harried police officers on the platform slugging it out with a passenger who had been left behind. Then, as the train began to rumble through Tai'an, the dozen men around me lit up cigarettes, and soon I was enveloped in a thick blue haze.

Excellent, I thought. I was finally having an authentic Chinese experience.

It was miserable, and as I reflected on my many attempts at quitting smoking, it occurred to me that this experience right here, stuck in a cramped, airless corner of an overflowing train next to a filthy squat toilet, breathing in the lung-searing smoke of Chinese tobacco, had I had it years ago, would have cured me instantaneously of any tobacco cravings, saving me the hundreds—no, thousands of dollars—I'd spent on nicotine patches and gum.

Soon, a conductor slipped through. I handed him my ticket. Regrettably, he felt the need to ask me a question.

"Uh . . ." I said. *"Duibuqi. Wo tingbudong."* This was my guidebook attempt at explaining that I didn't have the remotest idea of what he had just said. Sadly, however, I could not even convey my lack of understanding and be understood in China. The conductor barked something else at me.

"I'm sorry. I don't speak Chinese. You wouldn't happen to speak English, would you? No? *Parlez-vous française? Sprechen zie Deutsche? Español? Nederlandse? Cesky? Rusky?"*

So useless, these European languages. I recalled my time in Melanesia.

"Me no save Chinese. Yu tok tok Pidgin?"

Finally, my interlocutor gave up, and as he moved on he muttered something that made my train companions laugh hard and merrily until they were seized by lung-splattering hacks and coughs.

And so it went, my journey through Shandong Province. Every hour or two, the train would pull into a station, and I'd count the number of people getting off the train and compare them with the number boarding, until finally I sensed that there was a reasonable likelihood of an empty seat and I leapt into the cabin, only to discover that not only were there no free seats, but that I had lost my place among the smokers, where at least there had been a wall to lean on, and that the remainder of the trip would be spent lurching and swaying in a narrow aisleway, peri-odically apologizing to the people around me as the shifting train sent my elbow into their faces. Soon, the sun descended behind the murky haze outside and we rolled on toward Qing-dao in the darkness. I was lost in the fog of my mind, doing everything I could to resist the urge to look at my watch yet again, when suddenly I felt someone tapping on my arm.

"Come," she said.

It was the woman whose ticket I'd noticed back on the platform in Tai'an. I followed her as she led me to an open seat across from her.

"Thank you," I said. "I mean, *Xie xie.*"

"I'm sorry," she said with fluttering hands. "My English is very bad."

"No need to apologize," I said, trying to imagine an American apologizing for his poor Mandarin to a befuddled Chinese tourist in New York. "It's me who should apologize. I probably should have learned a little more Chinese before deciding to travel through your country."

Not that it would have mattered. Every attempted utterance I'd made in Chinese was met with quizzical glances.

"Your ticket?" she asked. "May I see it?"

I passed it to her.

"Yes," she said, glancing at the piece of paper. "Your ticket is for tomorrow."

"Ah . . . so that's what everyone's been trying to tell me." I reflected for a moment. Apparently, people did have assigned seats, then. So why the mayhem of boarding? As I was pondering this question, my rescuer tapped me on my knee.

"My name is Cinderella," she said.

Another curiosity! Many young Chinese had assumed Western names, but I hadn't yet encountered one quite so evocative as Cinderella. I glanced at this Cinderella, who, unique in my experience in China, had inexplicably decided to subject her hair to a perm, and tried to remember the name of the prince in the fairy tale. If the Chinese can assume new names, perhaps I could too, and then all sorts of red flags popped into my brain and I introduced myself as the man I am.

"Maarten," she repeated, uncomfortably rolling the word in her mouth. There was that pesky *r* in the middle. "What do you do?"

"Do you mean for a job? I'm, uh, a real estate investor," I offered, inwardly chuckling in a demented manner.

The train rolled on through a black night and I spent the time in stilted conversation with my new friend Cinderella. She was from Tai'an and worked in a factory in Qingdao, where she made handbags, an occupation she called "very boring." I asked her to teach me Chinese phrases like *I'll have the dog special* and *I think President Hu Jintao is very sexy,* but when it became apparent that vocalizing the Chinese language was clearly a physiological impossibility for my mouth, we settled on learning how to count to ten with my hands, which is completely different than the Western way, and learning it left me feeling giddy and triumphant.

It was nearly midnight when we pulled into Qingdao. Outside the train station, the air was cool and a mist hinted of the sea.

"Well, it was very nice meeting you, Cinderella," I said at the taxi stand.

"You are going to your hotel?" she asked. "I will go with you."

"It's all right," I said. "I can manage."

"You are a *laowai*. He will overcharge you," she said, hopping into the taxi and immediately beginning to haggle with the driver. Well, okay, I thought. Did I really seem so utterly incapable? Yes, probably.

As we pulled into the hotel driveway, I paid the driver and turned to Cinderella. "Well, thanks so much and good luck to you at the handbag factory." But she had leapt out and marched onward to the check-in counter.

I checked in. The front-desk attendant fetched the key and I turned to Cinderella. "Well, thanks so much for all your help . . ." But Cinderella had taken the key and had forged toward the elevator. Now this was getting to be a little awkward. Surely, I could be trusted to find my room.

"Well, thanks so much," I said again as we reached the door to my room. She used the key to open the door.

"This is a nice room," Cinderella noted. She turned to me, her perm billowing on her head. "It is very late."

"It sure is."

"I am locked out of my room. I have no key."

"Oh, well, I see," I stammered, trying very hard to understand the Chinese context of this particular situation. Perhaps she regarded it as auspicious that we shared a seat number on the train. Perhaps she'd concluded that her destiny lay with this *laowai* from the West who would sweep her off the factory floor and take her onward to a life of romantic intrigue. Or perhaps this was normal, accompanying a random foreigner from a train all the way to his evening hearth. Are Chinese women really so very helpful? And Cinderella was nothing if not helpful. Should I chivalrously offer to sleep on the floor while she claimed the bed? In the Chinese context, would this be the right thing to do? I had planned on calling my wife. *Hi, Honey. I'm*

*in my hotel room in Qingdao with my new friend Cinderella.*
No, I reflected. I probably didn't want to make that call.

"Listen, Cinderella," I said, reaching for my wallet. "Let me help you find a room in another hotel."

Cinderella batted her eyelashes. "No," she sighed. "I will stay with friends. But I want to see you tomorrow. What is your cell phone number?"

"I don't have a cell phone."

"No cell phone? Everyone in China has a cell phone."

This was true. Imagine tens of millions of people screaming into their handsets—*Can you hear me now?*—and you have an idea what urban China is like. It's true. *Wei* is the standard greeting when answering a cell phone in China, and it does indeed mean *Can you hear me?* This alone struck me as a compelling argument for the return of the rotary phone.

"This is my cell phone number," Cinderella said, writing it down. "And this is my e-mail address. Will you call me tomorrow? I will show you Qingdao."

"Absolutely. Look forward to it. Good night. Thanks so much for your help," I said as she left.

Then I bolted the door.

Now, what was that about? I wondered. I was very perplexed. Was Cinderella just a particularly helpful young woman? Or was she a seductress? I had no idea. Perhaps I was just a little dense. It wouldn't be the first time. So mysterious, this country.

---

In any event, I did not call Cinderella. It was a curious choice for a name. I'd observed that many Chinese had assumed

Western names. At first, I'd thought that this was just the Chinese solution to a sweeping epidemic of multiple-personality disorders. I imagined people waking up in the morning and, as they settled down with a cup of warm bean-curd milk and picked at their steamed buns, they'd decide who, exactly, they were going to be that day. Would they be Suyin, the factory worker in Lanzhou? Or was it time for *Lola*?

But, as always in China, things are not what they seem. It turns out that people in China choose Western names because there are so very few Chinese names. Like Western names, Chinese names are toponyms. They are essentially descriptive. The reason we have so many Smiths is that a long time ago blacksmiths were apparently irresistible, extremely hunky mates. And so, too, it is with Chinese names. But in China, of course, everything is magnified by the sheer number of Chinese. Li, Wang, and Zhang are the most common names. There are 88 million people in China named Zhang. There are more people called Chen in China than there are Canadians in Canada. Go to a typical school in China and ask to see Zhang Li and you will likely to be greeted by a half-dozen kids. It's become so problematic that no one knows Hu's Hu in China (Ha Ha Ha). And thus the Western names.

But the name Cinderella evoked aspirations I didn't want to go near. And so I'd explore Qingdao on my own. I'd gone there because I lived in hope of one day seeing the sun in China, and if ever I was going to see the great orb in the sky, it seemed likely that I'd find it on the coast. Also, I'd read that Qingdao was where Communists went to play, and I wanted to see them play, these Communists. Furthermore, Qingdao was the home of Tsingtao beer, and this, too, seemed like a compelling reason to visit.

To my delight, I found all this and more in Qingdao, a city of some 7 million people that jutted outward on a peninsula surrounded by the Yellow Sea. The city can roughly be divided into two parts—the old town, a little Bavaria with pagodas, and the new town, a forest of white and pastel skyscrapers with a proliferation of real estate offices and nightclubs like the Boys and Girls Show Bar and Disco, and Club New York, where patrons enjoy personal bottles of Crowne Royal, the drink of choice for those wanting to make an impression in China. To my eyes, this new Qingdao seemed like a comfortable, prosperous playground with stores devoted to golf and fashion, interspersed with an endless array of karaoke clubs. It is a place where inquisitive cabdrivers thoughtfully ask whether you'd like to *make love, Chinese girl,* and in case you don't understand, they'll helpfully circle their index finger with their thumb and stab at it with the other index finger. So romantic, the New Qingdao!

But it was old Qingdao that I'd come to see. For the first seventeen years of the twentieth century, Qingdao, or Tsingtao as it was then known in English, found itself under Imperial German control. The Kaiser had wanted to base his Far East squadron in Qingdao and the Qing Dynasty said sure, fine, whatever, and ceded the city to the Germans. This, of course, was not Imperial China's finest hour. The Germans arrived, built a city of *strasses* and *schusses,* beer gardens, and churches, and not long after finishing the city's masterpiece, the Tsingtao Brewery, the moment when their re-creation of a quaint Bavarian town was complete, the Germans proceeded to screw everything up and lose World War I. Sadly for the locals, instead of *Guten Tag,* they soon found themselves learning how to say

*Konnichi Wa*, as the Treaty of Versailles turned the city over to the Japanese, who remained until 1922, before returning again in 1937, when they began to do really, really bad things to China. Upon reflection, the Chinese probably had some more choice words for the Japanese than *Konnichi Wa*.

Nevertheless, by the time Mao finally wrested control of the city from the Nationalists in 1949, Qingdao, despite being bopped around by the vicissitudes of history, remained essentially intact. One misty morning, I set off for the old town, following a scenic waterside pathway that led me past the Marine Beasts Performance Hall and Aquarium and the city's famed beaches. The air was redolent of the sea and fried seafood. As the sun burned through the morning haze and the giant containerships offshore blew their fog horns, I watched people fishing from the bluffs and noted a few hardy old-timers out for their morning swim. I was on the Number 1 Bathing Beach, and I settled down to watch them, these Communists at leisure. Many officials, I'd been told, had their villas in Qingdao. I wondered what they did to amuse themselves.

"You want Jet Ski? Parasailing?" asked a man sporting flashy shades as he sat beside me on the stony beach. "Special price for you."

"Maybe tomorrow," I said, trying to imagine the Politburo parasailing.

"Today is Saturday. Tomorrow everyone go home."

Excellent, I thought, envisioning riding a train while actually seated.

My companion moved on to try his luck elsewhere and I wandered down the beach, now and then stopping to watch people waiting for the waves to bring in clumps of seaweed, which they then bagged, because seaweed can be very tasty. In the distance, enormous vessels maneuvered in and out of Qingdao's port, the fourth largest in China, and I tried to ascertain whether the ships coming in rode higher in the water than the ones going out.

Soon, I found myself in a part of the city that reminded me very much of Nuremberg, a city in southern Bavaria where my father had lived for some years in the nineties. I walked up streets half expecting to find a sign informing me that I was ambling up the Kaiserstrasse, but of course the signs don't say Kaiserstrasse, they say . . . Well, I had no idea what they said. Nevertheless, were it not for the busy stalls selling dried fish and the tinny Chinese pop music and the soldiers in olive uniforms with red stars, you might think you'd found yourself in Germany. Okay, maybe in a German Chinatown.

I walked up a hill to St. Michael's Cathedral, which I was looking forward to visiting. A few months earlier, the Chinese Catholic Patriotic Association had appointed two new bishops. I'd found this a little vexing as I tried to recall exactly which provision was it in Canon Law that had designated the Chinese Catholic Patriotic Association as the appointer of bishops. Wasn't it the Pope who decided such things? The Pope thought so, too, and he had expressed his concern. Soon after, the Chinese government had released a statement asking the Vatican to stop interfering in Chinese internal affairs. *The selection follows the will of all clergy and believers in the Chinese Catholic Church, so stop creating obstacles in Sino-Vatican relations.*

But, but, but . . . the Vatican exclaimed. Protests, however, were futile. This is because the Chinese Catholic Patriotic Association, a government agency, is the titular head of the official Catholic Church in China, not the Pope, which is why one will never hear a Chinese bishop utter a peep of protest on matters of interest to Catholics elsewhere, like abortion. It's not just the Catholic Church, however, that the government picks on. There is also the Chinese Patriotic Islamic Association and the Three-Self Patriotic Association, which monitors the Protestants. For the Tibetan Buddhists, they've dispensed with associations altogether and simply settled on the People's Liberation Army as the preferred means for keeping the followers of the Dalai Lama in line. Falun Gong has been assigned to the secret police. Clearly, the government has some issues with organized religion. And it is no wonder. In 1999, 10,000 members of Falun Gong silently surrounded Zhongnanhai, the walled compound of the Chinese Communist Party in central Beijing, to demand freedom to practice their beliefs. Communists don't like that, this stealthlike organization by a group outside their control. A short while thereafter, the government unleashed the violent crackdown on Falun Gong that is now grimly documented by protesters outside nearly every Chinese embassy abroad.

I paid a small entrance fee and made my way inside. The cathedral had been thoroughly looted during the Cultural Revolution, but today it has been restored to a polished luster. I was the only visitor, and I stopped in front of a statue of Joseph. Very helpfully, signs had been put up to explain who exactly these people were, Jesus, Mary, and Joseph. "Joseph is the legal paternity of Jesus, who played an important role in the salvation history." Technically true.

Afterward, I had lunch at a modest restaurant on a side street with tables outside. In the corner, a man stood grilling seafood. The proprietor, an unusually burly man with a friendly disposition, indicated that he didn't speak a word of English, which was just fine, because every meal I could see looked lip-smacking good. I pointed to a table where a waitress was setting down a bowl of small clams. "I'll have one of those, please," I said, pointing to the clams. "And some of that," I said, pointing to a plate of braised cabbage. We must remember our greens. "And one of those," I said, nodding toward an enormous mug of beer, which seemed to be the beverage of choice in Qingdao. I didn't normally drink beer with lunch, but I had a *when in Rome* moment, and if I were to understand the essence of Chinese culture in Qingdao, it seemed important to drink the beer.

I am a master with chopsticks, I thought, plucking the clams out of their shells. This was fine food indeed. The clams came in a fragrant, sweet-and-spicy broth, and as I finished the clams I thought that this might be an excellent time to introduce the idea of bread to China. It seemed like a small crime to let that broth go without sweeping a crusty piece of bread through it. I finished my beer, a large half-liter mug of Tsingtao straight from the keg, and suddenly I felt very pleased to be here, right now, in Qingdao, that fine city on the sea, and then, as I was overcome by a deep yawn, I remembered why I don't drink beer with lunch.

I felt an unshakable urge to nap. But the sun had finally burned through the early mist and now danced brightly across a blue sky, and the air smelled of the sea, and it seemed really so enormously wasteful, so disrespectful of the sunny day, that rarity in China, that I resisted the call of the pillow and set forth anew into old Qingdao.

Must have coffee, I thought as I walked, zombielike, toward the glimmering sea. I found Taiping Lu, the broad seaside avenue, and headed toward the Number 6 Bathing Beach. As I walked past the Oceanwide Elite Hotel, I noticed the familiar green and white logo of Starbucks and, pleased to have found a place that sold coffee, joined the Elite and settled on a terrace with an Oceanwide view. Except, as I looked a little more closely at the green logo, I realized I wasn't at a Starbucks. True, it looked like a Starbucks. They may have even adopted the coy pretensions of Starbucks-speak, that peculiar language that insists that small is tall. But this place called itself SFR, and to my pleasant surprise, they even maintained a basket of light and harmless English-language magazines. I picked up a copy of *Redstar*, a magazine oriented toward expats and visitors, and as I inhaled a dose of caffeine, I read the horoscope page. I'm a rooster in the Chinese zodiac, and apparently I was having a bad month. *Frustrating. You got more failure than your success. You got some oral quarrel. And better not think about big amount investment. To try to do more exercises is very good for you.*

So true, I thought, though I did wonder about my oral quarrel. It's difficult to have an oral quarrel when you can't actually talk to people. The other horoscopes seemed to fixate on sex and money. As roosters around the world were brooding on their failures and waddling around with their fat butts in dire need of exercise, those born in the year of the sheep were reveling in their good fortune. *Lucky month! You will on fire with opposite sex!* Hopefully for the sheeps, they'd know to avoid the boars, the cads. *Trouble to love affair is also possible, but not big deal.* Evidently, the boars were having affairs with dragons. *A lucky star is shining above you. It goes really well with your money making and your marriage. You may get trouble with your girlfriend/boyfriend.* Meanwhile, the hares were laughing all the way to the bank. *You got the luck of making some money this month, so catch it up.*

The coffee, alas, did little to alleviate the postlunch, beer torpor I felt, and since, apparently, I was in need of exercise, I walked onward to Zhan Qiao, a long, broad pier that jutted far out into Qingdao Bay. I joined a sea of tourists ambling toward the Huilan Pavillion, which graced the end of the pier, and was amazed, yet again, at how quickly my disposition could change in China. I had been feeling rather mirthful on the terrace, idly flipping through the horoscope. Sluggish, but mirthful. Possibly, I was slightly drunk. It was a very large beer. And yet, ambling upon the pier, I could feel my light mood disappear. I wondered why it was that in China, alone in the world in my experience, when presented with a two-way crowd, the Chinese didn't naturally gravitate to the right. Why is it that crowds in China must always bash into each other like one enormous rugby scrum? I mean, it was Saturday. It was sunny even. Surely, we should all be mellow. And yet a walk along the pier was anything but. Thousands surged one way and thousands surged the other. I darted through the crowd, dodging the brown, gelatinous loogies that flew past me in every direction, and moved my wallet to my front pocket as I sensed the menace of young men in dusty, ill-fitting clothes moving through the crowd like vultures. It was like walking though a crowded hallway in high school where half the students were looking for a fight. No one twists a shoulder here to avoid confrontation.

Then, suddenly, the crowd parted as if it had stumbled

upon a lane divider. There before me sat a boy, not more than seven years old, though it was impossible to tell with any certainty. He was an albino with skin that was nearly translucent. He had no arms, and his ragged shirt had been pulled down to reveal the rough scars from where his arms should have been. His skin had been burned raw by the sun, and he sat there rocking and moaning with a plastic bowl before him that contained a scattering of coins.

Who was this boy? Who had done this to him? The scars on his stumps suggested that he wasn't born armless. Who was sending him forth to beg on a pier? It would be far from the last time that I'd find myself pondering a display of mind-boggling cruelty in China, and it was why, despite the whiz-bang, China-is-the-future vibe I felt in this coastal city, I'd likely never have warm and fuzzy feelings for the country.

Later, I found myself on a pedestrian square. Above me loomed the towers of New Qingdao. I had settled on a bench in front of a large JumboTron screen that displayed an NBA playoff game. As I watched Steve Nash feed the ball to Amare Stoudemire, I was approached by three little boys in filthy torn clothes who inquired whether I had any money, and would I perhaps like to give it to them. Perhaps they were three, six, and eight years old. Perhaps they were older. They were all smaller than my four-year-old son, and as I regarded them, dusty and hungry, I wished that one day they'd grow to be giants, tall and soaring, as big as Yao Ming.

*8*

One of the interesting things about living in the United States is that you know, just know, can feel it in your bones, that you inhabit the beating heart of the world. This isn't true, of course. (It's actually in Tuvalu.) Nevertheless, we take it for granted that when we have our Super Bowls, 3 billion people around the world upend their work schedules and forgo sleep so that they, too, can watch. We assume that as we view the colossal fuck-up that is the life and times of Britney Spears, people abroad care as much as we do when the sad, bloated Mouseketeer decides to shave her head. We are told that when our economy sneezes, Canada, Europe, Asia, wherever, catches a cold. When we screw up, it's the rest of the world we screw up. And when we triumph, the rest of the world stops to admire the great shining city on the hill. We are, we believe, the prime movers and the rest of the planet just rolls along on the ride that is America.

Which is why it's so very interesting to be in China. Here, too, is a place that feels, knows in its bones, that it is the beating heart of the world. Indeed, there's nothing subtle about its self-assurance. The Chinese word for China is Zhongguo, or Middle Kingdom, a name that implies that there is China and then there are the sticks. The great emperors of China spent much of their time ensuring that other countries kowtowed toward them, and when these dynastic emperors periodically retreated behind their walls, it certainly wasn't because they were humbled by the outside world. Instead, it was because they couldn't deign to be concerned about the unlucky barbarians living beyond their borders. It is perhaps unsurprising, then, that most Chinese regard the incursions and interventions of Western powers in the nineteenth century, and the chaos unleashed by the opium trade, as profoundly humiliating. Indeed, modern Chinese history can often be read as the story of its reaction to the West.

The Chinese, of course, as a people are immensely proud. As well they should be. Theirs is an ancient culture, and for much of the past 5,000 years, few civilizations could claim to be as advanced as the people living behind the Great Wall. In science, art, literature, and astronomy, and culminating in the wonder that is the steamed dumpling, the Chinese have contributed much to the betterment of humanity—at least when they felt like sharing, which, apparently, wasn't very often. For many Chinese, who despite Mao's best efforts to smash the old culture remain steeped in history, the tribulations of the past two hundred years, when Europe humbled it with its drug trade and Japan bloodied it with its occupation, are regarded as an anomaly. But now that the tumult of those years is behind them, and China is emerging to what many Chinese would regard as its rightful place atop the economic and geopolitical food chain, I'd begun to wonder how this pride, this nationalism, would manifest itself.

If you spend any time on an Internet message board frequented by Chinese, you'd know that this nationalism can often come across, to put it kindly, as a little prickly. Type in something relatively innocuous like *I'd like to find some dog food that isn't flavored with pesticides. Any suggestions, gang?* And be prepared to be viciously flamed. *Do not criticize great country China!!!! China development very strong!!! We make you China bitch!!! We eat you!!! Sincerely, Henry Chen, Wuhan.*

But it's not merely on the Internet that one finds this prickliness. When Mattel was forced to recall millions of toys because of lead paint and safety concerns, the CEO of Mattel was compelled to very publicly apologize, or kowtow, to its leading Chinese supplier. True, there had been lead paint, but for one of the toys recalled, which had come with small magnetic balls that could do some severe damage to a child's stomach, the problem had been a design flaw, which, technically, wasn't the fault of the Chinese manufacturer. As parents around the world rummaged through their kids' toy boxes, tossing out everything from Thomas the Tank Engine locomotives to Polly Pocket play sets, the Chinese seized on this design flaw and demanded an apology. Some might say that this is simply a reflection of the importance of preserving face in China. Perhaps, although I don't think there is anything uniquely Chinese about the concept of face. In the Arab world, it would be called honor. In American culture, we'd call it respect.

But in truth, I wasn't interested in face, honor, or respect. I was interested in nationalism, and for nationalism to really start galloping ahead, it needs an enemy. For a while, way back in the nineties (can we have that decade back, please?), it seemed likely that the United States would fulfill that role. Every year, when China's trading status as a Most Favored Nation came up for renewal, members of Congress from both parties would loudly denounce religious oppression in China or the appalling work conditions of its factory workers or, with the Cold War still a fresh memory, the inconvenient fact that China was still Red China and confidently ignoring the bells of freedom ringing elsewhere in the world. And then they'd vote to grant China Most Favored Nation status. Business is business, of course. Nevertheless, these annual denunciations of China did little to engender soft and fuzzy feelings for the U.S. among the Chinese, except possibly among the religiously oppressed, exploited factory workers, and political dissidents. Then, during NATO's bombing campaign against the Serbs, the U.S. very accidentally bombed the Chinese Embassy in Belgrade, killing three diplomats and injuring twenty. Oopsie, said the U.S. So sorry. We had the wrong map. Belgrade, Belgium, so hard to keep them straight.

The Chinese erupted. Hundreds of thousands took to the streets in dozens of cities throughout China. The American Embassy in Beijing was pelted with rocks and diplomats were forced into the bunker. *It was an accident. Honest.* No one in China believed this. How could the government of the United States, the last superpower still standing, be so inept? The protests continued. American flags were burned. And throughout China, Americans everywhere found themselves sewing

Canadian flags on their backpacks. As the protesters raged, the government encouraged them onward, until finally, after the American Embassy's windows had been shattered and the diplomats inside had been thoroughly terrified, and President Clinton had issued his twenty-fourth public apology and promised to wear a hair shirt and flog himself daily, the Chinese government called the protesters off. The point had been made. *Do not fuck with us.*

Three years later, a hot-dogging Chinese fighter pilot collided with an American spy plane above international waters just outside of China. The fighter pilot tumbled into the South China Sea and the stricken spy plane limped toward the nearest airfield, which, most inconveniently for a spy plane spying on China, was a military airfield on Hainan Island. What a bonus, thought the Chinese government as they pondered what to do with this high-tech surveillance plane that had been eavesdropping on electronic communications and phone calls in their country. Here were secrets to be deciphered. Technology to be reverse-engineered. Though they let the crew go after eleven days, they held on to the plane for another three months, and when they did finally return it to the U.S. they handed over a bill for a million dollars. See, the plane didn't actually have permission to land in China. Thus the fine. But more important, the U.S. had delivered another propaganda gift, wrapped in a pretty bow. The Chinese insisted that the spy plane, a slow-moving, snub-nosed, propeller-driven EP-3E, had recklessly smashed into the fighter plane on purpose, a novel and exhilarating tactic for a prop plane to take when confronted by a missile-laden fighter jet. Nevertheless, that was the official line and newspapers in China reported it accordingly. *American*

*Aggressor Downs Peace-Loving Chinese Aircraft in Chinese Territory. Chinese Plane Was Delivering Toy Bunnies to Orphans.*

This was the first crisis faced by the newly elected President Bush. Diplomats burned the midnight oil. They sent telegrams to one another. Then they sent more telegrams. Experts in acronyms were called in to decipher the telegrams. What would the President do?

"We should invade China," urged the Vice President. "We'll be regarded as liberators and greeted with savory dumplings."

"It's a slam dunk," agreed the Director of the CIA.

But President Bush ignored them. Instead, he did something he had never done before, something so painfully challenging that few thought him capable of it. With his fists clenched and his jaws trembling, he squinted in that squinty way he has and said, *Sorry.* It was the hardest thing he'd ever done.

Not good enough, said the Chinese government. How sorry are you?

More telegrams were sent. New acronyms were created. The President stayed up deep into the night, to 9 P.M. even, and felt the weight of his awesome responsibilities. *How sorry was he?*

Again he squinted into the middle distance, and with a steely resolve, declared that he was *very sorry.* It was the most trying day of his life, and he determined that never again, under any circumstances, would he ever say sorry again.

Since then, of course, relations between the U.S. and China, while not a high-fiving lovefest, have been remarkably cordial, all things considered. True, there are still articles in American newspapers detailing the political repression, torture, appalling work conditions, etc., etc., but no one gets on the floor of Congress today to denounce Red China. Similarly, in China, people are hardly reflexively anti-American. While technically not American, I do occasionally travel like one (Can I have French fries with that? And a fork too?). Not once, however, did I detect any ill will toward me because of my nationality. True, I did sense condescension, but that was simply because I was a *laowai,* and many Chinese believe that anyone with the misfortune to not be Chinese is inferior. The general attitude among the Chinese toward Americans is similar to that of a young, hotshot quarterback waiting for the tired, banged-up veteran to step aside so he can lead the team.

Still, while Americans might be pleased that nationalist rage is no longer pointed directly at them, it doesn't mean that China doesn't have an outlet to display some good, old-fashioned nationalist fervor. And the country that currently finds itself the target for this vehemence is Japan. It's an anger that the Chinese government has learned to finely calibrate. On most days, newspapers will carry stories highlighting the villainy and treacherousness of the Japanese. Indeed, these anti-Japanese stories can appear in some surprising locations. Waiting in line for the cable car to see the Great Wall at Badaling? Bored? Looking for something to read while a hundred people cut in line in front of you? Well, the government has thoughtfully created a display highlighting Japanese wartime atrocities in the area. Now and then, such as when new history textbooks in Japan are issued sugarcoating the country's role in World War II, the Chinese government will allow the country to erupt in righteous indignation, then backpedal furiously when the protests threaten to spiral out of control. When in 2005 Japan issued a textbook that referred to the Nanjing

Massacre as a trifling "incident," tens of thousands of protesters took to the streets. The Japanese Embassy in Beijing was besieged by rampaging mobs. *Japanese pigs come out!*, they hollered. Sushi restaurants were torched. And throughout China, Japanese people everywhere found themselves busily sewing Canadian flags on their backpacks.

The rage that the Chinese unleashed against Japan had become so unhinged that, finally, the government felt compelled to impose a media blackout. Nationalism, of course, is the trickiest of dragons to ride. The protests eventually burned out, but not before revealing that for the vast majority of people in China, Japan is enemy number one.

To learn a bit more, I thought I'd head toward Nanjing, which had been the capital of the Republic of China early in the twentieth century. It's the war, of course—the long struggle of World War II—that lies at the root of anti-Japanese sentiment in China, and no place suffered more under Japanese occupation than Nanjing. During what came to be known in China as the War of Resistance Against Japan, more then 20 million Chinese soldiers and civilians lost their lives. In 1931, Japanese forces had seized a broad swath of land in the bitterly cold northeast of China and installed Puyi, the last emperor of China, as the puppet leader of what they called Manchukuo. China, lost in its own struggle among Nationalists, Communists, and assorted warlords that followed the collapse of the Qing Dynasty in 1912, could do little to resist. By 1937, in a quest for more resources to fuel its war machine, Japanese forces turned south toward Shanghai and Nanjing, where in the winter of 1937–1938 they committed one of history's most unparalleled atrocities, brutally murdering upward of 300,000 civilians. Inexplicably, not even today has Japan managed to say sorry, much less very sorry.

If ever there was a place to grasp anti-Japanese sentiment in China, Nanjing was it. I considered my travel options. I could take a fifteen-hour overnight train—hard seat only, I was confidently informed—or I could fly. For all the hours I'd spent in rickety tin tubes elsewhere in the world, I remain a fraidy-cat when it comes to flying. And yet, as I contemplated a night wedged into the fetid space between two train cars, an airplane suddenly seemed a little less terrifying. I took a taxi from Qingdao and arrived at the airport, where I soon found myself marveling at the polished sheen, the courteous English-speaking check-in people, the lack of lines, the broad, expansive views, and wondered, Why can't we have airports like this in the U.S.? I had expected the anarchic tumult of a train station, and yet this glimmering, multilingual, hyperefficient airport reminded me of Singapore. Of course, I'd never been to Singapore, but when I think of Singapore, which isn't very often, I imagine something very like the airport in Qingdao.

I wandered around the departure terminal. The majority of passengers appeared to be businessmen in trim, dark suits. At a bookstall, I perused the books for sale. Most were concerned with management and leadership and effective team-building and all sorts of other topics to help the businessman get ahead, including *Wine for Dummies*. There were biographies of Hu Jintao, Mao Zedong, and Ronald Reagan, and for the randy businessman, the bottom shelf offered a selection of soft-porn DVDs.

As I watched the aircraft pull into the gate, I was pleased to notice that it was a new plane, an Airbus of recent vintage.

Excellent, I thought, trying to settle down my preflight butter-flies. New Airport. New Planes. And then I looked at the pilots. New pilots too, apparently. In the United States, pilots tend to be in their fifties, ex–fighter pilot jocks, comfortable flying a plane upside down. In China, pilots are barely old enough to shave. Earlier, I had read an article in *China Daily* that noted that while aviation in China has grown exponentially over the last few years, there were now acute shortages of mechanics, aircraft controllers, and pilots, and that flying today, even on a snazzy airplane taking off from a snazzy airport, is, apparently, a very risky thing to do. And that even though there haven't been any major accidents lately, it was really just a question of time. I did what I could to completely forget what I had read just days earlier in a newspaper not particularly known for being critical of anything pertaining to, well, China, but as I boarded, I couldn't help but note that something was certainly a little off here. What was it? I wondered. What was causing the electrons in my brain to buzz so strangely? I'm boarding a plane. It's just like any other plane. What's different? It's . . . the music.

Instead of Muzak, there was American Christian Country Music. I am, frankly, not very familiar with American Christian Country Music, and as the plane taxied down the runway, it felt just a little funny listening to a deep, drawl-y, baritone voice strumming a guitar, sharing his musings on the Lord and what He means for the good ole U.S. of A. Cool, I thought. I'm in China. I'm on an airplane listening to the red-blooded, God-fearing songs of the Confederacy. But soon, as we reached our cruising altitude, my attention turned to the bathroom, which was apparently the smoking lounge. Did the pilots just ignore the alarm? Or had the passengers disabled it, and would this tinkering with wires affect the plane's hydraulic system? Was it possible to reach into the No Smoking in Bathrooms alarm system and very accidentally disable the rudder on an Airbus? At that moment, the pilot turned on the seat-belt sign. The flight attendants urged everyone to take their seats right now. The aircraft began to shake. Was it the rudder? Were we rudderless 27,000 feet above Jiangsu Province? The flight attendant spotted me, the lone *laowai*. "If turbulence causes feelings of airsickness, please vomit in bag." And I clutched the bag, and I held it tight.

I am quite likely the only member of my generation who still watches the evening news on national television. Our culture is committed to satisfying the needs of the old and the young, and those in between are often forced to choose. I once considered Facebook, but after spending a few minutes idling through its pages (they are called pages, yes?), I could never get beyond the Why of it. Scrolling through the walls of pithy comments, I'd wonder who, exactly, are these "friends" and why don't they just call? And so I'd tossed my lot with the old, and begun to watch the *Nightly News* with Brian Williams on NBC. In between the pressing news items of the day—the quest for female Viagra, the perils of missing the annual colonoscopy— Mr. Williams would inform us of the day's events in Iraq, a country where, apparently, we were fighting a war. Invariably, there would be footage of the grim results of a car bomb, and as the sirens wailed across the screen, my eldest son would scamper over, because nothing quite interests four-year-old boys like vehicles with sirens.

"What happened, Daddy?" he'd inquire.

"Well, it's like this," I'd say, assuming the measured gravitas of Mr. Williams. "In a place far, far away, there was a car accident, a little fender bender. And Mr. Frumple—you remember Mr. Frumple?—hurt his knee, so the ambulance is taking him to the Busytown Hospital, where Dr. Lion is going to make him feel better. Meanwhile, Bob the Builder is going to come over with his heavy equipment and clean up the scene of the accident."

Lukas would scrunch his nose and ask: "Is that true? Or is that another fairy tale?"

"It's true. Just ask your mother."

It's what we do, cosset the kids behind thick barricades where they can enjoy the wonder of childhood without being disturbed by anything so troublesome as reality. When I sensed Lukas was troubled by the ladybug he'd just squished with his bike, I'd take the time to explain the phenomenon known as the Great Reincarnation of Ladybugs, and that right now, at this very moment, the ladybug was being reborn as a horse, and soon this ladybug would be galloping across a broad, golden meadow, so grateful to have been squished by a bicycle.

This is a perilous form of parenting, of course. It is very possible that as the hard truth of the world begins to seep in through the barricaded doors, the kids will become bitter and twisted, distrustful of their parents, paranoid even, and eventually they'd start making furtive calls to AM talk radio stations.

"We've got a caller from California."

"Hi, Rush. It's me, Lukas . . ."

Nevertheless, we persist with our NeverNeverland, and if the boys end up in counseling, at least we will have provided them with a few years in which nothing bad happens. Ever.

Chinese parents, apparently, think differently. True, kids in China today are often regarded as spoiled, the pampered lone offspring of the One Child system. Of course, most of China is predominantly rural and poor, where a pampered child is simply a fed child. But for the little tykes of the newly evolving urban middle class, no sacrifice, no indulgence, is deemed too small. So perhaps they are spoiled. But if the hundreds of uniformed little kids visiting the Memorial Hall for Compatriots Killed in the Nanjing Massacre is indicative of anything, it is that children in China are certainly not sheltered.

I'd arrived in Nanjing during a spring storm, the kind of squall that tosses airplanes in bracing, sickening ways, leaving certain passengers profoundly grateful to be back on terra firma, even though it was pouring rain—sheets of it—the kind of nighttime maelstrom that makes it exceedingly difficult to see the bicycles on the road, which led to a groan-inducing collision with a cyclist, and though I bled from a gash in my foreleg I didn't care, because I was no longer on an airplane and that alone gave me cause for jubilation. Plus, Nanjing is surprisingly nice. There are, for instance, trees, lots of trees. It is a verdant city. And it is no wonder. Clearly, it could be extremely rainy in Nanjing.

The city lies on the Yangtze River, the river system that carves China into north and south. The north gets heating. The south does not. The south gets rain. The north gets the Gobi Desert. Sun Yat-sen, universally regarded as the father of modern China, made Nanjing the capital of the Republic of China in that difficult era between the fall of the Qing Dynasty in 1912 and the triumph of the Communists in 1949, thus restoring the privileged position of the city that had been lost when the Emperor Zhu Di moved his capital to Beijing. Temples and gates and walls from the Ming Dynasty still grace the city's lush hills. But within those old walls there is a modern city, where taxis come with little flat-screen televisions, and the streets are all glimmering and neon-lit, and the buildings, too, come with enormous screens featuring gyrating girls, and it's hard to believe that you're not somewhere deep in the world of Blade Runner.

And yet the city does not seethe like Beijing. Bargaining, for instance, is just far easier in Nanjing. I'd slowly adjusted to the need for haggling in China. At first, I moseyed about like a walking ATM, a convenient place for vendors and cabdrivers to extract a brazen *first price* from a dim *laowai* not yet familiar with the need for bargaining for the *special price,* much less the *Chinese price.* It was only after I discovered that I was paying approximately four times what anybody else was for a bottle of dodgy water that I'd begun, tentatively at first, to dicker for the *special price,* and I lived in hope that one day I'd be able to negotiate down to the *Chinese price,* the holy grail for foreigners. I'd found a Web site that offered discounted rates on hotels, and while there was no way I was going to input credit-card details on a computer in a dingy Internet café in China, I would take note of the discounted price at my target destination and make that my bargaining ambition whenever I needed to haggle for a roof.

"*Nihao,*" I'd said at the front desk of my chosen hotel in Nanjing. I was pleased to notice a sign that read, *Today's Hotel*

*English Lesson #86.* "*We have many amenities to satisfy all our guests.*" "How much is a room?"

"Six hundred eighty," he said, pointing to the listed price.

"But it says on the Internet that it's 280 *kuai.*"

"Okay. Two-eighty."

So easy!

Earlier that day, at a small newsstand, I'd stopped to purchase an umbrella. The proprietor typed 70 onto his calculator. I typed 30. Sold. True, the typical Nanjinite could probably get it for 6 yuan, but I took my triumphs where I could. I'd then found a cavernous restaurant where, beneath a ceiling of lanterns and birdcages, an elderly man plucked at a traditional instrument—*toing, toing*—while a woman dressed in silk sang old-school Chinese songs. The available dishes were wrapped in cellophane before an open kitchen, and I simply had to point at the dish that my heart desired, and the chef would rustle it up and deliver it to my table and stool, which was an excellent table and stool for a leprechaun but made me feel like Gulliver. As I inhaled a steaming bowl of clams, shrimps, and cabbage, and sipped at my Tsingtao, I thought, Gosh, I like it here. Nanjing is a fine city. But I had not come to Nanjing to enjoy myself; I had come to understand the serious antipathy for the Japanese that seems to lurk deep within the Chinese soul. Which is why I found myself the following morning in Jiangdongmen, a neighborhood not far from the Yangtze River, and the site of the Memorial Hall for Compatriots Killed in the Nanjing Massacre.

And I was not alone. No. There were hundreds of schoolkids taking a field trip into the grim past. And grim it is. Right where we stood, thousands of people had been slain when the Japanese marched into Nanjing late in 1937. Their bones are even visible, jutting through mounds of dirt that are encased behind glass. Outside, on the Mourning Square, I had encountered a statue of Iris Chang, the author of *The Rape of Nanking,* a book published in 1998 that demonstrated that the Nanjing Massacre wasn't simply one of those really, really bad things that happened during World War II, which had started a little earlier for China when Japan invaded during the summer of 1937. This was something far, far beyond bad. The Nanjing Massacre attained a level of murderous cruelty that makes you wonder not only what exactly went on inside the head of a Japanese soldier as he bayoneted a child but, more broader still, how it is that human beings can do this to other human beings. For six weeks, the Japanese brutally slaughtered 300,000 unarmed, defenseless people. It was a sadistic barbarism without equal. As Iris Chang recounted in her well-documented book, soldiers competed to see who could decapitate the greatest number of people in the shortest amount of time. *Kill and count! Kill and count!* they encouraged one another. With bayonets, they ripped open the stomachs of pregnant women, pulling out the fetuses. Tens of thousands of women were raped before they were killed. "Blood was splattered everywhere as if the heavens had been raining blood," recalled one of the few survivors. And strangely, so much of it was photographed, not only by the handful of Western missionaries who had remained in Nanjing, but by the Japanese soldiers themselves. These photographs were now on display, and as I peered at these images of rape and murder over the heads of murmuring schoolkids, I wondered what exactly these images would do to the psyche of a child, because they were certainly messing with mine. Toward the end of the exhibit are photographs of the Japanese officers who oversaw the butchery, and I watched the kids dutifully jot their names down. They might not have had a beef with Japan earlier, but they certainly did now. And with good reason, of course. The commander in chief of Japanese forces in Nanjing, Prince Asaka Yasuhiko, would go on to live out his days as a prosperous golf course developer.

It's remarkable that relations between Japan and China today are as civil as they are. The two countries are bound together by mutual economic interests. The Japanese are major investors in China, and now that China has become an economic power in its own right, the Chinese government, too, is concerned about global financial stability and is unlikely to allow domestic protesters to derail the money train. But take away the money, and what remains is simmering hatred. As a Japanese friend once explained: "In Japan, people are ashamed about the war. They are ashamed they lost." Unlike Germany, Japan has never accounted for its wartime atrocities, and it is this lack of remorse that feeds the well-justified hostility most Chinese have for Japan.

Later, I found myself in the hotel restaurant. A hard, sweeping rain had returned, keeping me in. Hotel English Lessons hadn't yet reached the waitresses or indeed the menu, and I tried to convey that I'd like to have whatever they thought was good. "I leave it up to you. I am at your mercy." Whereupon they returned with a bowl of tomato soup, which is very possibly the last thing I expected to eat in China. Meanwhile, I had written a postcard to my son.

*Dear Lukas,*

*I miss you very much. I am in Nanjing. It is a very big city with lots of cars, buses, mopeds, and bicycles. It's just like Busytown.*

*Love,*

*Daddy*

# 9

One day, I found myself musing about China. This often happened, of course, because when in China there is much to ponder. But, possibly because the coffee in the Temperance Lounge at the Nanjing train station was strong enough to induce a cardiac event, I found myself having deep thoughts, which, inexplicably, occur only when I'm hypercaffeinated. Despite a jaunty hike to the summit of Tai Shan and excursions into the Chinese past, I felt like I still didn't *get* China. Not even close. Say what you will about the U.S., but it's easy to *get*. It's loud and brash, and it stands up for liberty and commerce, and it wants the rest of the world to be like it. And very often this has been good, this zeal for liberty and commerce, and much of the world did indeed cheer for America (you can Google it), which is why when George Bush was elected and proceeded to completely fuck everything up, the rest of the world felt the outrage it did. In the international papers one reads mournful articles about America, this country of renditions and Gitmos and waterboarding, and how it is finished as an idea, an aspiration, and as we move deeper into the twenty-first century, new models and new ways of organizing society will supplant the American ideal, now battered and tarnished. Maybe even the Chinese Model, the papers declare. It is always expressed thus, the *Chinese Model.*

But what is this contemporary Chinese Model? It is usually, very simply, described as unfettered capitalism combined with authoritarian rule. Give us power, says regime X, and we will give you economic growth, opportunities to become rich, and stability, just like the Chinese Model. There is, of course, nothing uniquely Chinese about such an arrangement. Chile, under Augosto Pinochet, combined authoritarian rule with capitalism. So, too, did the city-state of Singapore. But this isn't quite what China feels like. Singapore is settled in its ways. So, too, was Chile until, of course, it wasn't. China, however, is anything but settled. When in Beijing, I had asked a Chinese engineer, a friend of Dan's, what he thought China might be like in fifteen years. "I cannot say," he said. "If fifteen years ago you had asked me what China might look like today, I never would have imagined that it would look like this. And so I cannot answer your question. Everything is changing so fast."

*Everything is changing so fast.* That's exactly what China feels like. Even I could pick up on that, and as this was my first trip to China, I didn't even have a frame of reference to compare. All I had were the books I'd read, which, now that I was in China, all seemed hopelessly dated. But from what I could see, there is no Chinese Model. There is only movement, a wild, hurtling movement, like a speeding train barreling down the tracks, the brakes shredded, and somewhere down the line is the train station, but no one knows which station, exactly, is it that this train, barely in control, is hurtling toward.

Once, not that long ago, there was a Chinese Model. It was called Maoism, and China was interested in exporting Maoist revolution. Today, of course, China is interested in exporting everything but revolution. Red guard fanatics may have had their uses, but they made for terrible consumers, and no one needs consumers more today than China, with its mammoth factories and pressing need to keep hundreds upon hundreds of millions of people employed. Now there must be growth in China. There must be building. There must be consumption, everywhere. The train can't be allowed to slow down.

But where is it going? Not even the government knows for sure. True, they still have their Five-Year Plans. And Hu Jintao speaks confidently of building a harmonious society. That will be his contribution: harmony. But the government today doesn't really plan with a big *P*. Instead, at least to the lightly informed eyes of this traveler, all one can detect is improvisation. There is no gold-plated Big Book of Rules and Laws in China. Or perhaps there is, but it's irrelevant. Old neighborhoods are destroyed, villages bulldozed, all to make room for the barreling train carrying China toward some vision of modernity. Sometimes residents are compensated fairly; sometimes not. It depends. Throughout China, factories defile rivers, contaminate land, foul the air, sicken the people. Sometimes these factories are fined, sometimes not. It depends. Every year in China, there are tens of thousands of mass protests of very angry people rising up against corruption, pollution, or even the impervious insouciance of a Party official or businessman. Invariably, these protests are quickly crushed. But sometimes, in the end, there is justice. And sometimes there isn't, and everyone is told to lighten up and remember what really nasty people the Japanese are.

The one constant, however, in this new, evolving China is money, both its despairing absence and its increasing abundance. A walk through a Chinese city is to experience this particular dissonance in overdrive. I'd look up at the buildings seemingly taking flight, each one reaching higher than the other, and I'd look down and find the most hideously disfigured, dismembered, burned, or otherwise heartbreaking displays of human suffering, lying on a sidewalk, sometimes with a beggar's bowl, sometimes just huddled there. I'd pause and gawk at a Ferrari dealership—every city seemed to have one—and soon my sleeve would be tugged by an old man with a wispy Fu Manchu beard and a blue cap shaking a tin cup lightly filled with twinkling coins. At construction areas—and urban China is really one vast construction site—I'd admire the big poster boards with the artist's renderings of skyscrapers and shopping malls filled with happy people with pockets full of disposable income, and then I'd peek through an opening in the wall and see the migrant workers bustling over bamboo scaffolding, welding a building together without welder masks, busy like ants, desperate like ants, doing what they could to hold on to a job that offered an on-site shantytown shack for a home.

Money seemed to be the link that bound China together. Economic growth was the beginning and end of the Chinese Model. There is no vision of a shimmering city on a hill, a bastion of liberty and inalienable rights. So, too, the Commie-speak of yesteryear, this language of class enemies and proletarian revolution, has largely faded into the history books. Indeed, I had spent May 1st, May Day, the most revered holiday in Commie World, ambling on Tiananmen Square, fully expecting to trip over soldiers on parade marching past the members of the Politburo carefully arrayed on a display stand beneath the portrait of a smirking Chairman Mao. But there was nothing. A few more flags. A few more tourists. Actually, a lot more tourists. But it certainly didn't feel like a celebration of revolution and the glorification of all things red. It felt like Columbus Day.

And so I thought I'd have a closer look at money, and Shanghai seemed like a good place to find it. I'd moved on from the Temperance Lounge in the Nanjing train station, and with a caffeinated jitter made my way to the Soft Seat Lounge, where hundreds of besuited businessmen sat in comfortable, ergonomical seats, tinkering at laptops and barking into cell phones. Once again, I sputtered at how very delusional my preconceptions of China had been. Sacramento might be a heatblasted backwater in America, but surely I wouldn't feel like a poor, disconnected yokel missing out on the money train of globalization inside a train station in Nanjing. But I did. It's a new train station, gleaming and shiny like the airport in Qingdao, with enormous windows offering panoramic views of Lake Xuanwu and shimmering high-rises soaring above the green hills. Again I wondered, Why couldn't we have infrastructure like this? Are we not richer? Are we not more—quote unquote—advanced? Not for long, I thought, if this waiting room is somehow indicative—or if not indicative, predicative—of where, exactly, the train called China is heading. And then the announcement came that the train to Shanghai was departing imminently, and as several hundred businessmen raged toward the doors, battering one another to get on board, I allowed myself a brief contented moment of cultural smugness.

But this does not last long in China. A train ride from Nanjing to Shanghai is the Sino equivalent of the line connecting Philadelphia with New York. Whereas the Phil-NY run is very often a sad reminder of what midcentury America once was—a decaying sign on a passing bridge reads TRENTON MAKES. THE WORLD TAKES—the line linking Nanjing with Shanghai is, well, it's blighted too. But it's not a dead blight, it's a living blight (except around Tai Hu, which was once a living lake, full of fish, but is now a dead lake full of dead fish). But this industrial furnace of a train route, with its belching factories and eye-popping destruction/construction of towns and cities, is unquestionably an industrious area, providing the funds that keep the crisply dressed businessmen around me tapping and yapping into the latest wonders emanating from the world of telecommunications.

And then, a short three hours later, I arrived in Shanghai. It's always very exciting arriving in a city of 20 million people where you can't speak the language and you can't read the signs. Naturally, I had prepared accordingly. *"Nihao,"* I'd said to the taxi driver.

*"Nihao,"* he'd said, and I was pleased because apparently I could communicate my greetings in both Mandarin *and* Shanghainese. Proud that I'd bridged the communication gap, I handed him a note describing in crisply written Chinese characters my intended destination.

"Shanghai," he said, pointing to the ground after reading my note. "Shanghai."

"Ah. Yes. So it is. Sorry. Wrong note."

I searched my pockets, pulling out tattered scraps of paper.

"Qingdao?" he said, arching his eyebrows. *You want me to drive you to Qingdao?*

"Er . . . No. Sorry. Here. Try this one."

I didn't understand his response. "Er, what's that?" I said, offering the familiar big dopey grin.

With his hands, he pointed to the sky.

"Yep. That's the place," I said, and then as we made our way to an expressway leading toward Pudong, the gilded district that resides across the Huangpu River from the Bund and old Shanghai, I wondered if I'd very accidentally handed him the note that said, *Please take me to the airport.* Long inward sigh. Then I remembered that there's a super-fast, state-of-the-art bullet train connecting the airport to Pudong, and I decided that this would be interesting too, to ride this train back into Shanghai, and so I settled back and relaxed into this ride toward I-didn't-know-where. I'm flexible that way.

But I had handed him the correct note. The driver pulled up in front of the Jin Mao Tower, an enormous skyscraper that looks like an accordion that's been stretched to its snapping point, and yet still looks really striking. It's the tallest building in China, though not for long. Next door, cranes were already crafting a steel skeleton that would become the Shanghai World Financial Tower, an immense cone that would scrape the sky at 1,614 feet. The designs for the tower had to be altered at the last moment when protesters noted that the huge, circular aperture at the building's peak reminded them of the Rising Sun, the symbol on Japan's flag, which wasn't exactly what leaders in China wanted to see on the world's second-tallest building. The Jin Mao Tower was a trifle shorter, but for the moment it still dominated the glass-and-steel canyons of Pudong. Twenty-five years ago, Pudong was swampy farmland. Today, it is the glittering center of finance in China and its buildings tell the story of that transition. It was here that the new China first emerged, and in its architecture you can see the early struggles with confidence. There is the Oriental Pearl Tower, reminiscent of Seattle's Space Needle, with its mutant, galactic orbs, screaming *Look at me! I'm modern too!*—a sort of Space Age Sixty–ish towering architectural relic where you just know that the restaurant inside sells Rocket Burgers. Or maybe Rocket Dumplings. And then there are the early sky-scrapers, the ones built in the eighties, plain inverted rectangles topped with a golden pagoda: Modernity with Chinese Char-acteristics. But it's the newer buildings that suggest that China is feeling pretty cocky these days. The Jin Mao Tower is also meant to convey a pagoda, but it doesn't at all look silly and ill-conceived. It looks really cool.

I had gotten all crazy and reserved a room at the Grand Hyatt Shanghai, the world's highest hotel, located on floors fifty-four to eighty-seven of the Jin Mao Tower. I figured that if I was going to look for money this would be an excellent place to find it. Then, as I handed over my credit card at the check-in counter on the fifty-fourth floor, it occurred to me that this was a profoundly addled way of thinking. I wasn't going to find money here. I was going to go broke here. I hadn't stayed in a hotel quite so august since my days as a consultant to the World Bank, when I traveled as the Official Carrier of the PowerPoint Projector. The Grand Hyatt is the sort of hotel where, if you're not wearing a suit, you feel a little sloppy, a heretofore unexperienced sensation in China. It is very likely that I was the first guest to wander into the lobby with a backpack. It is also the only place in China where I felt acutely self-conscious in seeking the customary 50-percent-plus discount off the listed price. And that was a very odd sensation indeed. By now I was hardwired for bargaining, and when vendors tried to overcharge me, the dumb *laowai,* I'd haggle with glee. But not here, deep inside the Grand Hyatt Shanghai, where everything was hushed and graceful, and guests exuded an overwhelming sense of richness that precluded them from even caring how many zeros there were on their hotel bill.

I hesitated before taking the key. There was still time to find a room a trifle less lavish than this, but then they offered an upgrade to a Super Deluxe Executive Suite at absolutely no additional cost and I thought, What the hell, go on, spend a night living like a Master of the Universe. I took the key, swiped it into the Guests Only elevator, and proceeded upward to the seventy-fourth floor, where I found my room, a sanctuary in the sky with soft woody colors and a top-of-the-line king-sized bed and a bathroom that evoked an extremely weird sensation of desire. I wanted this bathroom, this haven of chrome—no, not chrome, platinum probably—with the multinozzled immersion shower. But most impressive was the view, the kind of view that left my jaw scraping against the floor. There below me, far, far below, swirled the Huangpu River, choked with boats of every variation, and across was the Bund, evoking the Shanghai of yesteryear when the city was famed as the Whore of the Orient (now, there's a moniker), and beyond that the thousands of buildings, the swarming immensity of Shanghai, just beginning to light up a crepuscular dusk. Even in my hermetically sealed Super Deluxe Executive Suite, I could feel the intense drive and pluck of the city, and compelling as the city was, more compelling was the exorbitant amount of money I was spending for this view, and I figured for that kind of money I better have a little look-see at the rest of the hotel.

If you ever happen to find yourself on the fifty-sixth floor of the Jin Mao Tower, make a point of wandering toward the middle of the floor, where you'll find a lobby-type bar and a bunch of tables thoughtfully spread out to give businesspeople—and they're all businesspeople, mostly of the male persuasion—enough room to conduct deals and discuss strategies without having solo travelers in jeans eavesdrop on them, and then cautiously look up. And I do mean cautiously if you are at all susceptible to vertigo. Here you'll find a staggering thirty-story atrium, and if you're unprepared it's very possible to feel a sort of reverse vertigo, this sudden overwhelming awareness of an immense void. Sort of like being in a *Star Trek* movie, but with better lighting. Then, if you're curious to know what weeks of nothing but vividly flavorful Chinese food will do to your taste buds, head on over to The Grill, the hotel's Western restaurant, where every seat offers a window view of the shimmering city beyond the glass.

The restaurant was filled with businesspeople—Chinese, American, European, Japanese, Arab—and sitting in an opulent restaurant in bustling Shanghai is to be reminded of just how much money there is sloshing around China today. The government is sitting on a roughly $1.4 trillion reserve, and if you think China is just going to idly rest on a big pile of dollars while the U.S. government does everything possible to depreciate the dollar, you're wrong. The Chinese government started a sovereign fund, and in its first big move bought a stake in Blackstone, the private equity firm, which together with hedge funds is representative of the parts of Wall Street that have gone feral. They did this not merely to make some money—which they haven't since share prices in Blackstone have tumbled more than 50 percent—but to learn how the sharks operated in international finance, which is an interesting skill set for the Chinese Politburo to learn.

Of course, it's not only the government that sits on wealth in China, though they do have their hands in an awful lot of it. There are now more than a hundred billionaires in the country itself. And it's no wonder. Forty percent of all goods imported by the United States comes from China, and the United States, of course, is hardly China's only customer. More than $500 billion of foreign investment has found a home in China, and it has finally become the massive consumer market that businesspeople have been salivating over for decades. There are more than 500 million cell phones in China, and it's now the second-biggest market in the world for cars. Ditto computers.

And there are stock markets. Two, to be exact—in Shenzhen, near Hong Kong, and Shanghai. The Chinese, among the most prolific savers in the world, have more than 17 trillion yuan in household savings. Investors, however, are permitted to invest only on the domestic exchanges, which they do with manic glee; 69,000 people open brokerage accounts *per day* in China. Indeed, pawnshops have even started accepting houses and apartments as collateral for loans. The thrill of investing has become so pervasive that the government had to pass a law making it illegal for high school students to invest in shares, which they'd been doing with about the same measured restraint typical of sixteen-year-olds everywhere. But you can hardly blame the Chinese for throwing everything they have into the stock market. In 2007, the market rose 97 percent. In 2006, it rose 130 percent. Few markets in the world have ever approached the gains of the stock market in China.

Real estate, too, has experienced a similar manic appreciation. "Do you see that building there?" said the waitress, pointing at an apartment building far below us. "It's more than 20,000 yuan per square meter."

"Really," I said, mulling the Tuna Tartare. "That's terrible. How do people afford it?"

"Its too expensive. It's very difficult for most people. I think it is mostly overseas Chinese who are buying."

She was wrong, it turns out. Eighty percent of homes in China's cities are owned by private citizens, and just as in the U.S., some have turned to property flipping. But while in the U.S. that bubble has burst, leaving a grim trail of foreclosures and bankruptcies, in China the real estate bubble has continued merrily along, with some cities, like Shanghai, experiencing a doubling in home values every year. As with the stock market, investors have convinced themselves that nothing bad will be allowed to happen, no crashes, no depreciation, until the Olympic Games have passed, and so meanwhile the party continues.

As I finished my steak, which was a very good steak, nicely marbled, seared just so, and to my evolving taste buds, which had adjusted to Chinese fare, completely flavorless, I wondered if it was at all possible to lose money in China. And then I considered the bill, which was hideous. I looked around the room, listened to the businessmen in murmured conversation, and realized that there was probably just one person in this room who was not coming out ahead from his stay in the Jin Mao Tower. But I consoled myself and figured that if all went well, my wife would never learn just how much I squandered in one evening in Shanghai—unless, of course, I decided to write about it. (So, Honey. It's like this . . . )

The yin and yang of my budget had been thrown into disarray, and so to restore cosmic balance to my fiscal world, I moved across the river the next day and into a dilapidated hotel. Drunks in the lobby? Check. Dirty green shag carpet in the room? Check. Seat missing from toilet? Check. Bed that looked like the scene of a gruesome crime scene? Check. View of trash-strewn alley? Check. Harmony was returning to my fiscal world. True, it was the kind of hotel with the cracked walls and the chipped paint that suggested sinister things were afoot, but it was cheap, and even more important for my interests, it was well-located, within walking distance of the Bund, which is where I found myself on one gloriously crisp, radiant sunny morning.

No, I jest. The air was breathtakingly foul and I could only assume that for the people of Shanghai sunshine was now nothing more than a dim memory sometimes recalled in elegiac detail by an elder old enough to recall the Qing Dynasty. But still, the swirling clouds of particulate matter did little to deter my enthusiasm during my stroll on the Bund. This little corner of China across the Huangpu River from Pudong and extending through the leafy tangle of villas and avenues in the French Concession is quite likely the easiest place for a Westerner to feel at home in China. This is, of course, because it was built by Westerners. Before they arrived, Shanghai was a sleepy port city of little importance, but its status changed considerably after China lost the First Opium War in 1842 and the city was opened up to the barbarians, who sought to re-create a splendid European burg of Art Deco and Neo-Classical edifices. The fifty-two buildings that comprise the Bund are reflective of the apogee of that era in the early nineteenth century, when the city was quite likely the very coolest place to be for an expat. It wasn't suffused merely with British, American, and French seekers of wealth and adventure, but also with those displaced by the galloping hoofs of history, mostly White Russians and European Jews who had discovered how very quickly things can change. This was an era of intrigue and champagne, when fortunes were won and lost, gambling dens thrived, and so, too, prostitution, and an Englishman could stroll along the river and dismissively wave off the locals as nothing more than coolies. Things changed, of course. There was the war. And then, in 1949, red flags flew over Shanghai, too, as Mao Zedong marched into power. Somehow, Mao managed to make glittering Shanghai both bland and terrifying, which is a tricky feat to pull off.

Today, Shanghai is no longer bland, of course. There's a transcendental hipness to the city. It's a happening place. There is groove music. There are lounges. And spaces. There are restaurants, like M on the Bund, that rival any restaurant anywhere. It is the sort of place where, if I were a restless, unattached, childless man of twenty-some years with lungs of steel, I'd perhaps make it a point to learn the Shanghainese dialect of the Wu variation of the Chinese language, then hightail it pronto for this city on the coast. Because there is action here, even on the Bund, where stores line the cobbled streets offering the latest from Givenchy and Hermès, and bankers can be seen in slick suits and skinny ties driving BMWs, the 7 Series, on their way to lunch at Jean Georges.

But I was just a visitor in Shanghai, and as I viewed the goings-on on the Bund from the River Path across the road, I experienced exciting first-time-visitor encounters with the path's local denizens.

"You want Rolex?" asked a woman, displaying her wares on her arms.

"A Rolex? Really?"

"It is very beautiful."

"Yes. It sure is beautiful."

"I give you special price. Hundred dollars. Good price."

"Gosh. That sounds like a real bargain. But tell you what. Let me help you today." I showed her my traveling watch. "Let me give you a special price—say, $50. It is very beautiful. See, it even has Mickey Mouse on it. It's very valuable."

She laughed and pulled out a pen. "Mont Blanc. Good price."

I pulled out my pen. "Bic. Very good quality. Made in China. Ten dollars for you."

This was fun for the first three Rolex sellers, but then I grew bored and instead I replied to their inquiries with the all-time most useful Chinese words I had yet learned in China: *bu yao*. I don't want it. But if I'd had a pressing need for a Rolex, I now knew where to find one. Of course, the watches on offer here were poor imitations, but if I knew what I was doing, and I didn't, shopping in China being one of those things best left for professionals, I have no doubt that somewhere in Shanghai I'd be able to find a top-of-the-line, can't-tell-the-difference genuine imitation Rolex of sufficient craftsmanship that not even a watchmaker in Basel, Switzerland, would be able to tell them apart. The Chinese not only produce mountains of fake products, they also produce mountains of very good fake products. And the aspirations of fake-product producers had moved far higher than watches to include such things as, incredibly, cars. The Chinese automaker Shuanghuan Automobile even went so far as to produce a knockoff of the BMW X5, an SUV, and if you think they felt a little shameful about shamelessly copying a BMW, you'd be wrong. They unveiled the car at the Frankfurt Motor Show, just up the autobahn from the home of BMW. Now, that's gumption.

But, apparently, the Chinese regard counterfeiting a little differently than people do in the West. "The Chinese believe they can make the same thing, same quality, at lower cost, and pass the savings on to consumers, while making a profit," Dan had explained one afternoon as we perused the DVDs for sale on a Beijing sidewalk. "So it's a win-win for everyone. That's the Chinese view. No one is going to spend $100 or whatever buying an operating system from Microsoft, when they can buy a counterfeit operating system for $10. It's just inefficient."

But hadn't they been forced to crack down since joining the World Trade Organization?

"Sure. It's not as blatant as it used to be. There aren't as many people selling counterfeit DVDs as there used to be, though, as you've seen, there are still a lot of them. In the Silk

Market, you used to be able to buy fake Armani. Today, you can still buy fake Armani. But it doesn't say Armani anymore. Same jacket. Different label."

The result being, of course, that it is nearly impossible to ascertain the authenticity of anything in China, and while I walked around magnetically attracting every peddler of Rolex watches or jade pendants, the Chinese, too, could find no assurances that the baby powder they bought was really baby powder or the High-Quality DVD Genuine Imitation Mission Impossible III was, in fact, High-Quality, and not, in fact, the recording of some guy with a camcorder sitting in a theater. Near the river, in the warren of alleys that is the Yuyuan Bazaar, between the clusters of old men playing mah-jongg, I'd spotted absolutely everything ever made for sale—buttons, cloth, yarn, fans, belts, sunglasses, beads, tea, antiques, so alleged—and I even beheld in my hands a carved mammoth tusk (!), which has to be just about one of the finest things one could ever have on a shelf of curios. Mammoths, of course, have long been extinct, which solved any potential moral qualms I had. And while I wasn't at all certain whether the global ban on ivory trading extended to mammoth tusks, I did very seriously consider beginning bargaining proceedings with the proprietor, who assured me that it was very real. But I didn't completely believe her. You can't in China.

After I'd been accosted by the twentieth watch peddler, I began to wonder if there was anything else of interest on the Bund. I'd popped into the Peace Hotel, the home away from home for luminaries like Charlie Chaplin and Noël Coward. I'd turned to glance up at the apartment of Victor Sassoon, bon vivant of the Shanghai of yore. I'd pondered the boundless river traffic, the trawlers bearing coal and trucks beneath the steel-and-glass facade of Pudong. And then, as I ambled onward, I came across the Bund Sightseeing Tunnel and I thought, Hey, I'm a sightseer on the Bund, so why not have a gander?

All I can say is that if you happen to find yourself in Shanghai with a bag of magic mushrooms and you were looking to maximize the sensory overload of your magic mushroom ride, the Bund Sightseeing Tunnel is just the place for you. I was led to an underground monorail that called to mind a Jetsons cartoon, and soon I was experiencing one of the trippiest journeys I'd ever made. There were flashing lights and lasers, and then suddenly balloonlike figures, like the ones you see fluttering in suburban car dealerships, appeared, followed by a film screen with sharks on it, which quickly rolled up, and all the while a strange, female voice would murmur *space swirl, magma, fossil variations, shooting stars,* and as I stepped off with a baffled air—*what the hell was that?*—I soon found myself confronted by a big sign that read "China Sex Culture and History Exhibition: First Time in 5,000 Years," and I began to wonder, What doesn't this tunnel have?

In the spirit of journalistic inquiry, I put on the proverbial raincoat, bought a ticket, and entered the exhibition, which could have been called The Art of the Dildo. I had assumed that China maintained a relatively repressed attitude toward sex, but in this, too, I was wrong. True, the government holds a prudish disposition and keeps a careful eye on the lyrical content of pop songs and the skin content of films, but Chinese society, at least its urban variation, seemed to have a rather Swedish disposition toward sex. Whereas the French suffuse sex with romance and eroticism, Swedes have a much more matter-of-fact approach. It's just something people do. No big deal. The Chinese, thus, are the Swedes of Asia (you heard it here first), and nowhere is this more evident than in the sweeping proliferation of dildo shops in urban China. Every neighborhood seemed to have one. It's true. You can't buy *Playboy* in China, but should your sexual needs involve battery-operated devices, just head on down to your friendly neighborhood sextoy emporium and pick up the new and improved Deep Thruster—made in China, of course, which has pretty much cornered the global dildo market.

And, as I was now being informed, China has a long history with dildos—5,000 years apparently. There were jade dildos and ivory dildos and wood dildos of every size and shape. And there was also ancient porn. I'm partial to an illustrated Kama Sutra. (Have you seen the ancient Hindu goddess of fertility? Hot, even with four arms.) But, as I peered a little more closely at these crudely rendered porcelain depictions of intimate acts, I gathered that these images were not meant to arouse but to inform, and I can only say that if I were an ancient Chinese lass on her wedding day, spending a few minutes with Mom, who was informing her daughter of what exactly was expected of her on her wedding night, I'd flee. Though I did note that the evening would end with cuddling.

Toward the end of the exhibit, near the plaques commemorating the awards won by China's leading sexologists, was a sign that pretty much summarized the purpose of the items on display.

> *The sex medicine and sex tools were popularized in ancient age because men needed sex medicine to*

*strong their sex ability and women needed sex tools for masturbation because the women had to keep their chastity and couldn't remarriage, and the wives and concubines couldn't satisfy their sex desire from their husbands.*

Which is just so thoughtful.

Soon thereafter, I found myself in a restaurant, gratefully perusing an English-language menu, which informed me that I might want to consider the Bullfrog. It's not very often that I ponder the wonders of a bullfrog, but this one would come barbecued. I have a soft spot for barbecue. Not so much for its Southern porky manifestation (too sweet), but for, well, pretty much everything else that's grilled over smoky embers. Purists and semanticists, of course, would argue that only a pig cooked in the Southern manner can be considered true barbecue and any deviation should be called grilling, to which I say *whatever*. On many a fine evening, and even those that are not so fine, I can be found standing over a Weber, barbecuing fish, shrimps, hunks of flesh, and myriad vegetables. It is, frankly, the only way I know to make squash taste good. I do it because I like it. And it makes me feel like a Man.

But never had I considered the possibility of grilling a frog. Not once. Clearly, when it comes to barbecue, the Chinese are out-of-the-box thinkers. I was in a busy restaurant on a side street near the bustling pedestrian arcade known as Nanjing Lu. I was intrigued by this barbecued bullfrog, and then I noticed that the menu also offered a barbecued goose, my all-time favorite bird for eating, and I thought, Why not? Let's have both. I'm crazy that way. "And some vegetables in supreme broth too, please?" I said to the waiter, very carefully pointing to the correct Chinese translation lest I accidentally commit myself to a heaping platter of sheep gonads. "*Xie xie* very much."

As I waited, I noticed an Englishman sitting with an attractive Chinese woman at a nearby table.

"Would you like a drink?" he asked her. "Rum and Coke? Do you know where rum comes from? The West Indies. Scotch? Scotland. Vodka comes from Russia . . ."

And on and on he went.

". . . in France, people drink wine. Wine also comes from Italy. Slivovice comes from Serbia . . ."

What a dork. Here he was in a restaurant in China with an actual Chinese person who could speak English—though this might have been a fanciful presumption; she hadn't uttered a word—but still, presumably, a person who could unlock the mysteries of the Middle Kingdom, and he'd decided to educate her about Europe, which we all know is a totally irrelevant region that's about to be subsumed into the Muslim caliphate (I watch Fox News occasionally too). Here he was with a person who could resolve some of the most curious Chinese puzzles—like why, for instance, every day in China there are tens of millions of toddlers piddling on sidewalks. Why is this so? I understood the reluctance to use disposable diapers. It's the eco-friendly thing to do. But for those little ones that aren't quite babies and aren't quite ready for potty training—or squat training, as the case may be with Chinese toilets—why have them waddling around in split pants? Are the results not regarded as a little messy, a wee bit unsanitary? I could understand the reluctance to use a public toilet in China. They're hideous. There are few things more disturbing to the soul than the sight of thirty men squatting side by side in open stalls, smoking and shitting. But still. Every day, toddlers in split pants unleash rivers of pee and dollops of poo on the streets of China, and this seemed strange and peculiar and in need of questioning, though possibly not in a restaurant.

Meanwhile, as I sampled the frog (legs only, like chicken with Chinese characteristics) and savored the goose (excellent, but why so many bones? And difficult to eat with chopsticks), the Englishman next to me continued to prattle on about Europe.

". . . Italy is known for art. Germany for music. England for literature . . ."

Truly, a nitwit. I paid the bill, and as I walked past them, I noticed that he'd become a little more expansive in his sharing of knowledge.

". . . Suits are single-breasted or double-breasted . . ."

And this was interesting how?

". . . there are two countries famous for silk, Thailand and China . . ."

And you don't think she knows that, Romeo?

Really. I had never encountered such a pedantic clod in my life. I left, and as I turned the corner, I nearly tripped over a dead pig on the sidewalk. They're perilous places, sidewalks in China. It's not just leaky toddlers one needs to watch out for. But I sidestepped the carcass, and as I digested my bullfrog I refused to let my mind linger on food-sanitation issues because, really, in China it's just pointless.

I returned to bustling Nanjing Lu, noting the bamboo scaffolding climbing up the sides of these modern buildings, and far above me the window washers dangling on swings cleaning the facade of the Marriot Hotel next to the Ferrari dealership. Hordes of shoppers were going through the 10-yuan bin at the Shanghai Number 1 Department Store. Soon, I was encountering all sorts of friendly people again offering to sell me a Rolex or a Mont Blanc pen, or inquiring whether I'd like to *make love Chinese girl* or possibly visit their art studio. I talked to everyone who approached me, whether loathsome tout or earnest art student, simply because it's good to talk now and then, and in China I made do with what few opportunities came my way. *A Rolex? Is it real? Make love Chinese girl? Gosh. Sounds intriguing. But how about make love Chinese man?*

My conversations with pimps were brief.

I made my way across the expanse of Renmin Square, declining friendly offers from pretty women to enjoy a traditional Chinese tea service with them, knowing as I did so that this was not actually an invitation to experience traditional Chinese culture in a flirtatious environment, but simply an opportunity to drink highly overpriced tea with a woman counting the minutes until she can bolster her commission by luring another befuddled *laowai* inside. Instead, I wandered onward to the Shanghai Museum, the contents of which once needed to be hidden under banners of Maoist slogans to prevent the Red Guards from smashing its collection of old culture. Today, however, the museum was offering an exhibition titled "From Cezanne to Pollock: Master Drawings from MOMA," which was interesting—but not nearly as interesting as the game show being played live on national TV right there in the lobby. There was an enormous

JumboTron television that featured game-show participants and a studio audience who were apparently watching the goings-on inside the museum, where a cameraman was filming a game-show host in TV makeup asking questions to several museum visitors. I spent a moment watching them tape this show inside the museum. I didn't really know what was going on, though it seemed strangely loud and raucous given that we were in the general hushiness of a museum. I made several attempts to try to get into the picture, where I hoped to avail myself of the opportunity to make silly faces and peace signs on Chinese national television, but there were twenty guards minimum and they did not look like the sort of people one should trifle with, so I headed onward to the Chinese Calligraphy Hall.

I really don't have any particular expertise or insight into the dominant trends affecting the calligraphy of the early Tang Dynasty or the dreamy landscape paintings from the late Song era (except to say that they're kind of dreamy), so we'll dispense with Olympian-like art criticism and just add that the Shanghai Museum is a very fine museum and that my appreciation for Chinese art was very much uplifted by my wanderings through its thoughtfully lit halls and corridors. Also, I'd add that when it comes time to update my current furniture situation, which is presently under siege by two enthusiastic little boys with a proclivity for fort-building and toppling sippy cups, I will definitely be looking for teak furniture in the Qing Dynasty style, maybe when the boys are in the sullen teenage years when they just want to sleep all day and refuse to believe that their parents really do understand them. That's a good time for new furniture. And I liked this furniture in the Qing Dynasty style very much.

There was also an exhibition detailing Buddhist influence in China, and as I peered at the display, I listened to an American man explain its contents to the Chinese woman beside him.

"And what is this? This is the bodhisattva. He received enlightenment under a tree. I have a leaf from the actual tree. It's in Sri Lanka. Remember? I showed it to you. And now," he said, pointing to a statue. "You know what this is? Yes? We've discussed this before."

What is it about Shanghai that elicits this need in the Western male to inform, to enlighten, the locals? I could not understand it myself. Indeed, my general state of being in China could best be described as one of bewildered ignorance. But perhaps this resort to pedantry was simply their reaction to a similar sense of befuddlement. *I can't tell the difference between the Ming and the Qing Dynasties, but did you know that suits come either single-breasted or double-breasted?*

I walked out and followed Nanjing Xi Lu toward Jing'an Park, and all the while tried to remind myself that the average monthly income of a typical resident of Shanghai is only about $300. In this sparkling stretch of Shanghai, it appeared one would need to add a few zeros to that income. There were Chinese fashionistas tottering down the sidewalk wearing Prada and Armani. On the road, there was a preponderance of Mercedeses. I even saw a limousine. At Jing'an Park, I had expected to find a quiet temple, but instead I'd found four statues of punk rockers next to a plaza featuring a basketball demonstration game played to the thumping beats of American gangster rap emanating at sonic levels from a massive boom box. It really is so easy to be weirded out in China. As I watched these ball players dunking and competing to see who could get their head above the rim, I spent a few minutes deciphering lyrics. *Motherfuckin', hustle, guns, shit, homicide. Women in my life causing me confusion and shit. Sell my weapon. Fuck you. Fuck you.*

Excellent, I thought. The Europeans could take confidence in the allure of their products in China, but Americans could at least take pride knowing they were winning the battle for hearts and minds here.

But there were more curiosities to be found. On the sidewalk, an elderly woman with a headband inscrolled with Chinese characters and a sign pasted to her shirt, was loudly and theatrically complaining about something. I stopped to watch. So, too, did others. Nothing stops a crowd in China like a really angry person. I approached a fashionably dressed woman, thinking that the wearing of fine clothes might have some correlation to knowledge of the English language.

"Yes. I speak a little," she confirmed.

"May I ask you something? What is this lady saying?"

"Her dialect is difficult to understand. But she is saying that she is not happy with the Party. She says they are not fair." Pause. "She says that they murdered her husband."

"Ah . . . I see. And does she say why the Party murdered her husband?"

"I am sorry. She is very difficult to understand. She does not speak the Shanghai dialect."

"Do you think the police will bother her, or is it okay in China today to stand on busy street corners and accuse the Party of murdering people?"

"No. The police will bother her. I must go now. Thank you."

I waited at a discreet distance and watched three plain-clothes policemen take this elderly woman, screaming mightily, into an unmarked minivan. Well, maybe there is something Westerners can teach the Chinese, I thought. And then I thought of events in the U.S. over the past few years, where it is now acceptable to jail people indefinitely and without charge as long as the President says so. Perhaps I'd approached this wrong. Maybe the Chinese aren't working toward some vaguely American-type model. Maybe it's us who are moving toward the Chinese Model, and this realization caused a fleeting moment of despair, and then I remembered that it was time to search for sustenance again, and I walked onward into the Shanghai night.

# 10

In the year 1298, a romance writer by the name of Rustichello found himself sharing a prison cell in Genoa with a man who called himself Marco Polo. Bored, they got to talking and the results of the encounter eventually became the book known as *The Travels of Marco Polo,* which was the Harry Potter of its time. Well, not quite, as it would still be another 120 years until Johannes Gutenberg invented the printing press. Nevertheless, the book captured the imagination of the medieval literary world, which was composed of the approximately eleven people who could actually read in medieval Europe. But for these eleven people the book was a sensation. And it is no wonder. In it, a young and intrepid Marco Polo leaves Venice with his father and uncle, crosses the Black Sea, and follows the Silk Road all the way to the summer court of Kublai Khan in the pleasure dome of Xanadu. Young Marco clearly made a fine impression on the emperor, for he remained a part of his court for the next seventeen years, during which time he was frequently sent as a diplomatic emissary to the far-flung lands of what we now think of as China. During one such mission, he was sent to Hangzhou, a city that so enchanted him he referred to it as the "finest and most splendid city in the world," full of stone bridges and charming lanes and winsome women leading an idyllic life on the graceful shores of West Lake.

Of course, these winsome women would have been tottering on bound feet, an observation that seemed to have escaped young Marco, and the beverage of choice in Hangzhou, and indeed throughout much of China, would have been tea, another detail somehow overlooked by Marco, leading some to believe that *The Travels of Marco Polo* was really a fabulist's dream. Perhaps Marco Polo did really spend an eventful seventeen years in the court of Kublai Khan. Or perhaps he simply had a keen ear for the tales told by the Arab merchants who traded along the Silk Road. In any event, someone somewhere in the late thirteenth century once described Hangzhou as the "finest and most splendid city in the world," and this alone seemed like a compelling reason to visit.

I'd boarded a train in Shanghai, where, as I tumbled among the multitudes of travelers, I was quickly reminded that Shanghai is not all money and glitz. There are 200 million migrant workers in China, and I do believe they were all migrating together through the Shanghai train station on that same day. And really, these migrant workers with the disheveled hair, clutching worn bags, economic refugees from a rural China that has seen none of the prosperity of the cities, remain representative of the vast majority of Chinese. There is an enormous gap in China between the women in Chanel on Nanjing Xi Lu and the migrant workers washing windows high above the city. These workers sat behind me on the train, in hard-seat class, while I stretched in relative comfort in a soft-seat car, watching vendors wander the aisles selling drinks, food, trinkets, toys, bracelets, and even golden commemorative plates graced with the visage of Chairman Mao.

Next to me sat a nattily dressed elderly man.

"You are traveling in China?" he asked in flawless English, a linguistic feat that startled me, as I had to yet to hear a soul over forty speak English during my travels here.

"Yes," I said.

"Where have you been?"

I told him.

"You have not seen much yet. China is a big country."

This was manifestly true.

"Where are you going now?"

"To Hangzhou," I said.

"You must walk around West Lake. It is very beautiful."

"I will. May I say that your English is excellent?"

"I studied English as a boy, and I always remembered it. Later, I had to study Russian, but I've already forgotten most of it. I was a professor of chemistry in Shanghai."

"Ah," I said, trying very hard to think of a question or observation that pertained to chemistry, but before I could ask him to explain the mysteries of the periodic table, he asked me what I did.

"I do some writing," I said.

"And will you be writing about China?"

"Maybe. It's a very complicated country."

"You need to live here if you want to understand China."

Yes, well, I would, I thought, if I could find someplace in China that didn't feel like a biohazard zone. Until I found such a place, I was beginning to realize, I couldn't in good conscience bring two little kids to live here. I could imagine them years later; *I'm glad you had a chance to understand China, Daddy. Cough, cough. Don't worry. It's only the emphysema.*

"I'm thinking about it," I said noncommittally. It seemed impolite to suggest that I found the air in China so abysmally foul.

"Hmm." He nodded. "You are an American?"

"I live there."

"I think many Americans believe we still shave our foreheads and wear long ponytails."

"Do you think so?"

"Yes. American movies portray the Chinese very unkindly, like Charlie Chang."

"That's true. But I think that's changed."

Surely he'd be proud to have his culture represented by Jackie Chan. And then I thought about it for a moment, and as I recalled the Chinese stereotypes in the latter *Star Wars* movies, and the evil agents on *24* and so on, I had to concede that he did have a point and that for Hollywood, when it comes to the Chinese, there is only Bruce Lee and Ming the Merciless.

I asked him if he'd traveled to the United States.

"I have been to Berkeley, Seattle, and Omaha," he said.

*And Omaha?* An interesting choice for a travel itinerary in America. And a good one. I wondered where I could find the Chinese Omaha.

"My son works for Microsoft," he added.

"Is that right?" I said. "You must be very proud of your son." It's a long, hard journey from the streets of Shanghai to the gilded campus in Redmond. "But I would think that today there are as many, if not more, opportunities in China as there are in the U.S."

"Maybe," he said, shrugging his shoulders. And then he nodded off to sleep.

Pity, I thought. In a way he reminded me of my grand-mother, born in the hills of Moravia, a place where over a life-time, without once leaving the village, one could find oneself living in four separate countries. History looms large for the seventy-plus crowd, and while the sands of time have largely been benign for the last generation or two, I sensed that we were on the cusp of something momentous and unprecedented, and I hoped to be able to ride it out so that I, too, decades later, could greet foreigners on a train while resplendent in tweed.

It is but a two-hour journey from Shanghai to Hangzhou, and I left the train for a grubby train station, where the taxi drivers weren't at all confident where West Lake was.

"Bloody hell," fumed an English backpacker. "What, is it not far enough? They don't think they'll make enough money?"

"No," I said to her. It's interesting how quickly China can reduce the traveler to a state of rage and confusion. "In all like-lihood, the driver is from some distant town and has never encountered a foreigner before and probably doesn't know how to read a map."

I felt like an old China hand.

At last, with map in hand, a note with my hotel's name in Chinese characters, and with my big dopey *laowai* grin that suggested I could be easily overcharged, I finally convinced a taxi driver to take me onward. I had assumed Hangzhou, on the shores of famed West Lake, to be a town of modest size. It is one of the most popular destinations for Chinese tourists, and I had expected that it would be cutesy quaint, possibly even a seasonal town, the sort of place that quietly shuts down at the end of the summer. I'm not sure why I was so fantastically misinformed. Hangzhou is a humming city of 7 million people on the forefront of the tsunami that is the Chinese economy. Indeed, as in Beijing and Shanghai, should one have a compelling need to buy a Porsche, Ferrari, or even a Bentley, there are dealerships in Hangzhou only too happy to assist you. Though how anyone could be brave enough to drive such a gilded car in a country with 200 million hungry migrant workers was something I could not quite understand.

Eventually, we made our way through this teeming city to the very edges of West Lake, which shimmered appealingly in the hazy light of late afternoon. We drove along Hubin Lu, and then we drove back down Hubin Lu, all the while with me beside the driver, sputtering, *No, this way . . . no, no, turn there . . . it should be right there . . . okay, just stop here and I'll find it myself.* Which I did thirty seconds later. It was an unusually fine hotel for me in China. It was no Grand Hyatt, of course, but there were Chinese men in golf shirts in the lobby pondering the purchase of a condo from a sales group offering luxurious abodes in the sky in a place called Upperclass. This must be like what Miami felt like in 2004, I thought. I wondered what the Chinese word for "subprime" might be.

I checked in, pleased that while the dollar might be slipping into the abyss elsewhere in the world, in China, which pegs its currency to the dollar, $35 and a bit of haggling gets you a mighty fine room in Hangzhou. I dropped my bag off and walked toward the lake, where I soon found a statue of Marco Polo himself. There was a walking path beside the lake, and beside it were speakers piping in ambient traditional Chinese music, which is rarely ambient, but did seem so here. On the footpath, a policeman was chasing a man pedaling a heavy black bicycle. He reached for the back grille and grabbed it and then the two men began to argue violently, which seemed interesting to me, this lack of deference to policemen, until finally and unhappily the cyclist turned around, muttering darkly as he sped by.

There must be some sort of code enforcement here, I thought. So far this footpath was the only place in China where I hadn't found myself beseeched by beggars and hounded by pimps. I found a sedate restaurant that offered superb crab dumplings and mushrooms, and thought how amazing it is what the Chinese can do with fungi. We just squander them on top of pizzas or ignore them in our salads, but here in China the mushroom gets the respect it deserves.

It was dark when I finished, and I wandered back toward the general vicinity of my hotel. Now, in the dark gloom, I was approached by the familiar touts and purveyors of counterfeit shoes.

"Nike, Adidas," said one. "Good price. You buy?"

"*Bu yao,*" I said, and stepped inside a well-lit convenience store to buy some water, since the likelihood of finding tap water anywhere in China that isn't contaminated—either with parasites or industrial waste—is approximately nil. As I went to pay, a man pushed his way up before me and demanded a pack of cigarettes.

Now, I want to be clear about this. I am very open-minded when it comes to other cultures. By this time, it did not trouble me—well, okay, it troubled me less—that men in China would hawk enormous globs of phlegm and send it hurling forth before you like a wet, gloppy fusillade. But this cutting-in-line business? It continued to steam me. I took a deep breath and reflected on the Chinese context here. Perhaps if I'd been raised in a country of 1.3 billion people, a country that on the surface seemed to be organized on largely Darwinian principles, I'd be a pushy line-cutter myself. And then I extolled myself for my cultural empathy.

Outside, I cooled my temper with a refreshing gulp from a plastic bottle of what I hoped was clean-ish water—you really can't hope for more—and soon found myself enmeshed in a gaggle of little beggars.

"Do you not have parents?" I asked the little girl, three, maybe four years old, who tugged at my sleeve and who looked upon me with giant saucer eyes. There were four, five, six little ones now, all pleading *money money*. "Seriously, you are very little people. You should be at home reading Chinese fairy tales. Really, you are just way too young for this. Who takes care of you?"

*Money, money.*

In the shadows I saw an old, hunched woman with a weathered face. She waved and smiled. I waved back and wandered off to search for a place to drink a beer. Inside the Party-Time Disco and Bar, I found myself bathed in a dim blue light listening to trance music. *Who are you people?* I wondered, glancing at the dozens of figures around me. They must have been eighteen, tops, and they sat on couches listlessly playing games with dice as the tables filled with bottles of Crowne Royal and 35-yuan Tsingtao. I sipped at my beer and watched these young Chinese hipsters, the girls sucking on lollipops, and thought, You kids are just way too young for this. Really, ennui at eighteen. It's just not right.

As time went on, I had begun wondering about sports in China. The Chinese, of course, are fantastically good at gymnastics, Ping-Pong, swimming, particularly diving, soccer, especially women's soccer, basketball, and badminton (it's a sport, really), but you never actually see the Chinese doing sporting endeavors. Not once in China did I see a jogger. Of course, the mere thought of jogging in China made me laugh. Few endeavors strike me as more absurd than running in China, a country in which people routinely wear surgical masks while conducting their errands. Nor did I see anyone playing soccer or volleyball or even badminton, which, judging by the television coverage on the Chinese sports channel—a knockoff of ESPN, incidentally—is a sport in which the Chinese kick serious butt in international competitions. Beyond the basketball players and the gangster rap in Shanghai, I never actually saw anyone in China play sports as just a sort of fun thing to do on a Saturday afternoon. And yet they excelled at so many sports at the international level. How could this be? I wondered.

In China, sports are not meant to be fun. Like in the East Germany of old, China has sports factories where youngsters who have demonstrated an unusual aptitude for a sport or a particular body type, like being a six-foot second-grader, are sent for rigorous training. Sports are seen as an extension of China's strength and swiftness. It's not about you, these youngsters are told. It's not about the team. It's about the great nation of China. To see a Chinese woman lose a badminton match is a searing experience. She is crushed, humiliated, embarrassed. You can barely look. You can tell that she feels she has shamed the nation. And while I couldn't understand the commentators, I sensed they believed likewise. *You did not try hard enough, Liling* (which, incidentally, means Beautiful Jade Tinkle). *You have shamed the Motherland. And after China has done so much for you, you dare to lose? Shame!*

Sports are seen in an almost martial light. Indeed, as they prepared for the Olympics, the Chinese national basketball team trained by going to boot camp. They lived together in communal barracks. They were given military uniforms. Chinese military uniforms, alas for the players, did not come in the size XXXXXL required to cover a seven-footer, and so the team went through their paces in pants that flopped around their shins. But did they complain? They did not, except for Wang Zhizhi, a seven-foot-one center who was the first Chinese player in the NBA, and who refused to join the team for the hard drudgery of boot camp. Then the shame campaign began. Newspapers denounced his selfishness. Television commentators bemoaned his lack of national pride. After all, look what China had done for him. In the end, sputtering his humblest apologies and reaffirming that he would endure any hardship for the Motherland, Wang Zhizhi joined his team for the rigorous training that followed.

Though few Chinese participate in sports themselves, they

are not without activities that they turn to as sporting endeavors. There is, of course, bargaining. The Chinese excel at bargaining. They live and breathe it. This game of parrying back and forth is not played with hostility, it's just mindlessly played every day for almost everything. For spectator sports, however, the options are more limited. To be sure, there is professional soccer. And there is professional basketball. It's a good league too. The Chinese, in general, are not the tallest people in the world, but in a land of 1.3 billion people, there is bound to be a large number of statistical aberrations. Indeed, the tallest person in the world is Bao Xishun, a seven-foot-nine Mongolian herdsman famed for once being called upon to use his lengthy arms to reach deep into the throats of two dolphins who had swallowed bits of plastic in an aquarium in Fushun. But other tall people have found their way to the sport academies and now play some really good professional ball. Indeed, Americans, those who were good enough to play college ball but not quite good enough for the pros and just can't let go of the dream, have found themselves playing in the Chinese league, and as I watched them on television I couldn't help but wonder what on earth it must be like to be big and black in China.

For everyday spectator sports, however, the Chinese have turned to arguments. Nothing attracts a crowd in China like a good quarrel. This was my observation on the shores of West Lake the following morning. Two elderly women had stopped before a park bench where they were engaged in an argument of epic proportions. They screamed. They mocked. They waved their hands in threatening manners. They did not strike each other. But they wanted to. You could tell. All around them, people had stopped to observe the commotion. They had halted their lakeside perambulations to view the goings-on. There were dozens of people, then a hundred or more as the ladies argued. It was a flash crowd. I could imagine the text messages: *Two old women going AT IT beside West Lake. 9:47 AM. Be there.*

I had come to West Lake because it was said to be serene, and I wanted to see what that felt like, serenity in China, and so I kept walking. In the botanical gardens, there were temples and pagodas and ponds full of goldfish. They were all replicas; not much of Hangzhou survives from its glory days as capital of the Southern Song Dynasty. What wasn't razed during the Taiping Rebellion of 1851 was finally destroyed during the lunacy of the Cultural Revolution. Indeed, not much of old China can be found anywhere, since so much of it was built with wood. But that's okay. The Chinese are very good at replicas. In fact, the shoreline walk around West Lake seemed sort of ideal from a Chinese perspective: It was both tranquil and fake, but not fake in a bad way, fake in a new and improved sort of way. At the eastern shore of the lake, I came across a woman on a bench who was feeding dumplings to her Western boyfriend.

"You will be a sex maniac," she said. It's what I do in China. Eavesdrop.

Shortly thereafter, I opened my wallet and discovered that I was in need of money. China is largely a cash-only economy and so I headed over to the Bank of China, where I hoped to find an ATM that could manage an international transaction. I found one, which asked me for my pin number in English, but after I'd entered it the next screen appeared in Chinese, making it a trifle challenging. Was I getting cash or was I transferring my entire savings to an account in Laos? I fumbled with the keypad, and afterward, flush with cash, I walked toward the streets of downtown Hangzhou.

Suddenly, a man with a wild, leering expression appeared beside me. "German?" he said mystifyingly. I told him no and kept walking.

"Money," he said. I ignored him and walked on. Suddenly, from behind, I was struck hard.

"WHAT THE FUCK!" I yelled. Pain seared across my ear. I whirled around to face this man. My ear was ringing mightily.

"What the fuck are you doing?" I demanded.

He began yelling at me, smiling, leering. He was with others, young men with cruel expressions. A crowd had stopped to watch. They stood silently, just watching. I didn't like this. None of it. I didn't understand what was going on. I had been hit. I didn't know why. The man continued to yell. And he smirked. He leered. The scene was incomprehensible. I decided to walk away. I turned to go. I started walking.

*SMACK.*

"WHAT THE FUCK, YOU MOTHERFUCKER," I shouted.

He had hit me with an open-handed slap to the back of my head. Now he was taunting me, smiling maniacally, yelling. There were hundreds of people gathered around, staring with inscrutable faces. No one said a word.

"COULD SOMEONE TELL ME WHAT HE'S SAYING? WHAT DOES HE WANT?"

Adrenaline was surging through my veins. Being hit,

unexpectedly and without cause, had left me in a state of confused shock. And fear. What the fuck? I thought this was a police state.

"You," I said, addressing a man with an officious-looking name tag. "Can you tell me what's going on? Do you speak English?"

My assailant continued to scream and leer at me.

"Anyone?"

There was nothing, just hundreds of faces staring, utterly devoid of expression. Then I saw Mr. Sex Maniac.

"Do you understand Chinese? Can you tell me what he's saying?"

"No, man. But my girlfriend does."

But she refused to say anything. She demurred and turned away with blank eyes.

"Where're you from, man?" Mr. Sex Maniac asked.

I'm being stalked by a violent lunatic and you want to get all social-like? What the fuck!

"California," I muttered. *You useless, unhelpful shit.*

I decided I needed to get away from this as quickly as possible. I walked on. I turned to see what the lunatic would do. He continued to scream. When he saw me looking at him, he smiled and then screamed some more. I kept walking.

*SMACK.*

I kept walking. Walking. Walking.

So I was a little stressed. A little tense. Discombobulated. Should I have hit him back? Yes. Probably. I don't know. Maybe he knew that kung-fu voodoo magic. Perhaps he'd spent his formative years in the Shaolin Temple. I'd hit him and he'd drop me like Bruce Lee. Possibly he had a knife. It was a very long walk back to the hotel, as such walks are when, at any moment, you expect to feel the cool blade of a knife slicing through your torso. This was not typical of China, this getting slapped around at rush hour. In China, one gets the death penalty for far less. I simply had no idea what, exactly, had just transpired. Typically, in fights one knows precisely what they're fighting about. Was it because I was German? But I am not German. I am half-Dutch and half-Czech. Both halves have been invaded by Germany. Maybe he thought I was someone else. *Laowais* all look alike. Could be. Maybe he was insane. Very likely. Maybe it was an anti-foreigner thing. Possibly. As a foreigner, I wasn't exactly feeling the love in China. Perhaps it was a robbery attempt. He did ask for money. I don't know. It was just *strange.*

But what chilled me to the bone was the reaction of the crowd. There was nothing. Just hundreds of faces. And their expression? Dead. Lifeless. Nothing there. Just watching. All of them just watching with blank expressions, doing nothing, saying nothing, completely still. They would watch me die there. I would be stabbed. An artery would rupture, spilling blood. I'd be on a sidewalk in Hangzhou, China. Bleeding. Dying. And they would watch with lifeless faces. I would die. And they would watch as if it were a spectator sport.

But bleeding to death on a crowded sidewalk in Hangzhou was not on the itinerary. What to do now? I paced inside my hotel room, wandering from wall to wall. I was agitated. My adrenaline had surged and found no outlet. I felt like running for five, ten, fifteen miles. But I did not want to go back outside. And then I saw it. A little triangular card with an English translation. *Spa. Relaxing massage. Korea Massage. Thailand massage. Swedish massage. China Massage. 3rd Floor.*

I have had but one professional massage in my life, and it was on my honeymoon in France, in a seaside hotel in Brittany. There was a spa *pour hommes,* and I went, and I was oiled, and I was rubbed down by Philippe, who dimmed the lights and massaged me to the sounds of Enigma. It was okay, but it was also weird, what with scented candles and the Enigma and all. A man's hands. But I decided that now would be an excellent time for my second professional massage. It would be relaxing. It would relieve the stress. So I went to the third floor.

I was greeted by a young man dressed as a bellhop. He bounded forth and took me to a locker room. Off with my shirt. Okay. Away with my pants. Fine. Boxer shorts. Off, off, off.

All right. I stood naked before him. He handed me a pair of cotton shorts and a T-shirt. They were beige. They were also Chinese-size, and I am not Chinese-size. I would pop out of these clothes like the Incredible Hulk. One twitch of the shoulders and the shirt would shred. And the shorts were short, 1950s-style. I felt like I should be doing calisthenics, throw the old medicine ball around.

Still, I put them on and followed the spa attendant. This was China and things were done differently here. We entered a dimly lit room where there was a bed, a chair, and a dresser. The attendant left and a young woman entered, tall and lithe, dressed in white stretch pants and a T-shirt. We exchanged *nihaos* and I expressed an interest in the China Massage. Not the Thai or Korean Massage. The China Massage. This was China; thus, I should have the China Massage.

I lay down on the bed. She began to squeeze my shoulders. I was not familiar with the China Massage, but so far it was not pleasant. She kneaded my shoulders like dough. I am not very doughy, however, and neither were the Chinese, so this was bewildering, this gnashing of muscle and skin. Perhaps, I thought, it's one of those massages that are supposed to hurt but leave you feeling better in the end. I had a Japanese friend who gave massages like that, a karate-like massage that made you wince, but then afterward all the tension just seemed to have melted from your back. Maybe the China Massage was like that too. I'd hurt now but would feel better later.

She indicated that I should roll over, so I did. She squeezed my shoulders. She smelled nice. She moved down to my legs. She rubbed my thighs. And then her hands began to go up my shorts. My short shorts. Um, I thought. Er. I don't think so. I turned back over and pointed to my back. Men are not complex creatures. They are biological automatons.

Her hands returned to wringing my shoulders. Suddenly, her tongue was in my ear.

"Make love, make love," she suggested.

"No, no. No make love! China Massage," I exclaimed, startled.

"Make love, make love," she breathed.

"No, no, no. No make love. Massage. Massagee."

She reached for her cell phone. She typed *900*.

"No, no, no. I came for a massage. Relaxing China Massage."

She typed *800*. "Make love," she pleaded.

"Er . . . look . . . no! There's been a misunderstanding."

*750*. "Make love!"

It was all very embarrassing. I left and went to the locker room to change. And then I realized I'd forgotten my glasses. Once I'd dressed, I walked back toward the room to retrieve them. I encountered her in the hallway. There was bowing, many *xie xies*. Just totally embarrassing.

What an interesting day you're having, I thought. You found the brothel. Well done.

# 11

In the morning, I pondered the man dangling from the fifth-floor ledge of my hotel. It was a very exciting place, this hotel in Hangzhou. Clearly, this was a hotel that accommodated a wide variety of needs. There was, predictably, a large crowd below. There were also firefighters, all watching this man. Would he jump?

Typically in China, it's the women who jump. China has the world's highest suicide rate among women. And it's no wonder, really. In rural China, when a woman has a baby girl she is said to have delivered a *poyatou,* a worthless servant girl, instead of a *dapangxiaozi,* or big fat boy. As a result of the One Child policy, there is enormous pressure in rural China to produce boys, and as a consequence girls are often aborted. Though gender-based abortions are illegal in China, ultrasound scans are readily available and doctors routinely give coded signals to their patients, nodding if it's a boy, shaking their head if it's a girl. And if it is a girl, very often women will terminate their pregnancy. This is not good, of course. Decreeing that half of the population will never rise above mere servitude suggested a place that had more in common with the blight of Afghanistan than with the wealth of Norway.

And there are unintended consequences to enforcing a One Child policy in a society that diminishes women. Today, there are more then 40 million men in China who will never find wives. That's because the women just aren't there. They were never born. Forty million men will thus never have children of their own, will never settle down in the sociocultural arrangement that has spanned millennia—that's 40 million men who just aren't getting *any*—and yet women are still treated so abysmally badly in rural China that every year another 150,000 women go on to kill themselves, most often by swallowing pesticides. It's baffling, frankly. One would think that in a society with such an acute dearth of women, the remaining women would be swooned over, their every need catered to, that rural China would worship all things female, and yet, evidently, that is not the case.

I turned my attention back to this man on the ledge. Perhaps he had taken it upon himself to do what he could for gender parity in China. But did I want see how this ended? I did not. And I had an island to reach.

In contemplating my next move, I had set my sights on Putuoshan, a very small island in the East China Sea, about thirty miles off the coast of Ningbo. The bus to Ningbo was driven by a man with a fondness for swerving and blaring his horn, which could pretty well describe every driver in China. They are insane, these drivers; mad, crazy, dangerous. They drive angry, pissed off, aggressive. Cars, buses, trucks are just tools for them to say Fuck Off. That is how they drive in China: the Fuck Off school of driving. China has just three percent of the world's drivers, but has a quarter of all people killed each year by cars. They don't know how to drive in China. Really. Someone needs to teach them.

We passed a scene of rugged hills that appeared to have been chopped in half by a giant's sword, and more power plants nestled next to black, dusty slag heaps. We progressed past a mind-numbing array of factories, big and small, new and old, until near a cluster of umbrella factories we joined a traffic jam that had gathered behind a truck accident. It was a minor accident, a mere fender bender, but rather than move the trucks to the side of the road and clear the lane, the drivers stood in animated argument, and as we finally made our way past, our bus driver yelled at them too, then resumed the speeding, swerving, and horn-blaring that made driving in China such a lively, hair-raising, really awful experience.

In Ningbo, I changed buses and bus stations. I can say with some confidence that the part of Ningbo located around the two bus stations is hideous. It was filthy. It was, of course, teeming with crowds. Cigarettes and phlegm hurtled through the air in every direction. The buses droned by in a blue haze of exhaust fumes. Soon, however, I was joined on my new bus by four older, very chirpy Chinese passengers. They joshed and laughed, and this pleased me, because so far Ningbo was a soul-crushing dump and it felt good to suddenly be in the midst of innocent frivolity. He was funny, that old man with the blue cap and the twinkling eyes. I only wished I knew what he was talking about. But he could tell a good story, that much I gleaned. We rolled out of the city on our bus of mirth. Even the bus driver was laughing. And suddenly, the landscape had changed. It was lush and green, or rather it was lush and green in the areas that hadn't been paved over for factories and convention centers and office towers. BUILD A FIRST CLASS EXPORT PROCESSING ZONE, said a sign. And then there were more:

> CONSTRUCT AN ADVANCED
> MANUFACTURING SECTOR
> ADHERE TO SCIENTIFIC PRINCIPLES AND BUILD
> AN ADVANCED COASTAL ECONOMIC ZONE
> TIDING OVER DIFFERENCES TO
> ACHIEVE BRILLIANCE

Strange, I thought. I couldn't decide whether Maoism was truly good and dead in China, or whether these signs represented some mutant variation of it.

The bus stopped near a pier and I joined this elderly quartet of jocularity on board the boat to Putuoshan. It was a jet boat, an odd boat to use for ferrying people over open water that rippled with the wakes of giant containerships. It was sleek and made of metal, and it floated low in the water with a flat bottom that suggested that we wouldn't slice through the waves as much as fly over them. Unsurprisingly, the attendant on board handed out plastic barf bags, leading to another burst of mirthful joshing among the four travelers. Whatever meds they were on, I wanted some. On the shoreline, there was frenetic building: new factories, office towers, apartments, bridges. Huge containerships were being loaded with shoes, computers, televisions, sweaters, hats, mittens, toys that may or may not have lead, tables, chairs, and everything else.

We zoomed over the water, each ripple sending us into the sky. The water spray was brown. There were hundreds of fishing boats. On a television screen at the front of the boat, there was a short movie about Putuoshan, home of Guanyin, the bodhisattva of compassion, otherwise known as the Goddess of Mercy, and as the DVD turned to traditional music, the grandmas next to me sang along, which I found very endearing. These are fun people, I thought, these oldsters on the boat to Putuoshan. Soulful people. I wanted to hang out with them, have dinner. But I didn't speak Chinese and they didn't speak English. I had asked.

It was dusk when we finally arrived on the island. It was raining lightly, so I put on my windbreaker, heaved my pack onto my back, and started walking. Immediately, I had good feelings for Putuoshan. As I walked up a rain-slicked road, the surroundings reminded me of a village in Japan. I have not been to a village in Japan, but had always imagined it might be like this: tidy, orderly houses with happy families cleaning fish, laying out clams in buckets of water, waving kindly to passing strangers.

Now it was growing dark and it was beginning to rain harder. I found my target hotel, and as I didn't have a reservation, I steeled my mind for the ensuing bargaining, determined to get as close as I possibly could to the mythical, fabled, and ever-elusive *Chinese Price*.

"No standard room. Only executive suite," said the assistant manager, who had been called over to deal with the *laowai* who didn't plan ahead. *Executive suite,* I mulled. A bold opening move.

"I have no need for an executive suite," I explained. "Perhaps you have me confused with Zhengrong Shi," I said, referring to the richest man in China, who had made billions in solar power. "I am only a traveler. I simply need a roof over my head."

A standard room could be arranged, possibly. It would be trouble, but perhaps arrangements could be made, solutions found. Another assistant manager had to be called. And now the bargaining began in earnest. The calculator was brought out. We parried. Spectators formed around us.

"Would you accept this price?" I offered.

No, no, no, they said. This was a three-star hotel. See—look. There are our three stars. Your price is a two-star price.

"But I have stayed in official, certified by the People's Republic of China, four-star hotels for less than that price."

The crowd murmured. Who was this mysterious *laowai*?

I had stayed at only one four-star hotel, the Grand Hyatt in the Jin Mao Tower in Shanghai, and as I recalled the grim tally of my bill, I can say quite confidently that it wasn't a two-star price. But in China, white lies are perfectly acceptable in the game of bargaining.

Would I then accept this price? It is far lower than the standard rate, as you can see.

"Thank you for working with me. I am hopeful that we can come to a satisfying resolution. But that price? That is the price for a rich man. I am not a rich man. I am just a traveler. I am here to learn about China. I wish to understand China. I have a deep respect for Chinese culture."

The audience nodded approvingly, and this pleased me, because when haggling in China, it's important to have the crowd with you. By now, the manager had come out herself. She had taken control of the calculator.

"Will you accept this price?" I said, tapping in a number. "I will have to sleep in the streets for the remainder of my trip, but this is the best I can do."

She could not. No one had ever stayed in this hotel for that price.

"I am very sorry," I said. "I shall try the next hotel. Thank you for your time."

And I turned, and I made my way through the spectators, who had swelled five deep, and walked for the exit, and as I opened the door, I suddenly found my arm yanked by the manager. Yes, okay, she said.

"*Xie xie,*" I said, feeling exultant.

After depositing my bag, I made my way down a hallway, past a sign on a door that informed me that just behind resided the curiously named Department of S and M, and wandered into the hotel restaurant. As usual, I was the solitary diner at a table for twelve. All restaurants in China have tables for twelve. Very often, they only have tables for twelve, and this was such a restaurant. My table was in the center of the room and every other table was crowded with Buddhist monks in saffron robes. There were female monks too, I noticed, though somewhat belatedly, since every monk, the women included, had shaved their heads. They had come here because Putuoshan is considered holy. Or perhaps they lived on the island; of the three thousand people inhabiting Putuoshan, I had read that one thousand of them are monks.

The menu was in Chinese only. There were no translations, no pictures, and so I indicated to the waitress that I was amenable to anything she suggested. Perhaps seafood. Yes, seafood. I was on an island and I desired to dine upon the bounty of the sea. Whereupon she returned with Whole Jellyfish Head. Intriguing, I thought. I had not known that jellyfish had a part of their being that could discernibly be called a head. The victuals on my plate looked like diseased muscle tissue and managed to be both crispy and gelatinous at the same time.

Next there was shrimp, salty and deep-fried. And a platter of spinach. It was, as I had feared, far too much food. Restaurants in China, as the tables suggest, are not meant to be enjoyed alone. Dining out is a group activity and servings are sized accordingly. As I picked at my Whole Jellyfish, the waitress brought the next course, a large glass bowl capped by a plate. She set it before me. She removed the plate. Out leapt a squid. And then another. And another. There were three squids flopping about before me. The waitress quickly returned the plate to its place atop the bowl and decorously removed the rogue squid from the table.

Well, I thought. Well, well, well. And what am I to do with a bowl of live squid? CLANK CLANK went the plate, as squid after squid made sad, desperate attempts to flee. I slouched down to peer at them through the bowl. It was like having my own personal aquarium. There were a dozen or so, swimming and flopping, bewildered to find themselves in a bowl on a table in a restaurant. They looked like the peculiar offspring of a shrimp mated with an octopus. I flagged down the waitress and asked her to help me out here. What is it that I was meant to do? How, exactly, does one eat live squid with chopsticks? She indicated that I was to eat them by hand. I simply had to rip the head off the squid, tear its shell off, dip it into a vinegar-y sauce, and then enjoy this fine example of fresh seafood from Putuoshan.

"Ah . . ." I said. *"Xie xie."*

I pondered my squid. Could I do this? Could I, in a room of Buddhist monks who presumably were vegetarian, murder a squid? Could I take life away with the mere snap of a finger? Would it completely mess up my karma for the rest of my days? Was I a squid murderer?

Yes, I was.

In the years to come, tales would be told in the squid community of the epic carnage that occurred one dark and stormy night in a restaurant on an island in the East China Sea. Among the squid, it was said that this monster, this *laowai* from the West, found it difficult, initially, to eat them. His first victim, little Jimmy, squirmed out of his grasp and leapt back into the bowl, and there he remained for a long while as the *laowai* considered his course. But determination overtook him, and after little Jimmy had been disposed of—the cruel decapitation, the torturous peeling of skin, the body dipped in vinegar—the remaining squid were quickly subjected to a gluttonous bloodlust. The *laowai* decided that he liked his squid fresh, and methodically, efficiently, mechanically, he emptied the bowl, until finally nothing remained but a pile of squid heads with wet, black eyes staring blankly up at him. He then sat there contentedly picking his teeth with a toothpick, satisfied to have crossed this culinary Rubicon.

The new day began with sheets of rain and tempestuous winds. A squall had descended upon us. But this was fine. I like weather. I am intrigued by weather. Across the narrow road from my hotel were a few small shops where I bought an umbrella and an orange plastic anti-rain sheet that I draped over myself.

I had come to Putuoshan because, even after the beaches of Qingdao, I had been overcome by a serious case of urban fatigue and an island somewhere off the Yangtze delta in the East China Sea had seemed like an excellent cure. Putuoshan is a very small island; I could walk from end to end in an hour or two. But it is not an island for speed walking. It is an island for lingering. There are pagodas and gardens and warrens of alleys where shops sell dried fish and the joss sticks, or incense, that burn inside every temple. And there is greenery. Eighty percent of the island is forested, a verdant tangle composed of 1,800 ancient trees, including camphor trees, which are special, though I'm not entirely sure why.

It is said that in the year A.D. 916 a very naughty Japanese monk sought to steal a statue of Guanyin, the bodhisattva of compassion, from the Chinese mainland and abscond with it back to Japan. It's endless, really, the mischief of the Japanese in China. Guanyin, however, did not wish to go to Japan. And so when storms terrorized the young monk as he sailed back home, she appeared to him in a dream and informed him that if he would just leave the statue on Putuoshan he might live to see another day. Otherwise, it was Davy Jones's locker for him.

Putuoshan thus became an important sight for those of the Buddhist persuasion, and its most prominent landmark is a hundred-foot golden statue of Guanyin built in 1998 that overlooks the harbor. Indeed, the summit of Mt. Putuoshan, a small hill really, is considered to be one of the four sacred mountains in Buddhism (not to be confused with the five sacred mountains of Taoism, such as Tai Shan). Over the years, the island acquired a strong monastic tradition, and there are several prominent temples such as the Puji Temple, which is where I soon found myself, drenched despite the anti-rain gear. Inside was a large golden Buddha. They are the friendliest-looking deities I know of, Buddhas—there is just something about the big potbelly that encourages levity. You cannot imagine them smiting an idolater with a lightning bolt. Inside, monks and worshipers lit joss sticks and did their devotions. Two mothers stood nearby, teaching their slit-pants-wearing youngsters how to bow and pray.

Buddhism, I was pleased to learn, was enjoying somewhat of a revival in China. It had long been present in China, of course. The first Buddhist missionaries arrived in the first century, and with time Buddhism developed a sizable presence, particularly as it evolved to include facets of homegrown Confucianism and Taoism. But then came Mao, and as with all things old, he was determined to crush Buddhism. Temples were destroyed and monasteries padlocked as Mao turned his sledgehammer on the opiate of the masses. Today, however, the Chinese government, confronted with such profound social discontent, has decided that a little opiate might be good for the masses. President Hu Jintao wants a harmonious society. So, too, do the Buddhists. And while Tibetan Buddhists remain as repressed as ever, the 7 million Buddhists in China who are not Tibetan have regained considerable latitude in expressing their beliefs. According to the government, there are now 13,000 Buddhist Temples in China, with more than 200,000 monks and nuns, including the ones here on Putuoshan.

Outside, the temple was surrounded by branching alleyways where young monks leapt among the puddles in front of shops selling joss sticks, golden Buddhas, chicken carcasses, slabs of meat, eels, starfish, mussels, clams, shark fins, and seafood of a kind completely unrecognizable to me, though no doubt I would find it in my evening meal. Pelted by cold, wet drops, I walked on to the One Hundred Step Beach, which is nine hundred steps smaller than the One Thousand Step Beach a short distance farther on. My umbrella whipped inside out and then collapsed in the gale, and as I watched the foaming sea I began to wonder how exactly I was going to get off the island after dinner. I had planned on taking an overnight boat to Shanghai, but this now struck me as an unsensible mode of transport.

I found refuge from the weather inside a small restaurant with a leaky roof overlooking the beach. What I really wanted was coffee and perhaps a slice of pumpkin bread. Instead I had seaweed tea, and ordered a boiled egg with slices of tomato and cucumber, and received instead a plate of scrambled eggs mixed with diced tomatoes. Perhaps the waiter thought I was Australian. That's what Australians do, mix eggs and tomatoes with everything—an unholy combination, in my opinion.

The wind roared and the rain gave no indication of lessening, and so I decided that today I would just be wet. I made my way past streetlamps decorated with swastikas, a sight that always succeeds in startling me. But, in fact, in Buddhism it is a symbol for love and mercy, and to this day it strikes me as particularly twisted that the Nazis chose to appropriate this ancient image of peace and love. I made my way to the Western Paradise trail and climbed the stairs to a rock that was carved with calligraphy. Etched in stone was the character for love, and visitors had left thousands of padlocks linked to a low fence that lay before it, testimonies of someone's devotion to another. At this point, I realized that I could go no farther—water was now rushing down the stairs and soon they would be all be but impassable. The wind had picked up further, sending twigs fluttering across the steps and against my rainwear, and I decided that the yin and yang of wandering around in a maelstrom compared to being dry and warm tilted to the latter. I returned to the hotel to inquire about boats traveling back to the mainland.

"No boats," I was told. "Typhoon."

There are typhoons and there are super typhoons. Typhoon Chancu was only the second super typhoon to ever be recorded in the South China Sea. And somehow, I had managed to place myself on an island while it struck. Clearly, I really needed to learn how to read a Chinese newspaper. This was inconvenient, a small problem, as I had to be in Hong Kong shortly to meet a friend. But instead of leisurely making my way south through Zhejiang, Fujian, and Guangdong Provinces, I found myself marooned on an island while thunderous waves broke on its shore and gale-force winds buffeted the trees.

But this was my fault too. China is a big country, and you don't quite realize how big it is until you start plotting the time and logistics it takes to get oneself from here to there. Nothing is straightforward in China; there are *always* complications. And it is enormous, this country of 1.3 billion people. What I usually assumed would be a three-hour journey was invariably a ten-hour one. And so I found myself stuck on an island approximately halfway from my intended destination. And there was a typhoon.

Perhaps it was just one of those things. Typhoons happen. Even super typhoons, though not very often. Perhaps it was some deity in the sky who saw that this guy who had lived on islands was on an island again and so why not send in a typhoon. But I knew that was not the case. I am dust in the wind from a deitological perspective. I come from a Catholic tradition, and that God ain't personal.

More likely, this super typhoon was a harbinger of climate change. No single weather event, of course, is indicative of anything. Shit happens. Just because. But it's difficult to spend a moment in China and not be utterly awed by the scale of the ongoing environmental catastrophe. Today, there is one vehicle for every forty inhabitants in China. In the U.S., it's one vehicle per 1.25 inhabitants, so you can see where China is trending. Chinese oil companies are traveling to the ends of the earth to secure their oil supply: Sudan, Angola, Papua New Guinea. They even tried to buy Unocal, the eighth-largest American oil and gas production company. Together with India, there are now 2.5 billion people in the global economy that just weren't there fifteen years ago. The consequences for the environment are alarming. The U.S. has 5 percent of the world's population and emits 25 percent of the world's pollution. So what happens when the Chinese, and one out of every five people on this planet lives in China, start to live like us? Sure, they deserve it. Everyone should have the right to have a car, to have heating and air-conditioning, to have a job in an office or factory. But from an environmental perspective, this is a terrifying development.

And meanwhile China rumbles in discontent. There are thousands of protests. In 2005, there were 87,000 official, government-recognized "mass incidents" among the *laobaixing,* or common people. Many of those protests occurred due to land seizures or corruption. But, according to *China Daily,* 50,000 of those mass incidents were due to pollution. It's bad in China, really bad.

So I decided that I didn't mind being stuck on an island during a typhoon. Putuoshan was an escape from that China. I spent my time in a tea room, surrounded by monks and golden statues of Buddha and the bodhisattva Guanyin, drinking a bottomless cup of green tea, and periodically emerging to sample the menu at the hotel restaurant, which steered me to such offerings as Pork That Tastes Like Fish, which is quite likely the most hideously foul-tasting meal that I have ever come across.

Finally, the storm abated. The eye had hit a little to the south in Fujian and Guangdong Provinces. Dozens had been killed. The roads were washed out. The coastal cities had been flooded. The water was still too rough for the jet boats to Ningbo, but there was a larger ferry making a run to Shenjiamen, a fishing village on a neighboring island, where I could catch a bus to the other end of the island, then another ferry, then another bus to Ningbo, and then a taxi to the airport, where I hoped to buy a ticket for the evening flight to Hong Kong. This stretched my ability to get from point A to point B to point C through the chaos of China to its very limit.

At the airport thirty miles outside Ningbo—sleek and shiny like every other Chinese airport I'd encountered—I approached the counter to buy a plane ticket. I was informed that it would cost 1,100 yuan. I had 900.

"No American Express!" barked the woman when I took out my credit card.

"How about Visa?"

"No Visa!"

"Is there a bank machine where I can access an overseas account?"

"No! You must go to Ningbo!"

"But I don't want to go to Ningbo."

"You must go to Ningbo!"

"Can I use a credit card to buy a ticket at the travel desk in the airport hotel?"

"No! Machine broken! You must go to Ningbo!"

And so I went back to Ningbo, to a business hotel, where I bought the plane ticket for 800 yuan. I returned to the airport, irritated, a sentiment that soon gave way to the familiar, primal fear I felt as I flew through the turbulent remains of a typhoon.

And then suddenly I was in Hong Kong. What is this? I thought. Cars that remain in their lanes. Cars that do not honk. Who are you, Mr. Bus Driver, wishing me a nice day and to be mindful of the step? Are you trying to make me weep? Do you want me to hug you? Such kindness is overwhelming for the China traveler. And here, inside this hotel in Kowloon, is this, could it be, an orderly line at the check-in counter? Yes. No. There are mainland businessmen cutting in line now, marching up to the desk, insisting that they be served immediately, ahead of us, all of us. But the woman at the counter directed them: *Please join the queue.*

Oh ho ho, I thought. Sweet Jesus, take me home now. What is this place? *Please join the queue.* This is not China.

# 12

"Such is the end of Empire," wrote Prince Charles in his diary. The occasion was the handover of Hong Kong, the crown jewel of the British Empire, to China on June 30, 1997. It was, according to the Prince, the "Great Chinese Takeaway," but this was not what he was lamenting in his ode to empire's loss. It was the indignity of flying business class on British Airways while the English politicians, lowborn and common, who had attended the handover ceremony, were seated in first class.

Indeed, one senses from the Royal Family that they were only too happy to return Hong Kong to China. "If you stay here much longer," said Prince Philip, he of the golden tongue, to an English student, "you will go home with slitty eyes." But leave they did, and after 156 years of colonial rule, Hong Kong again became a part of China.

Except that, ten years later, it didn't feel like China.

It felt like a vacation from China.

To say that I adored Hong Kong would be a colossal understatement. After weeks navigating the mayhem of the mainland, I *needed* Hong Kong. I had assumed Hong Kong to be a vast, teeming city, but compared to the megalopolises up north, Hong Kong is but a quaint English seaside village. True, it boasts an impressive skyline that every night lights up the sky with a laser show, but it lacks the madness of a true Chinese city. Technically, of course, Hong Kong is part of China. Indeed, when I arrived, Hong Kong was preparing for the "Celebration of the 10th Anniversary of Hong Kong's Return to the Glorious Motherland." But while Hong Kong today might be a little less English than it used to be, it did not at all seem any more Chinese.

On my way from the airport, I had asked a taxi driver how things had changed since Hong Kong had reverted to Chinese rule.

"Not many changes," he said. "Hong Kong is still the same."

His grandparents had come to Hong Kong from Fujian Province long ago and he spoke both Mandarin and Cantonese. I asked if he ever traveled north.

"Yes," he said. "Across the border to Shenzhen. The shopping is much cheaper."

If anything, Hong Kong, ten years after the handover, is even more like New York or London today than it was when it was an outpost of the British Empire. To be sure, Beijing has been quietly exerting its authority in Hong Kong. Judges are accountable to Beijing, not to the people of Hong Kong. And yet one can still see members of Falun Gong humming and chanting in Kowloon Park, a practice that would get them a thrashing and a stiff jail sentence elsewhere. While the rest of the country lives in an information bubble, Hong Kong enjoys a lively free press, and most newsstands offer the *International Herald Tribune* and various other newsweeklies, papers, and magazines from abroad, which I gleefully consumed.

"One thing has changed," the taxi driver added. "The economy is different. All the jobs have gone to China."

It is the worldwide lamentation. *All the jobs have gone to China*. Even in China itself.

Once, Hong Kong had been one of the great manufacturing cities in the world. Today, it is centered on the alchemy known as international finance, and while it may be more difficult for the average resident to find a factory job, the city continues to attract an ever-revolving band of expatriates. More than 2,300 multinational firms have their Asian headquarters in Hong Kong, and with everyone from Merrill Lynch to the Bank of China competing for space, the Pearl of the Orient is perhaps the only place in the world that makes Manhattan seem cheap. And clearly, I thought, as I wandered among the lofty skyscrapers of the Central District below Victoria's Peak, which today was enshrouded in a damp, muggy mist, there is money in Hong Kong. Lots of money. The city had long ago ceased to be a bargain. I saw my first Maybach, among the world's most expensive cars, and I also spotted Lamborghinis, Ferraris, and Bentleys. True, one could buy a Ferrari in Beijing or Hangzhou, but they actually drive them in Hong Kong. A BMW in Hong Kong is like a Kia at home. But the real prize for the tycoons here was the personalized license plate. Millions of Hong Kong dollars had been spent on COOL, KING, and I ♥ U. Albert Yeung Sau Shing, the colorful chairman of the

Emperor Group, a media conglomerate, had spent HKD 13 million—that's nearly two million U.S. dollars—on the number 9, the symbol for longevity.

And there are perfumeries in Hong Kong, thousands of them. Hong Kong spends more than any place on earth on perfume. As a result, the city does smell better than the cities to the north—admittedly, a low bar—but here, too, the air remained foul despite the coastal locale. Indeed, the air pollution in Hong Kong had become such a deterrent that for the first time companies were having difficulty filling their expat slots from overseas.

Still, Hong Kong is nice, really nice. You should go. You'll like it. True, if you are an investment banker on Wall Street, you'll likely feel as if you'd never left home. But if you are just a traveler in China, Hong Kong feels like a holiday. I spent most of my vacation from China in the labyrinth of streets and alleys in Kowloon, a neighborhood that is invariably described as bustling—*bustling Kowloon!*—but it didn't bustle. Compared to what I'd seen before, it seemed languorous, sedate, calm. Kowloon, I reflected, is *easy*, and nothing is easy in China. So I wandered contentedly through the city, saw the sights, and ended my evenings in a convivial pub, where I exchanged China stories with English teachers who had popped into Hong Kong for a quick visa run and a dose of bangers and hash, before returning to their schools in Guangdong Province. And then I steeled myself for a return north.

Fortunately, for a couple of weeks at least, I wouldn't be traveling alone. This was because I had a friend. Yes, it's true. Not only was Jack my friend, Jack was my Republican friend. And not only was he a Republican, he was a professional

Republican—party hack, I believe, is the colloquial job description. We'd met on the first day of high school when I had just moved to the suburbs of Washington, D.C., from Canada, and while much of my new surroundings were familiar, there were, evidently, some things that were different in the United States. Our English teacher had asked us to chat with whoever was sitting beside us for a few minutes and then introduce that person to the rest of the class.

"I want you to tell everyone that I'm a born-again Christian," Jack informed me.

Huh?

What was this, a born-again Christian? When I thought of born-again Christians, I thought of Oral Roberts and Jimmy Swaggert and Jimmy Bakker, moronic televangelists and florid scammers blathering and emoting on the American television channels. These were not the sort of people that Canadians typically associated with. True, there were Christians in Canada, but they were quiet Christians. They're Canadian.

So perhaps Jack spoke in jest. It was a setup, I thought, something to make me look silly on the first day of high school, and so I refused to mention that Jack was a born-again Christian. When it was Jack's turn to introduce me, he said, "This is Maarten. He's from Canada. That's why he talks funny. But even though he talks weird, he's a really great guy. Maarten, stand up and take a bow. Let's all give him a great big hand."

I was fifteen, and fifteen-year-olds generally don't want to stand up and take a bow on the first day of high school. Jack, however, was different. He didn't care what anyone thought of him, and everyone liked him as a result. He'd somehow transcended the clique-iness of high school, and the jocks, nerds, cheerleaders, the AP kids, and the Introduction to Cosmetology students all gravitated to Jack, ultimately bestowing upon him the coveted award Best Car in the yearbook salutations. This for a 1977 two-toned brown Maverick, dubbed The Mav, because this was the eighties.

Like me, Jack was a political geek. Before we were old enough to drive, we'd ride the school bus and discuss House congressional races. When I hung out at his house, we watched *The McLaughlin Report.* On the day Republicans lost control of the Senate in 1986, Jack took a black-tipped felt pen to his chucks and covered his shoes with black ink.

"Because it's a day of mourning," he explained to our American history teacher.

In the years that followed, Jack became a political operative, managing campaigns around the country. We overlapped for a while in Sacramento, where he was able to procure for me an invitation to the inauguration of Arnold Schwarzenegger as governor of the state of California. If there is a finer moment in history to witness, I cannot imagine it. More recently, he moved on to Florida to manage a campaign and said he'd come to China if he lost. He lost. It had been a bad year for Republicans.

I took the train to meet him at the Hong Kong airport.

"That was a long flight," Jack said, looking around and stepping into the arrivals hall. "And I need a cigarette."

Political operative is one of the last professions in America where it is acceptable to smoke. Writing is possibly the other. Except in California. People there feel sorry for heroin addicts but save their loathing for smokers. With the kids I'd had to quit anyway, and once I'd convinced myself that it was okay to chew Nicorette for three years, quitting became easy.

"I'm still doped up from the vaccines," Jack noted.

"I'll bet. You made sure to get your shot for elephantitis, right?"

"Elephantitis? You didn't say anything about elephantitis."

"Did I forget that? Where we're going, elephantitis is as prevalent as the common cold. Most men carry their balls in a wheelbarrow."

"Shut up. You did not say anything about elephantitis."

"I thought I did. But there's nothing that can be done about it now. Just try not to . . . well, never mind."

"What? Try not to what?"

"Breathe. It's an airborne virus. Very contagious. But you know what? Don't worry about it."

"I'm starting to regret this trip already."

After a week or so, I suddenly found myself eager to return to the mainland. While Hong Kong had been a welcome respite, it was but an interlude to my larger trip.

"This feels like Sydney or San Francisco," Jack had noted earlier as we walked past the bars in Lan Kwaifung—the pub district—where Westerners in suits and rugby shirts downed their pints.

"Yeah," I agreed. "Isn't it great?"

"I was hoping for something . . . different."

"Different is over there," I said, pointing to the north and the Chinese border. "Very different. But first I thought we'd have a look at Macau."

"And what are we going to do in Macau?" Jack asked.

"We're going to gamble."

"Perfect. I'm unemployed. I'm in China. It only makes sense."

A day trip from Hong Kong to Macau will cost you three pages on your passport, all without leaving the country. At the ferry terminal in Kowloon, it's stamp stamp stamp as you go through Customs, Immigration, and Passport Control. They are one country, China, Hong Kong, and Macau, a renowned den of vice on the western side of the Pearl River delta. But they're not really.

I had looked at my map, discovered that Macau lay sixty miles away, and yet my guidebook assured me that it was a mere hour away by boat. I wondered how, exactly, we were going to get there in an hour. By jet hydrofoil, it turned out. It was Stanley Ho, who for decades controlled the gambling monopoly in Macau, who had brought the hydrofoils, reducing a five-hour journey to just one. Four times married with seventeen children, Stanley Ho was the man-about-town in Macau. Before his monopoly was broken, his gambling earnings had accounted for 70 percent of the city's income.

As we received our ferry tickets, I discovered that Jack, inexplicably, had been upgraded to the deluxe deck upstairs.

"How does this always happen to you?" I asked. "Is it because you are a Republican, a defender of privilege, and you are thus accorded deference and upgrades to Deluxe?"

"Maybe they think I'm a high roller and they're putting me in the whale section. Or they could tell that I was unemployed and they felt sorry for me."

We roared through the haze of Victoria Harbor, past cargo ships of every variation, past fishing boats rolling in the swell, past the last Chinese junk to remain floating in Hong Kong, then curved around the headlands of Lantau and flew past the Pearl River Delta and across the open waters of the South China Sea. It did not seem possible that one could travel so fast over water. Upon arriving in Macau, we again stood in long lines waiting to go through Passport Control.

"You're sure we're still in the same country?" Jack asked.

"Yes."

"Maybe they should let the people here know."

Outside the ferry terminal, we were greeted by the familiar fellows offering tours, gypsy cabs, or currency exchange services *at no cost to you. Absolutely free.*

"So where to now?" Jack asked.

"The old town," I said as we hopped into a taxi.

Once the oldest European colony in China, Macau had been administered by Portugal until 1999 but was in reality ruled by the triads such as 14k and Soi Fung. Like the mafia, triads earned their bread through money laundering, drugs, extortion, and contract murders—in other words, the usual mob fare. Except the triads are known, even among the global gangster community, as being exceptionally violent. Car bombs were a staple of life in Macau during much of the 1990s. Indeed, the violence had escalated to such a degree that the police chief referred to the mobsters as "professional killers who don't miss their targets." This was actually meant to entice tourists; mobsters never miss. Trust us. So come to Macau. Have a good time.

In the old town, I felt like I could be anywhere in the colonial world of the tropics. There were stately mansions lining the narrow, curving streets and inviting porticos through which we walked past shops specializing in spices. The city radiates nostalgia. It's an urban ode to the days when fleets from the Mediterranean ruled the world. Portuguese is still a living language in Macau, and many of its inhabitants are mixed race, something rarely seen elsewhere in China. We headed for the Protestant Cemetery, a serene enclave with chirping parrots. I am not a cemetery man myself. After all, it wasn't that long ago that I stopped holding my breath whenever I drove past one. But if I had to choose a favorite cemetery it would be the Protestant Cemetery in Macau. This is because the finest writer in the English language is Patrick O'Brian, the author of *Master and Commander* and the nineteen books that followed chronicling the naval adventures of Jack Aubrey and Stephen Maturin during the Napoleonic Era. Those books are like crack for me, and whenever I read them—and I have read them thrice—I depart this world for the HMS *Surprise* and a world of intrigue and adventure. Indeed, I am such a fan that my youngest son's middle name is Aubrey. It's a great thing being a parent, to have these little people to mold. They are canvases upon which to bestow your own whims and ambitions. *You carry the name of Jack Aubrey, Post-Captain of the HMS* Surprise, I tell my one-year-old. *Do you think Jack Aubrey refused his peas and scorned his applesauce?*

In the spirit of O'Brian, the cemetery held the remains of many sailors who had succumbed to the trials and tribulations of the colonial era, and their headstones were suitably evocative.

> *The Fort is reached*
> *The sails are furled*
> *Life's voyage now is over*

*By faith his bright chart*
*He has reached that world*
*Where storms are felt no more*

*Erected as a token of respect by his messmates*

It could have been penned by Jack Aubrey himself.

We then walked past the remains of the Church of St. Paul, which had been constructed in 1602 only to burn down more than 200 years later, leaving behind a haunting baroque facade, and wandered down cobblestone streets full of antiques shops to the Church of St. Dominic, where Jack popped in for a prayer, because he was now a Papist.

"You ready now?" I asked when he emerged.

"Hey, I'm a Catholic. It's bingo that keeps the Vatican afloat."

Lovely as Macau is, we had come to gamble, to toy with financial ruin. I had only gambled twice in my life. Once, when I was stuck in Reno due to a snowstorm that had closed the road over the Sierras, where I had intended to ski, I had stayed up the entire night and better part of a day playing blackjack. And I'd won, quite possibly because I was (if my children are reading this, proceed to next page) (I mean it, Lukas) profoundly stoned at the time. A decade later, flush with our savings for a down payment on our home, I'd stopped in Las Vegas after driving cross-country. This time I lost. And I kept losing, possibly because I was sober as a judge, until finally I had to stammer back from the table with the grim realization that sometimes you don't win it back, and the best thing to do, the only thing to do, is to walk away. I'd decided that the neurons buzzing in my head were way too fond of gambling, so I never did it again. Until now.

More than 25 million people a year come to Macau to gamble, most on day trips from Hong Kong or the mainland. Formerly, when Stanley Ho held his monopoly, gambling took place in smoky, dingy dens of vice. It was the anti-Vegas. But today, the plethora of new casinos are betting that the gamblers in China will want what those in Las Vegas do. Near the ferry terminal on the Cotai Strip, there were a half-dozen new theme-park casinos under construction. Everyone was there, Shangri-la, Sheraton, InterContinental, Raffles, St. Regis, all building casino hotels with swanky nightclubs and swanky stores that will happily take your winnings. This despite the fact that the vast majority of Chinese gamblers are day-trippers from Hong Kong or the mainland who rarely stay longer than a day. Still, the average table in Macau earns more than three times what a table in Vegas does, and this in a country where the average monthly wage is $150. Indeed, even now Macau already earns more in gambling revenue than Las Vegas.

We walked to the Wynn Macau, a top-end resort in the Vegas style with a golden facade and dancing fountains built by the famed casino magnate Steve Wynn. Frankly, I wasn't convinced that the Chinese were yearning for a Vegas-type experience. Not yet. Gambling is technically illegal in mainland China, so when the Chinese come to Macau they come with a mission. Gambling is the be-all and end-all of the trip, and I thought it highly unlikely, indeed deeply un-Chinese, that someone would take their winnings and blow it on overpriced jewelry and furs, rather than ply it into the family business back on the mainland. Nevertheless, there were crowds of gamblers swarming around the casino floor. There was a strange vibe among the tables, something dark and menacing. Perhaps it was the metal detectors and the mandatory bag check and the plethora of security guards that led me to expect an imminent raid by some triad displeased by their new competition for gamblers. Most Chinese play baccarat, and we stood alongside a table, quietly amazed to see a man in peasant garb pull out a fat wad of 100-yuan notes.

Jack's game of choice was roulette, so we set off to find a table.

"Isn't that the game with the worst odds?" I asked him.

"Yes, but when you win, you win big."

"I think this reveals something about your character."

"All or nothing, baby."

We finally found a roulette table, and as Jack laid his bets he explained the game to me.

"I didn't understand any of that," I said. "All I see is that you've just lost about $100 in a fraction of a minute."

"Yeah, well . . . but when you win, you win big."

Jack played a few more rounds, and just as the carnage was getting interesting, we decided that now might be a good time to head to the lounge, drink an overpriced Coke, and observe the action on the floor. I had, of course, witnessed hundreds of people in a casino before, mindlessly dropping coins into slot machines. They don't play for money in America. It's true. The big payout is incidental to most gamblers. It's the numbness they're after. Not so in China. No one had that look of glazed stupor often found in American casinos. The Chinese were nothing if not engaged over the baccarat tables. They yelled. They smoked. They bet. But no one seemed to be having any fun. And this is why I suspected that a Macau reborn as the Las Vegas of Asia wouldn't quite work. The expensive nightclubs would fail. The Piaget watches would remain unsold. Because gambling isn't fun in China. It's business, and no one takes business more seriously than the Chinese.

"You know," Jack noted, "this place kind of creeps me out."

"Agreed. Let's get out of here."

We moved on to the Sands, one of the first new casinos to open after the monopoly was busted. It had more of a Reno feel; the flash was ersatz.

"I'm getting a better vibe here," I said. "I think I'm more of a Reno kind of guy."

"Not sure I'd admit to that if I were you."

I found a blackjack table with a low minimum bet, while Jack wandered off in search of another roulette table. Soon, I was in the zone, that thoughtless place, reacting to numbers, calculating odds, playing systematically, and resisting those moments when I get a really good feeling that now would be an excellent time to throw it all in. A couple of hours later, Jack appeared.

"How'd you do?" he asked.

"I'm up . . . let's see, about 4,000 Hong Kong dollars. You?"

"I won a couple of hundred bucks."

"Let's do something really insane and quit while we're both ahead," I suggested. "The likelihood of both of us being ahead has got to be so infinitesimally small that we best run."

With an hour to kill before the ferry returned us to Hong Kong, we settled in a lounge to watch a cabaret show with dancers in sparkles and spandex and cowboy hats.

"See?" Jack said, watching the dancers. "Everyone still wants to be just like us. Even the Chinese."

It was time to take Jack to see the real China.

# 13

It was a swift transition. One moment we were in Kowloon discussing real estate with a taxi driver. "Those buildings there. Eighteen thousand dollars for one square foot. Too much money. In Hong Kong, no money, no honey." So true. And then, after a perfunctory stroll through Immigration in the sleek and modern Kowloon train station, we boarded a train that whisked us through Hong Kong's Northern Territories, a hilly and wooded expanse speckled with sudden bursts of high-rises, and suddenly we found ourselves in the bustling border city of Shenzhen.

A quarter century ago, Shenzhen had been little more than an anonymous fishing village. In the 1980s, however, Shenzhen became the Shenzhen Special Economic Zone, China's first foray into the exciting world of capitalism. Comrades turned into entrepreneurs, communes became factories, and tirades against the imperialists of the West gave way to trade with the world. In 1992, Deng Xiaoping, during his tour of southern China, is said to have proclaimed, "To get rich is glorious." It's quite likely Deng Xiaoping's most famous quip, and one can understand why. It's not, typically, the sort of thing often heard spoken by Communists. There's a disconnect between *Workers of the world unite! You have nothing to lose but your chains!* and *To get rich is glorious.* And yet no one actually heard him say it. No one. There is no record anywhere of Deng Xiaoping expressing these words. Nevertheless, Deng Xiaoping never countered the widespread belief that he'd uttered this paean to the veneration of wealth, and the expression—*To get rich is glorious*—became a whipsaw moment in China. To get rich was now desirable. It was permitted, encouraged. It had been officially sanctioned by the head honcho of the Chinese Communist Party. And what had started as a tepid stream toward capitalism became the tsunami that continues to this day. Except, of course, they don't call it capitalism in China. It's called Socialism with Chinese Characteristics. To which the Chinese say, *Who cares what it's called? I can be rich, gloriously rich.*

While Shenzhen is indeed richer than it was before—far richer—it is still, frankly, a dump. True, from the train platform we could see a skyline of cranes and glittering skyscrapers, but everything else built over the past twenty years had already become decrepit and forlorn. The Chinese are said to venerate the old. Perhaps this is true when speaking of people, but it doesn't apply to buildings. Still, there were millions of people now occupying these apartments. Most were women attracted to the region for the factory jobs, but more than a few had come to serve as girlfriends, professional and otherwise, to the wealthy businessmen crossing the border from Hong Kong. I had surmised from the daily offers for *messagees* and night ladies that every city in China had a thriving sex industry, but the one in Shenzhen had been deemed such a threat to public welfare that the government undertook a shaming campaign, rounding up the city's prostitutes and forcing them to march through crowds of people who hurled abuse and scorn upon the women, a tactic last seen during the Cultural Revolution. Within months, however, the prostitutes were back. They might not become gloriously rich, but they'd at least divest the rich Hong Kong johns of some of their wealth.

The train continued its journey onward. We passed rubble. Lots of rubble. It really is quite amazing how much rubble there is in China. "It doesn't feel like San Francisco anymore," Jack observed. "This is more like Tijuana."

As we traveled on from Shenzhen to Guangzhou, we passed vast numbers of factories and crossed over pools of still water bearing wholly unnatural chemically-induced colors. We rumbled past enormous mounds of trash and the ever-present piles of rubble. We began to think of a new slogan for China.

"China—A Giant Pile of Crap," I offered.

"China—It's Chinastic!"

A short while later, we arrived in Guangzhou. Jack knew someone who knew someone who knew someone in Guangzhou, and this alone had seemed like a good reason to visit. Also, I did not want Jack to be lulled by Hong Kong, to think for a moment that Chinese cities are anything other then bastions of swirling mayhem, and invariably, as expected, and as I had explained to Jack's disbelieving ears, after passing through Immigration, we experienced the assault upon the senses that is contemporary China. In the hallway, we were quickly surrounded by aggressive men yelling, *Taxi taxi!* Tour and hotel operators shouted at us. People clapped their hands in our faces. *Laowai! Laowai!* Beggars thrust their hands before us. *Money, money!* Touts marched beside us. *Make love Chinese girl.* The policemen looked stupendously bored. "No, Jack," I said to him when he moved to accept a ride with a gypsy cab. What was he thinking? Jesus. This is a train station in China. These are vultures, these people who linger here.

And then there was the taxi line, a long, snaking length of people—people who pushed, who jostled, who spat out wads of phlegm and clouds of smoke, people who cut in line, *goddamn it.* I am not the sort of person prone to going postal, but if ever it did happen, it would be in a line in China.

"Well, this is different," Jack observed.

"Good. I'm glad you found what you were looking for."

Finally, we made our way into a taxi. True, we could have avoided the line by agreeing to a gypsy cab. But while there was a one-out-of-four, maybe one-out-of-five, chance that this regular, state-sanctioned, official taxi driver would seek to overcharge the dumb *laowai*, a ride in a gypsy cab was a guaranteed rip-off. We tossed our bags into the trunk and the taxi left the train station to follow one of the many ring roads.

"Remind me to start investing in cranes," Jack said.

Guangzhou, of course, was huge, another of the megacities that China specializes in. Three quarters of the world's tall building cranes are in China, an unsurprising statistic for anyone who's been to China, but a source of wonder to first-time visitors like Jack, who'd encountered his first true Chinese city. On our way to the hotel, we passed enormous work sites, construction zones with on-site shanties for the migrant workers. Guangzhou is also a rich city; the per capita GDP is about $10,000, making it one of the wealthiest cities in the country. Like Shenzhen, it was favorably located near Hong Kong. But of course, as elsewhere, an endless layer of pollution hung in the air. We battled our way through mad, crazy drivers until we crossed over a small bridge and found ourselves on Shamian Island.

This island in the middle of Guangzhou had once been a Western outpost. Like lepers, early traders from Europe and the United States had been isolated here on this small sliver of land in the Pearl River, and even today the island retains a Western focus. On every corner, there are statues of American kids engaged in some Rockwellian endeavor—fishing, playing tag, reading a story on Grandma's lap, and otherwise carrying on like storybook characters circa 1931. It was, frankly, a little creepy.

But then we noticed all the American couples pushing strollers. The American Consulate was on Shamian Island, and this was the last stop for couples adopting Chinese babies. Laundry shops offered free strollers. A shop sign informed passersby that a jade pendant means Mother–Daughter. We counted dozens of new parents. Like so much in China, the scale could be unsettling. But, of course, this was good, this economy of scale in adopted babies. Fate was smiling on these children. Almost all were girls, and China, as we know, is a hard place for girls. So I was pleased to see hundreds of Americans pushing strollers with Chinese babies as we drove past. These children would have lives. They would be taken care of. They would be loved. So this was good.

Still, I'd never seen so many babies in my life. After checking into our hotel, we walked around the neighborhood and watched men console wailing infants and women prepare bottles. Most of these new parents looked to be a bit older. Things had changed in America; women had professions, dreams that needed fulfilling. Life was complicated. But biology had remained the same: *tick-tock, tick-tock,* and then the buzzer sounded. And so now hopeful parents came to China. And there were so many of them that China could now afford to be picky about where it placed its unwanted babies. There were income standards, of course. And marriage was required. And you couldn't be fat. There will be no fat parents of Chinese children, the government had declared.

We continued moseying around the island, which was strangely peaceful. We could hear women singing through an open window; boys played soccer on the cobblestone streets as if they were in provincial France. This was hardly the urban China I'd come to know. We wandered through the leafy streets, past the Guangdong Animal By-Products Import and Export Corp., until we reached a table of vendors selling watches, whereupon Jack decided to buy one.

"You're a brave man," I noted. "Buying a watch in China is not for the meek."

"How much for this watch?" Jack said, pointing to a huge, ornate timepiece that claimed to be a Bulgari.

"Four hundred yuan."

"Okay," Jack said, reaching for his wallet.

"You know," I interjected, "I'm going to go out on a limb here and say that now is when you're supposed to start bargaining. You're insulting his culture by agreeing to the first price."

The vendor, however, didn't look insulted. Instead, he looked rather annoyed at me.

"Well, I certainly don't want to insult Chinese culture. How about 300?"

The watch seller leapt at it before I could utter another word.

"Well, it's a very nice watch," I offered. "It makes you look like a very wealthy man. Which, of course, is exactly the image you want to convey in a bus or train station in the middle of China."

"I hadn't thought of that."

We left the island and walked across a footbridge that took us over a narrow channel of water and six lanes of traffic and headed toward the Qingping Market, where I hoped to introduce Jack to the peculiar wonders of authentic Chinese cuisine. It's different, I'd told him. He'd wanted different. Food is different in China. He'll love it for its *differentness*.

Whereupon we stumbled over a tiger paw.

At the entrance to the broad expanse of the Qingping Market, a vendor had laid out a red blanket upon which lay an assortment of animal parts.

"What's this?" I asked the surprisingly burly salesman.

It was the paw of a Siberian Tiger. An endangered species. And then he demonstrated how he'd saw the claw out. Two claws were already missing.

"This, tiger tooth."

I held it. "And this?

"Rhino horn."

There were tiger tails, monkey skeletons, lungs and other organs, and a plethora of horns, all from species that didn't have them to spare, and all arrayed on this red blanket at the entrance to the largest open market in Guangzhou.

"What price?" he asked me as I beheld the tiger tooth.

"Big problem taking this into my country," I said.

"No problem," he said. "I mail it." And then he imitated a plane.

Oh, sure. I'll look for my tiger tooth in the morning mail.

"Well," I said to Jack as we walked on. "That counts as one of the more appalling things I've seen in China, and that's a very high bar."

And then, as if we were lost in some grim Humane Society nightmare, we began to wander past stalls selling frogs, chickens, eels, turtles, cats, scorpions—big and small—dogs in cages, ducks in bags, and snakes in bowls. There were 2,000 stalls in this market, and this, apparently, was where Noah's Ark unloaded its cargo. If you were planning a dinner party and looking to tickle your guests' palate with a delicately prepared Cobra heart, perhaps followed by some bunny soup and sautéed puppy, the Qingping Market is the place for you. And if your needs should involve a tiger penis and a rhino horn, these, too, can be found in the market. Once relegated to medicinal uses, the consumption of endangered animals has become a mark of status in the new China. Siberian Tigers are rare, ergo they're expensive, which means they're valuable. Nothing makes an impression in China like Tiger Liver Soup.

We stopped in front of a crate of cats.

"You do realize we're still in the food section," I observed.

"I don't feel like I'm in Sydney anymore," Jack said.

As we turned to go, Jack tripped over the sidewalk and stepped into a fetid pool of water and animal waste and who knows what else. Jack, it should be noted, was wearing sandals. If there was one pool of water that one didn't want to step in, it was quite likely this one in the Qingping Market in Guangzhou.

"My feet are wet," Jack observed with a touch of panic in his voice. "I'm not going to get sick, am I? This isn't how you get SARS, is it?"

"You might have a problem."

"Seriously, I can feel something eating through my skin."

"That doesn't sound like SARS. Maybe gangrene."

"I'm really starting to regret this trip."

I vaguely recalled that SARS had begun somewhere in southern China before killing hundreds and leading to a panic when the government was slow to grapple with the problem. But I put it out of my mind as we made our way to a restaurant with an appealing courtyard facing the river. Chinese people were dining in private open booths. At the entrance, the hostess told us that No, we could not sit there, and seated us on a view-less terrace.

"That was weird," Jack observed.

"Not really," I said, feeling like an old, grizzled China expert. "Many Chinese look down on us. Thus, we're not worthy of riverside booths."

On the illustrated menu, we considered deep-fried whole pigeon, fried sliced swan, boiled frog in radish soup, stewed pig lung, and what was alleged to be boneless pig fnuckle.

"I'm having the swan," Jack decided.

"I'm leaning toward the pig fnuckle."

"You know," Jack observed. "This is different. China is different."

"Yes," I told him, "it is."

The next day, we again found ourselves strolling alongside the Pearl River. The opposite bank was lost in a shroud of toxicity.

"It's . . . apocalyptic," Jack observed, not without a little awe.

"Exactly," I said. "There really is no other word."

We'd been discussing the air in Guangzhou, because it simply could not be ignored. It was worse then Shanghai. It was worse than Qingdao. It was worse even than Beijing. The air in Guangzhou is brown. No, not brown. Yellow. No, not yellow. The air in Guangzhou is *sick*. It is unwell. The air has been poisoned and now the air is noxious. Today, the average life expectancy for a traffic cop in Guangzhou is forty-three. And remarkably, it's not Chinese drivers that kill them (at least not directly). But their fumes do. Ninety percent of those traffic cops still among the living have lung infections. And it's not going to get better anytime soon. There are 10 million people in Guangzhou and every year they buy 150,000 new cars. This boggled the mind.

Jack lit up a cigarette. "You know what I get from smoking around here? I get clean smoke."

"I don't think so," I said. "Those are Chinese cigarettes."

We had an hour to kill before we met Jack's contact in Guangzhou, and so we ambled to Lucy's Café, a restaurant that catered to Shamian Island's typical visitor. We joined the multitudes of American couples with their Chinese babies and listened to "Sweet Home Alabama" wafting from the jukebox.

Jack pondered the menu. "I'm having the hamburger."

"You don't want to do that."

"Why?"

"There is much in China that I don't understand. But this I know. You do not want to order the hamburger."

"I'm ordering the burger."

"You'll be sorry."

When it arrived, we spent a long while marveling at this alleged hamburger. We began with the bread. There are four regional schools of cooking in China and hamburger buns don't figure prominently in any of them. Having heard that hamburgers involve bread, the chef had included a spongy slice of Wonder Bread. But what was really breathtaking to behold was the meat. We had never seen meat quite so gray. Nor was the texture recognizable to us. And the smell? It was the sort of odor that would cause even a coyote to flee.

"I've never seen meat that looked like this," Jack observed. "Or smelled like this."

"Perhaps it's cat."

Is this where the unsold cats ended up, we wondered? Is this where cat vendors dispose of the really gnarly cats, the ones that not even a cat-craving Chinese customer would eat? Very possibly, I speculated. Everyone in this restaurant was a Westerner. They wanted hamburgers, I imagined the chef thinking. A cow was expensive. But cats are cheap. We'll give them cat-burgers. They're *laowais* with undeveloped taste buds. Ground-up cow on bread is their most celebrated dish; ketchup their most famous sauce. So we'll give them cat-burgers.

Next to us, a young Dutch couple asked if they could borrow our Lonely Planet guidebook. I spoke my mother tongue with them. Geert and Lois were from Utrecht and they'd spent nearly a year traveling through South and Central America, Australia, New Zealand, Laos, Cambodia, and points in between. They were hardy travelers, had seen the world, had climbed mountains and endured hardships.

"Have you been to the market across the river?" Jack asked them. His plate had remained untouched. "It's pretty interesting."

"No, we don't go there," Geert said. "I have an uncle who works here as a lawyer. He told us that whatever you do, do not go to that market. That market is where SARS began."

It's a remarkable thing watching the blood drain from someone's face. "You said come to China, so I come to China," Jack stuttered. "And what do we do on my first day here? We go to the market where SARS began! And now because I stepped in that puddle, I have SARS. What's the mortality rate with SARS? Fifty percent?"

"I think it's more like 10 percent," I said.

"Yes, about 10 percent," Geert agreed.

"So there's a 10 percent chance I'm going to die," Jack said. "And my trip is just beginning."

"Look, you don't know if it's SARS. It could be any number of things. But what I think you should do is just live for today. And I think we need to go. What time is it?"

"It says here on my brand-new watch that it's 6:23 A.M."

"As they say, even a stopped watch is right twice a day."

As we got up to leave, Jack gave the running tally. "Fake watches, cat-burgers, 'Free Bird' on the jukebox, apocalyptic air, and SARS."

"You got it," I said. "Welcome to China."

Before leaving for Hong Kong, Jack had called a friend who had provided a number of Chinese contacts for us to look up in southern China, including a woman in Guangzhou named Gallon. "She has a business on eBay. You might find it hilarious or deeply disturbing, but here's the link," his friend had e-mailed. I'd clicked on the link in a crowded Internet café in Hong Kong. It was something about Egghuggers. I'd expected knitted sweaters for Easter eggs. But then, as a half-dozen people waited for the computer behind me, my screen began to fill with photos of dozens of male genitalia bedecked in a variety of sacs. I desperately stabbed at the little X in the corner. Close, close, please close now.

Tragically, when we arrived in Guangzhou, Gallon's e-mail address no longer worked. But Kenny's did and he'd agreed to show us around Guangzhou.

We met Kenny in the lobby of the hotel after Jack had spent the better part of the afternoon with his feet under scalding water. "Whoa. You guys are big," he exclaimed. "Cantonese people are smaller than the Chinese up north."

This was true. The Chinese to the north were considerably taller, quite likely because of differences in diet. It's noodles in the north, rice in the south. Jack, in particular, towered over everyone in Guangzhou. Kenny wore a T-shirt with a kneeling woman in dominatrix leather. He had lived in Los Angeles and spoke flawless English. He told us he was involved in transportation; when a car-parts supplier needed a widget, he'd find a widget producer for them in China.

We walked with him from Shamian Island back into Guangzhou proper. On the bridge over the highway, we came across a young girl with a horrific leg condition. Her legs were split open to the bone and she sat on the pedestrian overpass with a beggar's bowl.

Since my encounter with the albino boy in Qingdao, I'd discovered that some people do such things to children in China. Children are burned, disfigured, and maimed simply to provoke pity and an outpouring of *kuai*. But Kenny seemed to anticipate my train of thought.

"Her parents are very poor," he said. "Don't assume that this was done on purpose just to make some money. Everyone pays for their own health care here," he went on. "No money. No doctor. It's not good for the poor. But in your country, you have what, 250, 300 million people? We have 1.5 billion. Not 1.3—1.5 *billion*. Many people are not counted. And it's very expensive to insure 1.5 billion people."

"That's not legal," he said as we passed the endangered-animal traders. "And that's a fake," he continued, pointing to an enormous root vegetable that looked uncannily like a man with an erection, which was drawing a large crowd. We walked back through the Qingping Market—despite Jack's fears, it was the only way into Guangzhou proper—and then crossed some invisible line where the animals were no longer meant to be eaten, but to be cared for as pets—turtles, cats, dogs, fish, rats. And then down we went into a gleaming subway station with flat-screen televisions.

The subway seemed the epitome of the new China, and as we rode we talked economics. "You see this part of your shirt,"

Kenny said, pointing to a button. "You probably think this was made in a factory, but it wasn't. It was made in a village, in a house. Much cheaper in the village. Millions of houses in thousands of villages, all making something. And you know what? No one can make it cheaper. You think maybe Vietnam or Malaysia? But no. To get around your quotas, Chinese people buy businesses elsewhere in Asia. Everything is still made in China, but assembled in Vietnam or wherever. Now you buy computers and cameras made in China. And do you know what we buy from America? Corn. Because we have to meet quota rules."

Walk through a Target or Wal-Mart and it's difficult to believe that there are indeed quotas on Chinese goods. Everything seems to have been made in China. And yet, while the U.S. government may have abandoned the country's textile mills, and its steel producers, and its television manufacturers, and its toy producers—really, what hasn't the government thrown under the bus—somehow, a few corporate farmers were able to draw a line in the sand with corn. It's miraculous, really. Nevertheless, Kenny had provided a succinct summary of the trade situation. In the U.S., we squawk about shoddy goods, poisonous toothpaste, contaminated toys. We bemoan the lost jobs. We point to the slave labor in China, like the unfortunate people, kids even, snookered or kidnapped to work in the factories. Or we lament what China is doing to the environment. But it's like blaming an addiction to crack on a poor, illiterate farmer in the highlands of Bolivia. We're the market. We decide what to buy. But do we decide to buy domestically made, high-quality goods manufactured in a well-regulated environment that ensures humane working conditions? We do not. We want it cheap, no matter what the consequences. And thus China, with its "millions of houses in thousands of villages, all making something."

We got off the subway in the gleaming new downtown. In front of an enormous shopping plaza, a gathering of uniformed security guards was being led through their paces, marching like a military regiment on parade.

"Now, compare these with the mall security guards at home," I said to Jack.

He shook his head in wonder. "We're so screwed, aren't we?"

Inside the shopping mall, I could sense Kenny's pride. There were seven or so stories of gleaming stores topped by an entire floor devoted to the amusements of kids, something I rarely saw elsewhere in China. Whenever I thought I had stumbled upon a playground, it was, in fact, an exercise yard for the elderly. But here, there was a haunted house. There was a movie theater.

Kenny suddenly turned to Jack. "How many pixels in your camera?" he asked. "Two?"

"Five, I think. I don't know."

"But I see that your camera is three or four years old. In China, we only use the new. Cell phones, cameras, computers, we only want the newest."

Slowly but surely, Kenny was confirming an incipient impression I had been forming. The Chinese were becoming the Americans of Asia. There was a sureness to the Chinese, a cockiness even, that not so long ago could be found among Americans. Today, of course, many Americans, even conservatives like Jack, would concede that the U.S. has lost its way. From endless war to the expensive absurdities of the health care system, onward through the colossal amount of debt that Americans have assumed, most of us can't help but begin to feel that things in the USA aren't looking particularly perky at present. The rest of the world, of course, couldn't agree more. China, however, was beginning to strut. And they were even beginning to assume some of our most remarkable characteristics, like buying shit they didn't actually need.

"When I was in the U.S.," Kenny continued, "I thought everything would be modern, state-of-the-art. But it's not. Much of it is actually very backward. Here in Guangzhou, we have flat-screen televisions and air-conditioning in the subway."

And crippled kids begging on bridges. And the foulest air this side of Venus. But I knew manners were important in China, and I didn't want to be disagreeable with our host. Kenny had offered to take us out for traditional Cantonese hotpot. We left this showcase mall and walked past the Starbucks in the New China Marriot Hotel. Nearby, we were besieged by hordes of young boys not more than twelve years old who began stuffing our pockets with the calling cards of prostitutes, many of whom appeared to be lingering in front of the Starbucks alongside a couple of animal-skin peddlers, including one who was actively hawking a tiger pelt. So, okay. Maybe Starbucks was a little different in China after all.

The restaurant we entered was encouragingly crowded. Kenny did the ordering. "I will tell you what it is after you have eaten it," he said. "In China, we eat everything with four legs except the table, and anything with two legs except a person."

"My only request," said Jack, "is no dog."

"You don't want to eat dog?"

"No dog."

"I better get the waiter again."

Soon, in a sizzling spiced hotpot, Kenny stirred the meat. "What do you think?" he asked.

"It's delicious."

"Good. This is goose intestines. And those are cow veins. And that is lamb."

Jack was sweating from the spiciness.

As we ate, we continued to talk economics. "American debt, both public and personal, now runs into the trillions of dollars," I said. "China sits on more than a trillion dollars in reserves. Should the Chinese Politburo choose to, it could blow up the American economy at will. This is something that is beginning to make many Americans nervous."

"Yes," Kenny acknowledged. "But what do we really have—paper, IOUs, nothing. We lend you the money, but we have nothing to show for it. Just paper. Nothing tangible. But you use that money we lend you, and what do you get? Tanks, fighter jets, aircraft carriers. You use that money that China lends you to secure your oil supplies. You get something very tangible, very important. We just have paper."

I must confess that I had never looked at things from that perspective. But Kenny was onto something. Official statistics suggest that the Chinese economy grows at roughly 10 percent per year. Unofficially, the rate is far higher, more like 20 percent. That level of growth can only be maintained by secure access to energy, and with oil depletion far outracing the discovery of new fields, it is inevitable that for the next decade or two—or even longer should we fail to move on to a post-carbon-based energy world—resource competition is likely to characterize U.S.-China relations. And that could get very ugly indeed.

But perhaps that level of tension might be offset by increased democracy in China?

Kenny scoffed. "In America, you are always talking about freedom and democracy. But China is a different place. We are not ready for that. We have fifty-six different minorities here. How do you think they'd vote? How do you think those guys who gave you the prostitute cards would vote? If some politician gave them one yuan, they would vote for them."

Provided, of course, that the voting age was reduced to twelve.

"In China," Kenny continued, "you will find educated people in the cities. But China is a very big place. Most people are not educated. Most people—900 million—live hand to mouth in the country. Their votes would be bought. So China needs to do this slowly, at its own pace. Now, what we need are opportunities."

Kenny paid the bill. We offered to pay but were quickly waved off. Indeed, we had been warned not to press too hard. In China, the distinction between host and guest is important.

"So what do you guys say? Are you ready to go to a nightclub?"

"Rock on. Let's party!" Jack enthused.

We walked a short distance to the nightclub. Though Guangzhou might be China's wealthiest city, this particular nightclub suggested that the city wasn't swaggering like Shanghai. True, inside the club, there were rap videos on the big screen. A lounge. A bar. Enthusiastic dancing. Loud, loud music. We could barely talk. But it wasn't *hip* like the clubs in Shanghai are. I'm not sure why this was so. But perhaps it was just us. Jack went to the bar and ordered Long Island Iced Teas for all. Then another. It wasn't really my drink, but what the hell, I thought, we were in a nightclub in Guangzhou. I did a yeah, yeah, let's party dance in front of a group of girls dancing on a couch. I was utterly ignored, shot down, a leper in the disco. Jack was beside himself with mirth. And then he sat down beside a group of young women who could very possibly have been prim librarians. He did something goofy. They got up and moved away. But still, he wanted to have another Long Island Iced Tea. He wanted to party like it was 1999.

"I don't know, Jack," I yelled into his ear. "We've got a really early morning tomorrow."

"TOMMORROW?" he yelled back. "THERE IS NO TOMORROW! I HAVE SARS!"

# 14

We escaped.

There really is no other word for it. We had awoken four hours later in the predawn darkness and congratulated each other on our good fortune. Surely we should have been hideously hungover. Our heads should have throbbed, our stomachs churned. There had been beer. There had been Long Island Iced Teas. All consumed on a base of spicy goose intestines. We should have been feeling wretched.

But we were not wretched.

We were buoyant.

"Let's hear it for watered-down drinks," Jack said.

And so with unexpected cheeriness we left Guangzhou. We said good-bye to the choking sprawl of urban China. And none too soon, either. I had begun to form dark thoughts about China. I wanted happy thoughts. China was the future, yes? The twenty-first century would be China's, no? But that thought alone filled me with dread. Perhaps it was the crated kittens in the Qingping Market. I do not object to the consumption of cats. If one can eat a pig, I don't see how one can morally object to a cat-burger. So *bon appetit,* I say. But must they be skinned alive? Or maybe it was that pervasive tingling I felt, a sense that at any moment, someone might accuse me of being German and proceed to bitch-slap me senseless. But mostly, it was a creeping awareness that there are no rules in China, that so much of life in China is essentially a flirtation with anarchy.

Oh sure, it's not all rioting and chaos. Things get done in China. Lots of things get done. This is because the system that prevails throughout the country—the system that has always prevailed from the Imperial days of yore to the Maoism of recent years to the hypercapitalism of today—is *guanxi,* the network of family, friends, and contacts that grease the wheels of life in China. Monarchism, Communism, and Capitalism have always been inadequate isms to describe China. *Guanxi* is what makes China go. It is a society based upon connections.

But above this *guanxi,* and below it, too, there is anarchy. The government, of course, would dispute this. Despite evidence to the contrary, there are, in fact, rules. Technically, slavery is illegal. But this doesn't stop brick-kiln-factory owners from kidnapping hundreds of boys to work in horrific conditions in northern China. Theoretically, it should be possible for a Chinese parent to buy baby formula with reasonable confidence that it won't kill Junior. But you can't. Hundreds of babies in China have died from counterfeit formula in recent years. Product safety, clearly, is not a high priority.* While stores from Canada to Chile were busily emptying their shelves of contaminated toothpaste, did shops in China do likewise? They did not. Once the deluge of contaminated exports became a trifle embarrassing for the government, however, they did do something: They shot the head of the Chinese Food and Drug Administration. But actually recall the toxic products within China? No.

From the madness of the roads to the endangered animals in the market, it was hard to discern the rule of law in China. And I kind of like laws—good ones, anyway. I'd spent enough time in the South Pacific, where laws are regarded as mere suggestions, to know that the absence of a fair and impartial application of law is a sure path to instability. True, somewhere there is presumably a big book of Chinese laws, but if no one enforces them, what does it matter? I had asked a lawyer friend of Dan's in Beijing about Chinese law and he had scoffed at the very notion that there was such a thing. "Look. Here's how it works," he said. "Lawyer Zhang is doing pretty well. He's a partner. He's making some money. He buys a Mercedes, a very expensive car in China—more than twice what you'd pay for it in the U.S. The judge notices Lawyer Zhang's shiny new car, so he says, 'Lawyer Zhang, you must be very rich to afford such a car. I would like to borrow it.' So what does Lawyer Zhang do? He turns over the keys. He doesn't see his car again. But he wins his cases before the judge. That's how law works in China."

And it has become pernicious, this gotta-get-mine, screw-you, get-out-of-my-way kind of thinking. The toxic brown sludge that the Chinese call air is only the most visible manifestation of this abandonment of rules designed to foster the common good. But it goes beyond the unregulated air and soupy rivers: Thousands of miners in China die each year in illegal mines. Almost every hotel has a brothel. A sidewalk stroll can quickly become a walk of misery; from the abandoned old to the criminally abused young, one can't wander twenty yards without needy hands thrusting out tin cups. The wonder I felt nightclubbing in Beijing or idling among the gilded skyscrapers of Pudong was increasingly supplanted by something far different. I was, in fact, appalled by much of what I was seeing in contemporary China. And I was beginning to feel like a bad host. I felt responsible for Jack.

"So what did you think of Guangzhou?" I asked him as our taxi sped toward the airport.

"Sing it with me: *I'm proud to be an American, where at least I know I'm free . . .*"

Few songs irritate me more. Somewhere in my formative years, I had heard something about scoundrels and patriotism. And that song in particular, with its love-it-or-leave-it pomposity, conjured up images of professional wrestlers, *Playboy* bunnies, and *American Idol* finalists leading the cheer as fighter jets swooped through the sky on their way to bomb some country few could find on a map. But that's the thing about China. Suddenly, the good ole U. S. of A. starts to look, well, pretty darn good. But surely there were parts of China where one didn't need a gas mask to breathe, where a China of quiet pagodas and babbling brooks could be found, a place where the country didn't seem quite so cruel. I'd decided to look for that China in Yunnan Province, in the far southwest of China, where steamy rain forests meet the soaring pinnacles of the Himalayas.

We flew to Kunming, the largest city in Yunnan, on China Southern Airlines. Kunming had recently begun to call itself China's most relaxed city. The competition for that title, of course, was not particularly stiff. But not even such an alluring moniker was enough to keep me in urban China for a moment longer than I had to be. From Kunming, we would fly farther west to Dali, which had come highly recommended by a well-traveled friend. Ordinarily, I would have taken the train, stopping for a few days in Guilin and Yangshuo to admire the karst formations, the jagged limestone cliffs that are featured on every Chinese postcard. But Jack was pressed for time and I was eager to start acclimatizing to the lofty heights of the Himalayas. Besides, the travel agent I had spoken to in Guangzhou had described Guilin as very touristy, and I did not want touristy. Okay, maybe a little touristy, touristy enough for picture menus. That would be good.

"You know, it's okay to let go of the armrests now and then," Jack said as we took off.

"We haven't flown together, have we?"

"No. I don't think so."

"Well, I'm not a really strong flyer."

"I see. And yet your work takes you to faraway places?"

"It does."

"Places that you have to fly to?"

"Yes."

"I think, maybe, you just might be in the wrong profession."

"Very possibly."

In Kunming, we transferred airplanes. This was the first airport I'd seen that hadn't yet been renovated into something glassy and shiny, and strangely this seemed good, to wander around a dingy airport. It suggested distance from booming coastal China. I noticed nursing rooms for mothers, which seemed like an unexpectedly thoughtful touch. On the runway, there were lines of blue fighter planes.

"So what's in Dali?" Jack inquired as we took off.

"No idea, really. But it's near the Burmese border. So I figure it's bound to be different."

I liked the sound of that—*near the Burmese border.* Surely, Dali would be exotic, intriguing, possibly even dangerous.

"Also," I remembered, "most of the inhabitants there are not Han Chinese."

Jack nodded. "And who are the Han Chinese?"

"Ninety-two percent of all people in China are Han Chinese. They're the Chinese Chinese. But the people living in Dali, while technically Chinese, are called Bai, one of the fifty-six minorities Kenny was talking about."

"Hey, wait a minute. You're not taking me to some separatist region, are you? This isn't going to be like Bosnia, is it?"

"Who can say for sure? But if there's trouble, we'll just cowboy-up and deal with it."

Of course Yunnan wasn't going to be like Bosnia. But I couldn't help myself. I was traveling with someone who knew even less about China than I did. Still, I had absolutely no idea what to expect, which was why I was so immensely pleased when we found ourselves at the airport in Dali, surrounded by rolling hills awash in that strangest of things: sunshine.

"Am I mistaken or is the sky actually blue here?" Jack asked.

It was. Stepping outside, our senses were flooded with clean air, blue skies, and golden sunlight. Never had I been so grateful to be in the presence of the great bright orb in the sky. Here it was at last, along with sweet, undulating hills and villages that—from the air, at least—seemed to be more than large piles of rubble surrounded by toxic ponds. We had finally found bucolic China.

We checked into our guesthouse, which was done in the Tibetan motif with thick wooden beams and carpeted doorways. There were a number of Tibetans in Yunnan, including the owner of this particular guesthouse. We deposited our bags and walked toward the old city walls, past portentous signs that read THE THOUSAND YEAR VALUE OF HONG-LONGJING STREET WILL CONTINUE AND LEAP IN THE CONSTRUCTION THINKING. What is this? I thought. This was not encouraging. I had not come to Dali to experience CONSTRUCTION THINKING. I was looking to escape from that China. And then, once we'd walked through the city's imposing East Gate, it soon became clear that we were not alone in our pursuit of escapist bliss.

Dali is tucked between Erhai Hu, a lake in the style of Tahoe, and the Jade Green Mountains, which are, in fact, green. Indeed, parts of them are even spray-painted green—the solution to the aesthetic problems posed by mining. Old-town Dali is small, with narrow streets bustling with people in traditional Bai dress, blues and pinks and soft knit hats, sitting on the ground selling walnuts. Outside the old walls is an ever-expanding Chinese city, but inside it feels like a village.

We walked around, absorbing atmosphere. From a window, we heard a child practicing her English "A, B, *xie*." On the street curbs, there were many Bai in their colorful garb, selling things, laughing. And there were many Chinese tourists too, some stopping to stare and gape not at the locals, but at us, the foreigners. We had come to Dali to look at the Bai. They had come to look at us looking at the Bai.

A sign pointed us toward the Catholic church. This pleased Jack, who gets a little shaky without his weekly mass. We followed an alleyway until we found ourselves in front of what appeared to be a stone pagoda on steroids. It looked nothing like any church I'd seen. It looked, strangely, like a boat in heavy seas, with flaming eaves parting like turbulent waves. We went inside and met a friendly woman named Irene. Jack inquired about mass and learned that they'd have one at 6 A.M. the following day, and we promised to attend.

"There's always someone named Irene in a Catholic church," Jack observed as we walked down cobbled streets toward Huguo Lu, which locals call the Street of Foreigners. Feeling hungry, we stopped and settled ourselves to eat at an appealing spot called The Yunnan Café.

"I'm having the yak," Jack announced after perusing the English-language menu.

"I think I'll have the same."

The culinary possibilities in China are endless. Why not yak? Or cat? Or swan? Or bullfrog? Or live squid? Why limit ourselves to pigs, lambs, and chickens? And why dine on cow but not their big, shaggy cousin, the yak? I'd been in China for a while and it seemed only natural to sample this new offering. *In China, we eat everything with four legs except the table, and anything with two legs except a person.* Splendid, I say, now pass the chopsticks.

We sat on a wooden terrace, idly enjoying our surroundings, watching the street life.

"So," Jack said after a while, "have you ever wondered where the hippies went?"

This seemed like the ultimate non sequitur. I hadn't wondered where the hippies went. I'd just assumed they'd rechanneled their narcissism and become yuppies, before evolving into the self-indulgent, squabbling baby boomers of today.

"No," I said. "Why do you ask?"

"Because," he said, "they've all moved to Dali."

Just then a pair of fetchingly bedraggled young Western women in dreadlocks wandered past. Shockingly, they were barefoot. I could not begin to imagine what kind of altered state I'd have to be in to wander around China barefoot. Considering the rivers of piss and phlegm that flowed down Chinese streets, these women were clearly insane. Or very, very high. And they were not alone. As I looked around, I saw that there were dozens, hundreds even, of Westerners in Dali who looked like they'd boarded the bus for Woodstock. What were they doing here? And what was it about Dali that had made it the go-to destination on the hippie trail?

"Ganja," whispered a voice.

I turned to see an elderly woman with a deeply lined face standing beside me. She was in traditional Bai dress and carried a wooden basket with a baby on her back. With a beatific smile, she leaned forward and whispered again, "Ganja?"

"I'm sorry," I said. "I don't understand."

"Ganja," she repeated, bringing her fingers to her lips in an imaginary toke.

"Ganja?" I whispered.

"Ganja," she nodded. *"Smokee, smokee."*

"Er—awfully thoughtful of you, but I think I'm going to

pass." And then, feeling helpful, I told her, "We're in China, you know. It's a police state."

"Ganja," she said again. I shook my head and off she finally waddled, with the baby bouncing behind her.

We had arrived in a place where kindly elderly ladies gently inquired whether your stay might be enhanced with a little *smokee* of the ganja. I suddenly admired the Bai for their entrepreneurial pluck. There was no better way of luring a steady stream of backpackers than by offering them the prospect of readily available weed. And clearly, the dealers themselves were among the most genial and solicitous in the world. What's not to like? We had solved the mystery of why the hippies had come to Dali.

*Reefer Madness.*

Jack looked at me, relieved. "Thanks for not buying a dime bag from grandma there. I don't want the Chinese police after us. It would suck to end this trip in a gulag in Manchuria."

I laughed. "You can relax. One thing I will not do is smoke weed in a country with mobile execution trucks."

It is true: There are Death Vans in China. And lest you think that mobile execution trucks are just a trifle barbaric, the roving Death Vans are, in the words of its manufacturer, a sign that China "promotes human rights now." Until 2004, all prisoners sentenced to death were shot, which can be messy and inefficient if the prisoner requires a coup de grâce. Now, for the lucky few, there are Death Vans that roam the country, going from town to town, efficiently and *humanely*—the Chinese really stress this—executing prisoners by lethal injection. No one knows for certain how many people are executed each year in China. Some say 2,000, others 15,000; the exact figure is a state secret. And the offenses can be something as simple as tax fraud. But the Chinese are also moving toward Death Vans because the government is involved in a profitable enterprise harvesting human organs from condemned prisoners, which is frankly much easier when the bodies aren't splattered with bullets. Members of Falun Gong, in particular, are said to be the go-to prisoners for organ transplants, and apparently the Japanese are big customers. So while back in the day I might have had a *smokee* here and there, if there was one criminal justice system in the world I wanted nothing to do with, it was China's.

That night after dinner, we passed a bar with a big dog slumbering at the entrance. "Tell me that doesn't look just like Osso," Jack said.

Osso was Jack's dog, his very big dog, the sort of dog who greets guests by barreling at them, chest level, to see whether the guest is to be played with. But the guest, of course, doesn't know this dog is being playful. All the guest knows is that there is a very large dog, a Rhodesian Ridgeback, about to knock him over.

"Have you ever seen a Rhodesian Ridgeback in China?"

"It's probably the local delicacy."

"Let's go in."

I looked up at the sign. The Elephant Bar. Inside, the air was redolent with a smoky haze familiar to anyone who'd attended a Berkeley sit-in in the summer of 1969. We took a seat at the bar and spoke to James, one of the dreadlocked owners, who explained that they'd rescued the dog from dog fighting. As we talked, a couple of Colombians walked in. "Shots?" they offered. It was a little early to set such a blistering pace. "It's on us."

Okay, then.

Soon the bar began to fill up. There was an Englishman in a straw hat who had spent the previous night sleeping there. Two brothers. Australians. Dutch. For a time, this was the crossroads of the world. The bar began to fill up with a crowd of convivial, determined drinkers. There were beers, shots. And then joints were lit up, and while we declined a proffered toke, it wasn't because we were trying to maintain a pretense of sobriety. No, with the first shots it was established that tonight we would get cheerfully hammered. But there was no need to actually smoke weed. In the sweet, fragrant haze, my eyes watered, I had a curious case of the munchies, and I couldn't stop laughing.

I turned to James, who was English. "So can I ask you something?" I said between chuckles. "How long have you guys been here?"

"We opened about three years ago. We had a place in Thailand, but Thailand became just . . ." He waved his hand languorously.

"And business is good?"

"Business is good."

"Has it always been like this?" I went on. "I mean, there's tons of Westerners here. Why are we here? What is drawing us to this town in Yunnan Province?"

"It's because of Lonely Planet, man. A couple of years

ago, they made a reference to the local herb. You've probably noticed the friendly locals selling weed. It grows wild up in the hills. So the writer mentioned it and voilà."

It is astonishing, the power of Lonely Planet. One off-hand comment by a freelance writer and suddenly a small town in Yunnan Province had become the Mecca of the hippie trail.

Just then James's attention was diverted by the arrival of a fierce-looking Chinese man in a suit. It is, of course, very difficult for a stoned man in long dreads to convey tension, but that is exactly what he exuded. They conversed with the aid of a waitress translating, and pointed frequently to the dog, which slumbered happily on a couch.

Afterward, I asked what that was about.

"He's one of the local mobsters. His boss's dog is missing, and since it looked a lot like ours, he came over to take a closer look."

"Is the mafia powerful here?"

"They control everything, man." He shook his head. "Don't mess with the mobsters in Dali."

We were not in Dali to mess with mobsters. We were here, it now seemed clear, to get positively *lit*. Not for a moment was there an empty glass before us. Not in this bar. This was a place for drinking, where the moment a glass was drained, another was placed before us. I was liking it here, this merry place where everyone was funny and quick-witted and where you could settle back and enjoy the secondhand cannabis. *No, Officer,* I'd say should I encounter one. *I didn't inhale,* I'd assert as he stared into my glassy eyes.

I soon found myself next to a young Chinese woman from Shanghai. Her Western name was Judy and she'd settled in Dali three months earlier but would join her boyfriend in Dalian, a city in northern China, when he returned from the United States.

"I want to be a housewife," she said.

This was a surprisingly popular ambition among young women in China. But then, I reflected, it sure beat working in a factory twelve hours a day.

"And where's your boyfriend from?" I asked.

"He's from North Carolina. He was my English teacher."

"And a fine job he did too. Have you been to North Carolina?"

"Yes." She scrunched her nose. "I don't like it there."

"Why not?"

She struggled to convey her thoughts. "People are very fat there."

"Well, that's not a good reason to not like North Carolina. It just means the barbecue is pretty good."

"There is no culture there."

"No culture? Have you ever been to a basketball game between Duke and the University of North Carolina? It's a tribal conflict that has its roots in the dim mists of time."

"I still don't like North Carolina. I just want to be a housewife."

"But what if your boyfriend wants to return to North Carolina? What if he becomes homesick? As an American, he can never truly become Chinese, can he?"

She nodded her head slowly, as if she'd never considered the possibility.

"But if you come to America, you can become an American," Jack chimed in. "It's what makes America great. Anyone can become an American."

"But I don't want to go to America."

"I know," I told her. "But I've seen this many times before. Your boyfriend will always be a *laowai* here. Maybe he doesn't want to be an outsider his entire life. Maybe, one day, he will want to return to North Carolina because he wants to be someplace that feels like home."

She began to quiver. "But I don't want to live in North Carolina. I want to be a housewife in Dalian."

"Dude," Jack interjected. "You're going to make her cry." He turned to her. "Don't listen to him. He's a bad man."

"I don't think he's a bad man."

"I'm not a bad man, but him?" I said, pointing to Jack. "He's a bad man. Do you like George Bush?"

She shook her head emphatically.

"He likes George Bush."

And just like that, all the goodwill toward us evaporated. Our barmates ignored us. Our glasses remained unfilled. The owners wouldn't even look at us.

I knew, of course, that George Bush wasn't the most popular of presidents. But still, simply because Americans had elected a psychopath didn't strike me as a sufficient reason for this denial of alcohol. True, we did it twice, but I think that would elicit the need for more drink, not less. And so here we were. We'd been 86'd? Cut off from ale. Cruel indeed.

"You don't think it's because we're completely drunk?" Jack asked.

"I don't think you get 86'd for that around here."

Jack tried hard to regain their good graces. He served up witty banter, to no avail. His attempts to rejoin the conversation around us fell flat.

"So, James, can I ask you something?" Jack finally asked, raising his voice so that James, who had slinked far, far away from the Republican and his guilty-by-association friend, could hear. Cautiously, he moved toward us. "So, James." Jack searched his mind for something that would alleviate this wall of bitterness. And this is what he came up with:

"Do you like the Grateful Dead?"

I snorted so hard I damaged my sinuses. But it was enough. James did indeed like the Grateful Dead. People were talking to us again. Soon, Jack was no longer regarded as a dangerous madman but as a peculiar alien, one called to explain his world. It helped that Jack had always thought that invading Iraq was a bad idea, and that his conservatism was of the old school, Reagan kind.

"No, I respectfully disagree," he said to the Englishman. "Gun control is bad. See, the reason we don't have soccer hooligans like you do in England is because we're all armed."

Soon, another group of foreigners arrived. Jack, eager to reclaim the warmth so recently lost, asked them where they were from.

"Israel," one offered cautiously.

"Israel! I've been hoping all night for a group of Israelis to walk in. *Mazel tov,* my friends. This round is on me."

And the night went on, leading inexorably to flaming shots sucked through straws and a long, endless stumble in the dark—*Which way? I don't know. Fuck. I'm drunk*—until finally we found the heavy wooden door of our guesthouse, and we pounded—so much pounding, had they never before had drunken guests needing an open door at 2 A.M.?—until, at last, a young boy undid the lock and wordlessly, loudly, we tottered in.

A knock on the door. Groan. I opened the latch. Jack stood in the darkness. "You're not going to church with me, are you?"

I was in that grim place halfway between gross inebriation and a head-shattering hangover. It was not a moment I wanted to be conscious for. And I certainly wasn't going to drag my sorry ass out of bed for predawn mass, though I did resolve to never, ever drink again if God would please, please spare me the hangover on the horizon. I had a dim recollection of a shot glass on fire. This was going to hurt. Please, Lord. I'll never touch a drop again.

"No. I'm not going to church. But pray for me. I am not well."

It was as if my head had been invaded by little men with jackhammers. They pounded. They drilled. And my mouth felt as if I'd swallowed a wad of cotton. My body felt as if it had been poisoned, which of course it had been. It's the first sign of aging, the crippling hangover. True, I'd had hangovers before. More than a few. But once, not so long ago, I could simply guzzle a couple of Gatorades, go for a run, sweat it out, and move on. Not so now. After thirty-five, hangovers *hurt*. Jesus, they hurt. Flammable shots? Good God, what was I thinking.

Some hours later, I stumbled downstairs to find Jack on a chair outside, smoking a cigarette.

"Tell me that you're as hungover as I am," I said to him.

"I am hungover," he said. "But I'm not the wreck that you are right now."

Enough of a wreck, however, to have missed the church

service himself. It turned out that we'd also missed breakfast at the guesthouse. I was, of course, in no mood for food. I was not entirely convinced I could handle food. But the cure, of course, could only begin with nourishment.

We walked into the old town in search of sustanence as the little men inside my head continued to pound away. I yearned for the sun to disappear. I wanted darkness. I wanted the grim twilight of Guangzhou. Anything to dull my headache.

Soon, we came across a pizzeria. Dali is that kind of place. There are pizzerias. I sat there in the tiny restaurant with my eyes closed, massaging my temples, trying to decide if I could manage to eat a slice without hurling. It was a very bad hangover. Somehow, I forced a few bites into my mouth and lived in hope that they would stay down.

Back on the street, we walked on to a large outdoor Bai market. There were dead pigs, dead chickens, blood, flesh everywhere, all over the place, all these carcasses being butchered. This was not a good milieu for someone desperately trying to suppress the spontaneous expulsion of a pizza breakfast. I had a vague notion that I should linger here, that there was traditional Bai culture here among the animal carcasses. Something to learn. But I was not well. And so we marched to the Three Pagodas, which are among the oldest pagodas in China.

In my surly state, the entrance fee to the pagodas seemed an offense of the highest order.

"A hundred and twenty *kuai*," I sputtered. "It's an outrage."

I fumbled with my money. My head throbbed. And then the fireworks began. The Chinese love their fireworks. *Pop, pop, pop.* Every Saturday in China—wedding day—the country explodes to the sounds of head-shattering booms. *Pop, pop, crack. Rat-tat-tat-tat.*

"I need to get out of here."

So instead of lingering at the pagodas, we walked back toward the West Gate, where we were convinced by a woman to follow her on the Number 2 bus to Erhai Hu for a boat trip to a temple and fishing village. This was more my speed. The bus was very crowded with women carrying babies on their backs inside wooden baskets, but the farther away from town we got, the better I felt. As as we ambled down a country road, we passed fields of hay and innumerable carts pulled by men or donkeys and a young woman walking alone in traditional white and pink garb listening to an iPod.

Lakes, I discovered, are the cure for hangovers. There was a freshness to Erhai Hu, a pristineness that soon purged the lingering effects of last night's revelry. It was blue. It was clean-*ish*. There were fishermen plying the waters, and in the near distance rippling hills, and beyond that the Jade Green Mountains that rose to a lofty 12,000 feet. We took a tour boat across the pleasant expanse, and soon I began to feel better.

We were let off below a temple, which like those on Putuoshan was devoted to the worship of Guanyin, the bodhisattva of compassion. There was a graceful pagoda on a promontory overlooking the lake, and we stepped in to pray for some compassion. Or rather, I prayed. Jack doesn't pray to bodhisattvas. I, however, was willing to seek help for my hangover wherever I could find it. Then the boat took us onward from the temple to a small fishing village on an island in the center of the lake. On its banks were nets full of tiny fish drying in the sun. There wasn't much to see save for a small outdoor market. Still, it was pleasant, quiet. We sat around a tree stump for tea. Nearby, on the shores of the lake, women were washing clothes by hand. Soon, we were joined by the villagers. We couldn't understand a word, of course, but they were very friendly. A fresh breeze blew and an elderly woman offered us a plate of tomatoes.

"You know what?" I said to Jack. "I'm actually feeling kind of content right now. It's not often that you feel the love in China. China, as you've probably noticed, isn't the warmest place on Earth. And so to be here, in some village in the middle of a lake in Yunnan Province on a clear day, and to be offered a plate of tomatoes, gratis, just as a kindly gesture to a visitor . . . it makes me happy."

"Well, good," Jack said. "It's about fricken time."

# 15

There are many places in the world I wished I'd seen thirty years earlier, but none more so than the town of Lijiang, nestled in the shadow of the Himalayas, in a lush valley beneath the looming majesty of Jade Dragon Mountain. It was here, in the 1920s and '30s, that the idiosyncratic Dr. Joseph Rock, a brilliant botanist, established his well-stocked base. He was born in Vienna but had moved to Honolulu in 1907, where he had found his calling in the study of plants. Possibly suffering from island fatigue (something I could totally understand), Dr. Rock made his way to Yunnan Province and arrived in Lijiang in 1922. He was no mere backpacker, however. He had taught himself Chinese at the age of thirteen, and brought gold plates to dine upon, opera records, and a bathtub that he insisted porters carry over mountain passes. His perambulations in the region around Lijiang, under the auspices of his nemesis, the National Geographic Society, led to his magnum opus, *The*

*Ancient Na-khi Kingdom of South-West China*, memorably described by the travel writer Bruce Chatwin as perhaps the most eccentric publication ever produced by Harvard University Press.

It was, in fact, Bruce Chatwin who had put Lijiang on my mental map. He is sometimes described as a travel writer; at other times, more unkindly, as a fabulist. When I read his work, back in my teens, I didn't care to make the distinction. Perhaps he wrote about a world as he wished it to be, but what a world. His essay about finding himself caught up in a coup in Africa remains for me the ultimate evocation of cool sangfroid. In the 1980s, he visited Lijiang and wrote a memorable essay about Dr. Ho, a Taoist healer, spinning a tale of love and magic and a history that never ends. So it was with uncommon enthusiasm that I boarded the bus for the journey into the high hills of Yunnan and the fabled town that some believe was the inspiration for the mythical Shangri-la.

"So, Lijiang," said Jack, trying to muster enthusiasm for the six-hour bus journey. "And what can we expect to find in Lijiang? More hippies? Maybe some anarchists? Crackheads?"

"We'll be visiting the Naxis."

"Naxis?"

"Uh-huh. Naxis."

"Well, okay. Let's party with the Naxis. Will the Israelis be joining us too?"

Naxi is actually pronounced *Na-khi*, but we did not know this then. Descendants of nomadic Tibetans who had settled in the verdant valleys and soaring mountains of northern Yunnan, the Naxis are the predominant minority in Lijiang. It is a matriarchal society wherein men are relegated to the status of useless dolts, henpecked ninnies, or, if they're lucky, dreamy slackers, which is good work if you can find it. In any event, such an arrangement seemed profoundly un-Chinese, and this, too, seemed in need of observation.

The bus was crowded, and we crossed the flat farmland alongside the blue waters of Erhai Hu on a two-lane road without an emergency shoulder, which would be unremarkable except for the fact that the road, this narrow slab of cement, was elevated ten feet above the farmland, presumably to deter farmers and animals from wandering across it. And naturally, this being China, there wasn't anything like a guardrail. Passing a truck, with no room for error, while oncoming traffic was barreling toward us at seventy miles an hour, is one of the more uniquely terrifying experiences I'd yet encountered. The drive was essentially one long cardiac event, and I tried to calm myself by watching the Bai farmers in their fields, hundreds of men and women, threshing wheat by hand. On a small television screen that rested above the driver, we were treated to a long loop of martial arts films and highlights from the Bruce Willis oeuvre. I had always wonderd what the movie *Die Hard* might sound like dubbed into Chinese. Fortunately, I now had the opportunity to hear Yippeekaya Motherfucker spoken in Mandarin. This pleased me to no end. Clearly, my threshold for entertainment is low, which is a good thing because it was a long bus ride.

Lijiang is situated above 8,000 feet, and as we climbed into the hills I began to notice an increase in soldiers and military garrisons. Traditionally, this area of China was the frontier. But the soldiers, of course, are not in Yunnan to guard against an invasion from the Republic of Myanmar. China has the largest army in the world and there's only one reason, of course, to maintain an army of that size: to keep the Naxis in line. And the Bai. And the Tibetans. And the Uyghurs. And anyone else who might have subversion on their mind. According to the Chinese government, there are three evil forces in the world: terrorism, separatism, and extremism. It's a broad group of evil forces and it gives the government a lot of leeway.

Despite the soldiers, however, the scene was an Arcadian paradise. There were forested mountains. There were the farmers threshing grain and people selling apples by the side of the road. There were wood-beamed farmhouses with yellow corn drying in the sun. Now and then we passed donkey-led wagons and the peculiar three-wheeled tractors that looked like choppers on steroids. I couldn't imagine leaving a farm in Yunnan for an urban cesspool like Guangzhou.

I was lost in my reverie when the man across the aisle asked me where I was from. "My name is Tam," he said.

Tam was from Beijing, where he worked as an engineer designing medical supplies. Or at least, that's what he used to do.

"I quit my job last week."

"Is that so?"

"Yes. Beijing is too big, too dirty. Everything is about money now. I don't want to live that way. I want to live in the mountains under a blue sky. I can get a job anywhere."

Tam's wife and young son had remained behind in Beijing. The nuclear family, as we know it, wasn't the norm in China anymore, as the booming economy had been scattering families to the wind. Not so long ago, it had been nearly impossible to obtain residency permits outside one's place of birth.

True, political realities might have taken you someplace new. Mention to the wrong person that you're going to spew your bean-curd milk if you have to read the Little Red Book one more time and soon you might find yourself farming stones on the barren steppes of Inner Mongolia. But like Judy in Dali, longing to be a housewife in Dalian, Tam was part of the new vanguard of Han Chinese moving westward. True, most were hunting for business opportunities. But Tam, and I sensed he was hardly alone, was moving to the west for lifestyle reasons, searching for his own private California.

"That sounds like a good plan," I offered. I understood; I'm usually first in line for the escapist bus. "That's great that you can do that in China today."

"Yes. There are many changes in China."

"All for the good?"

Tam shrugged. "China is very complicated. Everything is changing, but the politics remains the same."

"Yes, it strikes me as odd," I said, pleased to have met someone so open with his opinions. "I wasn't in China thirty years ago, but I suspect that the China of today looks vastly different. And yet the government remains stuck in another era."

"We need more democracy," Tam agreed. I hoped, for his sake, that there wasn't a government goon on board. "Today, maybe 500 officials have a say in government. But the people have no say."

"Yes. It's not right." And now I hoped for my sake there wasn't a government goon on board.

"People are very worried."

"As they should be."

"They think the government will start a war."

War? How now, what's this about war? War with who? Should I be digging bunkers in California?

"Er . . . what war?" I hesitated. "With America?"

Tam looked at me oddly. "No. Not America. With Taiwan."

"Ah . . . Taiwan."

Technically, of course, the U.S. has indicated that it would go to war with China should it ever attack Taiwan. Indeed, China was seen to be preparing for it by confronting the technological advantages of the U.S. China had been testing weapons that could take out satellites. They'd hacked into the Pentagon. But there couldn't be more than twelve people left in the U.S. who could muster any enthusiasm for an apocalyptic war with China over Taiwan. Of course, those twelve people probably all had jobs at the White House.

"So do you think it likely that there will be a war between China and Taiwan?"

Suddenly, I rocketed against the seat in front of me. The bus slid across the roadway, the tires shrieking. We were heading directly into the path of a chopper-tractor that had unwisely chosen that moment to make its turn onto the road. The bus screeched to a stop mere inches from the other vehicle. The bus driver emitted a well-deserved harangue at the tractor operator, who remained stoically perched atop his machine.

"Yes, I think there will be a war," Tam went on, nonplussed. "We have a one-country, two-systems relationship with Hong Kong. It should be the same with Taiwan."

Ah. Though a democrat, Tam too was a nationalist.

Several hours later, we rumbled into the outskirts of Lijiang, which I was disappointed to discover was made up of the usual collection of dirty low-rise apartments and shops. Chatwin, I thought, you've been making things up again, haven't you? True, we were surrounded by stone mountains capped with snow. And the lush terrain beyond the town itself was enchanting. And looking at a map, one would think we'd fallen off it. But Lijiang, at first impression, was just another Han Chinese city, an uninspired place, dusty and run-down.

We hopped off at the bus station, put our backpacks on, and started walking. "I know a place where you can get a room for 80 yuan," Tam offered.

This sounded good, we thought as we passed the obligatory hulking statue of Chairman Mao, who here had been immortalized with a *Deutschland über alles* salute. How could anyone find this charming? I wondered. But then we walked past the Yulong Bridge and Waterwheel and entered a maze of cobblestone streets and small canals that wound their way through the town center alongside timeless wooden buildings. It was, in fact, a lovely place, and fully deserving of its status as a World Heritage Site—a status, frankly, that I found regrettable since, as was quickly apparent as we approached the center of town, Every Damn Tourist in China, all of them, 300 million possibly, was in Lijiang on this Tuesday afternoon. Seriously. It has been said before. Often. But China is *crowded*.

Nevertheless, it was clear why we had all come here. A major earthquake had struck in 1996, doing considerable damage to Lijiang, except for the old town, which was largely constructed with wood. Here at last was someplace venerable, a place hidden in a high valley in Yunnan, far away from the destructive gaze of Beijing. Until recently, that is. The moment Lijiang was declared an official UNESCO World Heritage Site, the gold rush was on as thousands of Han Chinese made their way to this corner of Yunnan Province to earn their living as proprietors of tick-tacky souvenir emporiums. True, there were still Naxis in Lijiang attired in traditional blue aprons and sheepskin capes, and as they lured Chinese tourists into restaurants or encouraged them to join in on the traditional dancing in the village square, they seemed more like the hired help than the guardians of an ancient culture.

Today, tourism was the business of Lijiang, and also, strangely, the building of doors. On every corner, men were sanding doors, finishing doors, scuffing doors. As far as I could tell, there was no apparent need for these doors. Every doorway had a door. So this was mysterious.

After weaving our way through a twisting alley, Tam led us to a modest guesthouse with an appealing courtyard. I went ahead and coughed up the extra dollar for a room with a "river view," and was pleased to discover that this river was, in fact, a six-inch stream.

We thanked Tam for directing us to the guesthouse. But I was still curious about something. "Tam, could you do me a favor and ask the owner why, exactly, every man in Lijiang seems to be making doors?"

Tam exchanged a few words with the owner, then turned back to us. "Some months ago, there was a very rich foreigner, he thinks an American, who paid a lot of money for an antique door. So now everyone is making antique doors."

If there's a market niche anywhere, the Chinese will fill it. Do you need a very old door? No problem. The Chinese will make you a very old door. Good quality. Brand-new very old door. Special price for you.

After dropping off our packs, we joined thousands of other zombie-like tourists crowding the lanes behind umbrella-toting tour guides and found our way to a pleasant restaurant overlooking one of the canals. We had invited Tam to come along. Jack, possibly forgetting that he was in China, bravely ordered the sausage.

I turned to Tam. "So which part of the animal do you think they reserve for sausage around here?" I asked.

"I don't care," Jack said. "As long as it's not a dog."

"You don't eat dog?" Tam inquired.

"No dogs," Jack confirmed.

"You must try to be more open-minded," Tam said.

"He is open-minded," I assured him. "He's eating a sausage in China. For a *laowai*, this is a very brave, open-minded thing to do."

Afterward, Jack lit up a smoke, and because I had pre-pared for this just-in-case-I-felt-like-smoking moment, I reached for the stash of Nicorette I'd brought to China. "You don't smoke?" I asked Tam, who alone among us did not seem to crave nicotine.

"No," Tam said. "In China today, smoking is for the blue-collar or the poor. In an office, no smoking. If you go out-side to smoke, instead of doing your work, you are seen as very weak."

As we talked, we were soon joined by our waitress. She was, evidently, a genuine Naxi and not a Han woman dressed up like a Naxi, like many who had been lured to the money-making possibilities of Lijiang. She was friendly and affable, and now that we had a genuine Chinese person beside us, I asked Tam if he could translate.

"In Naxi society, it is the women who are the bosses, yes?" I asked her.

"Yes," she said through Tam. "I am the boss. I tell the man what to do. If I want a man, he comes to me. If I want him to go away, he goes away."

I had read about this earlier. In Naxi society, there is what is called the *azhu* system, which as far as I understood is similar to the Friends With Benefits system we have at home. A woman is free to choose her lovers and discard them as she pleases. Men provide support for any children they might sire, but otherwise paternity is insignificant. The child belongs to the mother.

"You know what she is, don't you?" Jack said as we paid the bill. He grinned. "A Femi-Naxi."

"Good one. Very good."

Tam expressed his need for an afternoon nap, and so Jack and I wandered on through the enchanted streets of Lijiang, enchanted streets that could hardly be seen through the teeming crowds. Not so long ago, Lijiang was an idyllic hamlet with a unique culture, the sort of place I would have been very happy to spend weeks in, retracing the footsteps of Rock and Chatwin. But, as yet another consequence of China's leap into the global economy, there are now 1.3 billion potential Chinese tourists. And when more than a billion people set their sights on something, invariably they crush it. There was little to do but give in, and soon we walked into a souvenir emporium specializing in leather, where Jack bought a cowboy hat. Every Chinese tourist in Lijiang wore one.

Eventually, we stopped at a café that overlooked the whimsical black-tiled roofs of the old town. In the distance,

Jade Dragon Mountain pierced the swirling clouds that floated near its top. We ordered something to drink and sat back to appreciate the easy-listening sounds of Queen—not "We Are the Champions" Queen, but obscure Queen. A fan's Queen.

Jack arched his eyebrow. "It's not surprising, is it? You just knew that the Naxis would be into Queen."

"Actually, I thought tonight we'd go to the Naxi Music Academy to listen to some traditional Naxi music."

"You know what that's going to be, don't you?"

"No, what?"

"Wagner."

It wasn't Wagner, of course, though the musicians were probably of the same era. The Naxi Orchestra is the local equivalent of the Preservation Hall Jazz Band in New Orleans. They're not the spryest bunch, most are in their eighties, but they are very cool with their wispy mustaches and long, flowing beards. The band was led by a charismatic man who spoke English.

"I am seventy-three, but look much younger. Happy spirit, but hard life. Twenty-one years in prison."

His name was Xuen Ke, one of the Three Eccentrics of Lijiang, according to the locals, together with the Dr. Ho, immortalized by Chatwin, and He Zhigang, an armless calligrapher who paints with his mouth in a park next to a portrait of Prince Charles. Xuen Ke continued to talk. And talk some more. And then some more. Mostly, he spoke in English, which I thought was interesting since the vast majority of the audience was Chinese, and they sat there, impatiently tapping their feet and generally looking really, really annoyed.

"We hate that word—minority. We prefer tribe," the bandleader said. And then he introduced the music. "And so the theme of this song is anger or hate."

It was a little ditty about Kublai Khan, sung by a chorus of women. It was a very moving song, very powerful, and when it finished, I, too, felt anger and hatred, and wished only to set out on the warpath. But Xuen Ke toned the atmosphere down by introducing a song played during the Yi Torch Festival. It consisted of a girl playing a small mouth instrument, and as I listened to these trippy, warbling sounds, I thought this must be what ancient techno sounded like. This was followed by a Tibetan man, a former hunter who kissed the amulet around his neck and sang, a cappella, a gripping song about a friend.

"He sing from the heart," Xuen Ke went on, "not from the face like Chinese pop singers. We hate them. This man only a grade-three education from mountain school. But his singing a Ph.D."

I liked Xuen Ke. There was a cheekiness to him. He ended the performance with some sage advice. "Don't eat the fish from the lake, or the heart of the animal. And don't drink beer or spirits. Then smoking no problem."

"So what did you think?" Jack asked me afterward.

"I'd be very curious to know what he said to the Chinese audience members. I mean, twenty-one years in prison for being a Naxi. I'd say he has cause to be just a trifle pissed off with the Han Chinese."

"That's the Chinese Chinese?"

"Yes."

"Well, there sure are a lot of them here."

All wearing cowboy hats like Jack. Yes, Lijiang was now very touristy and very Chinese. True, there were many who were Naxi. But most seemed to be employed to be the cute supplicant minority, with young women in traditional dress stepping out of the restaurants to do a dance on the canals at five-minute intervals. Ten kilometers to the north in the town of Baisha, Dr. Ho's home had become an extremely popular stop on the tourist trail.

We had dinner on a second-floor balcony, overlooking the hordes of visitors. And then, below us, through the bustling crowds, three young, very dirty pilgrims were lying down, touching their foreheads to the street, standing and bowing, repeating this devotional rhythm again and again, as they made their way forward through a crowd that pointed and laughed. They were Tibetan Buddhists on pilgrimage to the Yufeng Temple, a small lamasery outside of Lijiang.

"So," I said to Jack after the Tibetans had passed. "Are you feeling rested? Ready to do some hiking?"

"I'm not entirely convinced this is a good idea. The thought of marching into the wilderness in some remote corner of China with you kind of scares me."

"It'll be fun. Trust me."

"Okay. Now I'm really worried."

# 16

A week earlier, somewhere in the hills above Dali, it had occurred to me that hiking the high trail above Tiger Leaping Gorge might be a little challenging. This is because I was apparently traveling with the world's laziest man. Jack and I had gone to look at the Zhonghe Temple, perched upon Zhonghe Shan, a lofty eminence riddled with Bai cemeteries. It's above 7,500 feet, a good hike. But we did not hike up this mountain. From Dali we had taken the *chairlift*. Where we stepped off, there stood a sign pointing us to a café 100 meters upward.

"We are not going up," Jack had insisted. "It's 100 meters—that's, I don't know, a long way in feet."

"It's about 300 feet."

"That's a long way. And I'm tired."

"Don't be such a wimp. My four-year-old could run up 300 feet. Even my one-year-old could waddle up the hill."

Finally, Jack had relented and, with an astonishing display of gasps and labored breathing, followed by innumerable breaks, he managed to heave himself up to the café.

"There. You happy now? You've got a Coke, a plate of French fries, cigarettes. It wasn't so bad, was it?"

Jack was dripping in sweat. "Salt. I need salt."

"Look," I had said. "This is nothing compared to Tiger Leaping Gorge."

"Well, I'm not much of a hiker."

"Evidently. But you did bring hiking boots, right? You're going to need them."

"No, I didn't bring hiking boots. I've got running shoes."

"And clamp-ons," I had mused. "We'll need to buy some clamp-ons."

"Clamp-ons," Jack had sputtered. "What do we need clamp-ons for?"

"For the ice."

It was early October, far too early for ice. But as always in China, I didn't know what to expect of this hike above Tiger Leaping Gorge, a deep canyon carved by the Yangtze River and framed by spectacular 16,000-foot mountains. Once, long ago, a tiger was said to have leapt across the gorge, and the Chinese, who have a strong disposition toward poetic place-names, commemorated the event by calling it Tiger Leaping Gorge. Really, it is remarkable that Communism, with its deadening effect on language, lingered for so long in China. Mao, no doubt, would have called it Gorge Number Fifty-three, or some other buzz-kill of a name. The fifteen-mile, two-day hike above the gorge is said to be among the finest hikes in the world, offering breathtaking vistas of immense cliffs and the frothing river. This is what I knew. That is what I sought.

And this being China, which is still very much under the thumb of the Communist Party, this would likely be my only opportunity to see Tiger Leaping Gorge in its full splendor. This is because the government has decided to build a dam across what by some measures is the deepest gorge on Earth. Tiger Leaping Gorge, from Beijing's perspective, is the perfect place for another dam. And they love dams in Beijing. Indeed, nearly half the world's dams are in China, including the largest, the Three Gorges Dam, 1,500 miles downstream. Dam building begets dam building, and Chinese engineers, concerned about sediment buildup in the Yangtze River, have concluded that Tiger Leaping Gorge is the ideal spot to take some of the pressure off of the Three Gorges Dam. One would think, however, that the local government in Yunnan would object to Beijing's plans. After all, it would call for transforming Tiger Leaping Gorge, one of the natural treasures in China, into a big pond. But there is a saying in China—*Build a bridge and you'll get silver. Build a road and you'll get gold. But build a dam and you'll get diamonds.* There is money in dams. And money in China trumps everything else.

So I was eager to see the gorge before it flooded. The trailhead to Tiger Leaping Gorge begins in the village of Qiaotou, forty miles north of Lijiang, but sadly for us, the early buses from Lijiang had been full, and by the time we reached it, it was nearly noon. There didn't appear to be anything compelling in Qiaotou, and so we dropped off our backpacks at Jane's Guesthouse, where we encountered Jane—who may or may not have been a man. The guesthouse is located just before the gate at the entrance to the high trail that would lead us up to the lofty pinnacles, and we decided, since we were there, to fuel up on banana pancakes. Jack was surprisingly chipper.

"Let's go for the speed record," he said.

I encouraged this. We would climb thousands of feet today. There was no need for reality just yet.

It was a warm, sunny day, and we set off from the guest-house with our daypacks full of water, wandering past fields of grain and small wooden farmhouses. Jack had set a blistering pace but then suddenly stopped.

"Are you sure we're on the trail?" he asked.

"I have no idea. But you know what? It's a nice trail, what-ever this trail is, so let's just see where it goes."

Jack gave me a dubious look. "Okay, right, I'm feeling really good about this hike."

And then, just a few steps farther along the path, we did feel really good about this hike. For a half hour or so, we'd been following the Yangtze River as it meandered past the last rem-nants of Qiaotou and into terraced cornfields. And then, as the trail curved around a bend, we suddenly found our jaws drop-ping at the sheer magnificence of the scenery. There before us rose Dragon Snow Mountain and Jade Snow Mountain, mighty ridges rising 16,000 feet toward summits of jagged rock and snow. These were sheer walls, staggering cliffs, the kind of daunting cartoonish mountainsides that one climbed to find the lama who knew the meaning of life, cragged precipices that plummeted toward the raging river below.

"Wow," Jack said.

Wow indeed. Foreigners had only been able to enjoy this view since 1993, when China finally allowed outsiders into this corner of the country. And the view has come with a price: More than a few hikers have died along the trail above Tiger Leaping Gorge. Falls, rock slides, getting lost, a change in weather, these were among the things that could prove fatal on the high trail. I had concluded that it would probably be best to keep this sobering fact from Jack. And then I thought better of it.

"You know, quite a few people have died on this trail. Foreigners too."

"It doesn't trouble me. Because you know what? We are mountain men."

"Yes, we are. This is our milieu."

Of course, it was unlikely that a mountain man would utter the word "milieu." Nevertheless, we pressed on, following a trail that began to grade higher.

"It's called Tiger Leaping Gorge," I noted. "Kind of makes you think, doesn't it."

"What? That we're in tiger country?"

Whenever I was hiking in California, I couldn't get mountain lions out of my mind. I always expected to see one, perched on a ledge, a spring in its step, a big cat looking for lunch.

"After the market in Guangzhou," Jack said wryly, "I'd say that the likelihood of us encountering a tiger is zero."

Not quite, as it turns out. There were indeed still tigers in Yunnan Province. Scientists had, in fact, recently filmed an Indo-Chinese Tiger in the Xishuangbanna National Nature Reserve near the border with Burma and Laos. And indeed, in 2001, tigers near one village managed to kill six buffalo and twenty-four cows. In some parts of Yunnan, tiger prints are said to be a not entirely unusual thing to see. It's one of those things you like to hear in China: *Other* people have seen tiger prints. I, however, did not want to see them. I just liked knowing they were there, out there, somewhere—just not here.

The trail was becoming more dramatic. We passed a farm, beside which a boy had clambered up a tree and begun to sing. What a pastoral hamlet, I thought, nestled here in the gentle slopes below Jade Snow Mountain. This was China as I had envisioned it. A warm breeze stirred the air. The river below had the faint bluish color of ice. The sky had a deep, purple tinge and the mountains glistened with snow. And then, as I walked around a bend fringed by tall grass, I encountered a snake.

I am, frankly, a complete sissy when it comes to snakes. I do not want to say I shrieked like a little girl. So I won't say it.

"I think it's dead," Jack observed.

"Are you sure? Why don't you throw a rock at it?"

Gingerly, I made my way around the snake, which on closer inspection was indeed dead, extremely dead, had already been munched upon by some beast or bird. But perhaps there were others, a multitude of serpents in the grass, just waiting for some hiker to pass on the trail, and I began to wonder about the snakes of Yunnan Province, and whether they were venomous or not. It was a familiar sensation. I recalled my time in the South Pacific. You think you're in paradise, when, in fact, you're residing in a den of foot-long, poisonous centipedes.

I resolved to turn my mind off. There was too much beauty here to be savored. The awesome magnificence of the natural world was all around us. And so I settled into the pleasant rhythm of bringing myself ever upward, following this trail that carried us higher and higher above the river. We walked on until we stumbled into the village of Nuoyu, where we found the Naxi Family Guesthouse, a wooden farmhouse with corn drying from the walls, where we could replenish water and have a bite to eat. We settled ourselves at a table in a courtyard that offered a dramatic view of the mountains.

"Okay. It's been nice knowing you," Jack said, sweating freely and breathing hard. "This is where I leave. I've decided to join the Naxis."

I laughed, but in truth we were not even close to halfway. It would be about another 3,000 feet up before we saw another guesthouse, and we had about five hours left to do it before darkness.

"I can't believe we're doing this," Jack groaned as we got to our feet.

"I've been telling you all week that we're hiking Tiger Leaping Gorge."

"But I didn't think you meant it."

But I did.

We returned to the trail, which was becoming ever more interesting, switching freely from dirt path to stony cliff-side ledges that swiftly narrowed. It was ten feet wide. Not so bad, I'd think. Then it was five feet. Um. Three feet. And because we had already ascended a thousand or two feet in elevation, there was now genuine danger. Because it would be so easy to topple off a three-foot ledge, particularly if, like me, you might be susceptible to wooziness when confronted with perilous heights.

"You okay, there?" Jack inquired as we made our way over one such ledge. "I've never seen anyone hug a mountainside quite like that."

"I'm not so good with heights," I breathed.

"Well, you might have thought of that earlier, don't you agree?"

We clambered on, a pair of hikers on a mountainside high

above the torrent of the river, one suppressing his fear of heights, the other struggling through the debilitating effects of too much campaign food and cigarettes. There were other hikers strung out along the trail as we went on. Most were Europeans, though here and there we came across a Chinese hiker or two. And there were donkeys.

"Okay," I said as we found ourselves in the midst of a cluster of mules. "I think this is the beginning of the 24 Bends."

"What's that?" Jack asked.

"The 24 Bends are the really hard part."

"I don't know if I can do this," he said, panting and sweating in the warm sun.

A donkey keeper offered to take us up.

"No, thank you. But you might have a customer here," I said, pointing to Jack.

"I'm really thinking about it."

"I know you are. And the moment you get on that donkey, I'm getting my camera out. Republicans on donkeys. Always a good picture."

We headed up. The 24 Bends, as it turned out, are poorly named. There are not 24 Bends. There are about a hundred bends, steep switchbacks that crisscrossed the mountain. Perhaps there weren't actually one hundred bends. But it certainly felt like it. A few others struggled up the switchbacks with us, including a fashionably dressed Chinese woman who looked utterly miserable as she lagged behind her partner.

I put my head down and powered up the trail, which was covered with donkey shit. Hiking up steep inclines is all about momentum, and soon the two dozen hikers around us had clustered into small groups according to their speed. Jack, I noticed, had fallen behind with the slowest group. I did not linger. He's with other people, I thought. If he needed help, they'd help. Probably. I put my head down and marched on, switchback after switchback. After forty-five minutes or so, I stopped for a water break and settled down on a rock to take in the scenery, which was breathtaking in its awesomeness. Somewhere far, far below were the churning rapids of the Yangtze as it rushed through a chasm not more than seventy feet across. Four rafters had once tried to run these rapids. They were never seen again. I wondered what the tiger thought when he'd succeeded in jumping the river. Probably *oops*. The other side of the river was nothing less than a sheer, 6,000-foot, absolutely terrifying-looking cliff.

Finally, Jack arrived. On a donkey. I was beside myself with mirth.

"Didn't you see me waving?" he asked.

"Were you waving? I couldn't tell. You were so far below, I couldn't tell the difference between you and that really unhappy Chinese lady."

Jack paid the donkey owner. The donkey pooped. I had not read about the donkey poop on the high trail above Tiger Leaping Gorge, which is surprising really, because it is a trail of shit. Sure, the vistas are vast and beautiful. The hike is satisfyingly strenuous. Periodically, it can be very, very scary up above Tiger Leaping Gorge. All this I had read. I had never read, however, an account that mentioned the colossal amounts of donkey crap along the way. So I would like that to be my contribution to the literature on Tiger Leaping Gorge. There's donkey shit. Lots of it. Now you know.

We continued to climb, stopping often, but after twenty minutes Jack decided that he could go no farther.

"I can't do this. I don't know. I can't breathe."

"The air is a little thinner up here."

"I . . . My head hurts. I don't know. I can't go on."

"Look," I said. "This is the hardest part. But we're almost at the top, and then it should flatten out. If you're really struggling, we'll just hail another donkey."

Slowly, we continued to climb, until finally the trail evened out. And then, around a bend, it was my turn to fall apart.

The trail had been carved across a cliff that plunged thousands of feet to the river below. Every year, a few hikers go toppling off. Probably right here, I reflected. Because this looked like an excellent place to fall off a mountain. I was achingly familiar with the knowledge that, now and then, shit does happen. People do fall. Indeed, once while clambering on some rocks above a waterfall in southwestern Turkey, I'd slipped and found myself hurtling over said waterfall, landing unhappily on the rocks below. I spent the next six months waddling around in a tight-fitting corset waiting for my fractured vertebrae to heal. So I knew, painfully knew, that bad things do happen. People do plunge off cliffs. And thus the wooziness with heights.

"You okay?" Jack asked.

"It could be worse, I guess. There could be a waterfall too."

I couldn't take my eyes off my feet. I hugged the cliff. The trail was less than two feet in width, and beside me was air, a huge expanse of air, a terrible void, and far below, the river, utterly soundless. We marched on into an approaching dusk, noting the gathering clouds swirling around the mountains, and the distant rumble of thunder, and even Jack, poor Jack, poor tired Jack, began to walk, to climb, to clamber with urgency until finally, as the sun began its final descent, we entered the dusty courtyard of the Tea-Horse Trade Guesthouse, where we were greeted by a friendly English-speaking Asian man.

"So where are you from?" Jack asked him, breathing more evenly and comfortably now that the perilous climb was behind him.

"Korea," he said.

"North or South?" Jack inquired.

He looked a little oddly at Jack. "South."

"What, you don't get many North Korean tourists here?" I asked our jovial host.

"No," he said, and laughed. He was spending a month on the mountain, he told us, helping out the owner of the guesthouse.

"It is so beautiful here," he said. "And so quiet."

Except for the buzz saw. The guesthouse was expanding. Even up here, you couldn't escape the thrum of Chinese construction.

The sun had nearly set as we vacuumed our dinner, when in stumbled the fashionable Chinese couple. There was much to surmise. He, I discerned, a young Shanghai businessman. Founder of an environmental NGO perhaps. Someone who valued the natural world—a rarity in China—and wanted to share this world, this majestic scenery, with the woman he loved. She. The Girlfriend. The girlfriend from hell, apparently. I'd seen her riding a donkey up the 24 Bends. She was not in her milieu. And then, once they'd arrived and she'd been apprised of the toilet situation here high above Tiger Leaping Gorge, well . . . she went completely ballistic. And this was interesting, because now her boyfriend, the tree hugger, the one who had suggested a stirring hike up above Tiger Leaping Gorge, felt compelled to loudly berate the toilet situation up here, dozens of miles from anywhere. He didn't want this fight. We could tell. But fight he did, loudly, theatrically, in true Chinese fashion, yelling at the owner, who gave as good as he got. They screamed. On and on, into the darkness, beneath the glimmering light of a million stars. Until finally, the last shouts were made, the last curses were uttered, and the doors were slammed.

"They're nuts," Jack said. "But I don't care. I am going to sleep so well tonight."

There are few things more discombobulating than arising from a slumber and, as you shake the cobwebs loose from your head and try to answer the basic questions—who am I? where am I?—you step out and discover that you are facing a wall of rock, a wall like no other, a wall of Mordor proportions, dark and massive, a forbidding cliff of black stone rising to a cragged, snowcapped peak surrounded by wispy clouds. And a sky so blue that you are left so very awake, so very cognizant of everything around you, that you begin your day in a state of wonder, which is a good way to start a day. I was happy to be here, did not want to be anywhere else but here, somewhere far above the frothing Yangtze, in the mountains, away from everything.

Jack, too, arose in good spirits. Being here, high above Tiger Leaping Gorge, was an accomplishment, particularly for those with a fondness for fries and smokes, and we returned to the trail because that is what we did, walk like Mountain Men among the rocks. We had, I thought, hiked the hard part, conquered the ascent, and only had to follow an even trail until the descent to Walnut Creek, where we would end this hike. But, apparently, our troubles had not yet come to an end.

"Okay, you go first," I said to Jack.

"Why do I have to go first?" he asked.

We'd reached an impasse, an obstacle. The path had been blocked. By goats.

"Look at the way he's looking at me," I said. "The one with the big horns. He has ill intent. I can sense it. And now he senses my sensing his ill intent—a recipe for certain disaster."

"You're not quite one with nature, are you?"

"I am one with my nature, and my nature is telling me that I'm about to be rammed by a goat."

Jack strode boldly forward into this herd of goats, which scattered to the side of the trail. And then the goat, the one with the malevolent intent, returned to the trail, again blocking it. He stared. I stared. And then, resigned, I approached it buttocks first. If I was to be rammed, better from that direction.

"I had no idea you were such a pansy," Jack said as I joined him on the other side of the herd.

"I am a pansy," I agreed, "but not enough of a pansy to ride a donkey above Tiger Leaping Gorge."

And so we walked. Onward along perilous ridges, dusty trails, surrounded by mountains, fearsome mountains—not storybook Alpine mountains, or Let's Have a Coors Light mountains, but fearsome ones. Chinese mountains. Soon, we found ourselves at the Halfway Guesthouse, where we met the owner, the jocund Mr. Fang, who, after we'd professed our admiration for his accommodations and the fine view, announced that he, too, found his guesthouse and this view to be "smashingly good." He had with him a copy of the book *Himalaya,* by Michael Palin. A backpacker had left it with him, and he wanted to know what exactly Michael Palin had to say about the Halfway Guesthouse.

"Well," said Jack as he skimmed the chapter on Tiger Leaping Gorge. "He says that you have an exceptionally fine toilet."

"Smashing," said Mr. Fang.

"Oh, and you might want to read this," he said, handing me the book. "Go on," he urged. "Read it out loud."

I looked at the page. *The trek continues north clinging to the side of a rock face, the Yangtze a boiling froth 4,000 feet below. At one point a sizeable waterfall comes bouncing off the rocks above us, and we have to pick our way beneath over fifty yards of wet stone . . .*

"Mr. Fang, do you have any jobs for Maarten here? He can clean."

*. . . the stony, slippery path reaches its narrowest point . . .*

"All right," I said. "This is where I turn around."

And yet we did not turn around. We ventured forth. Ever onward. Until we came to a rush of tumbling water plunging over a cliff roughly thirty feet above.

"Do you think this is it?" I asked Jack.

"Could be," he said. "If it is, they've built a bridge since Michael Palin came through."

"Look. It's very clear. You can see it. That's where the trail used to go," I noted, pointing to a trail that ended in the water. "And now they've built a little bridge that avoids it. Yes. Excellent. No problem."

And so we walked on, mirthfully, in good humor, confident now that the beast known as the high trail above Tiger Leaping Gorge had been slayed. Whereupon we rounded the corner to see cliffs everywhere, a narrow trail—possibly four feet across—and below us, thousands of feet of air, empty air . . . and then we saw it.

"Okay," Jack observed. "So we were wrong,"

It was indeed a big waterfall, fifty feet across, and it cascaded upon a trail of mossy stones before plummeting thousands of feet into an abyss of rock. It was a Certain Death kind of waterfall, one misstep and it's over. No waddling around in corsets. Boom. Over. Done.

"I think I might turn around now," I said. "I would rather walk for two days than cross that waterfall."

But continue we did. We had come this far, after all. I made no attempt to stay dry. I crab-walked through it, heart palpitating, pants soaked, looking at nothing else but where I placed my feet and hands. The wet moss was slippery, and as I inched my way forward I felt like I was playing some horrifying game of twister. I'd never been more nervous in my life. People do slip. I'd slipped. I did not want to slip again. Ever.

Finally, we were off that cliff and we began our downward descent, gleeful, until we could see at the bottom of a rugged escarpment the village of Walnut Grove. Few places have elicited more ecstatic ramblings than this village near the terminus of the high trail at Tiger Leaping Gorge. So remote for so long, Walnut Grove was once *the* place to be in China to experience that remote, I'm-in-a-beautiful-setting-in-a-charm-ing-Chinese-village-without-electricity-or-telephones-though-there-is-beer vibe. It's what everyone yearns for in western China: authenticity mixed with beer. Today, however, Walnut Grove is essentially a truck stop. There is a low trail through Tiger Leaping Gorge, and whereas once it was a footpath, today it is a two-lane road, upon which tour buses and taxis and minibuses shuttle Chinese tourists to the very rock from which the tiger had made its leap. The road had finally reached Walnut Grove, transforming a hamlet of Naxis and backpack-ers into just another chintzy town of cement-block hotels and souvenir shops.

But while the road followed the low trail, it's all relative at Tiger Leaping Gorge. We'd made arrangements with a minibus driver to take us back from Walnut Grove to Qiaotou, where we'd left our packs, and as we sped over this road, hundreds of feet above the Yangtze, I noted the lack of guardrails, and the enormous potholes, and the huge boulders that had tumbled from above, and the fact that that the driver, driving one-handed as he barked into a cell phone, was of the Fuck You school of driving, and I made a mental note that however I got into Tibet, where I hoped to go soon, it would not be by car because it would combine so much of what I feared in China: heights and driving. And I saw that this mountain was looking to dislodge this road from its slopes, wanted nothing to do with it, and I thought there might be hope yet for Walnut Grove. Per-haps one day it would again be a simple hamlet. Because the road was evaporating, disappearing, tossed down into the river by a spiteful mountain.

When we arrived back at Jane's Guesthouse, it was too

late to go anywhere else. One would think that as the village at the trailhead of the famed Tiger Leaping Gorge there would be some charm in Qiaotou. Or at least something to do. But this turned out to not be the case. It was drab and dull, though as we found a restaurant overlooking the river, we noticed all the trash floating in the water, heaps of it, a colorful antidote to all this natural beauty, a depressive actually. No one would approach us to serve us, however, and so we moved across the street to a simple restaurant where we pointed at the dishes of other patrons.

"It's kind of a dump here," Jack observed.

"Yes, it is. But you know what? Tomorrow we'll be in Shangri-la."

In 1933, James Hilton published the novel *Lost Horizon*, a story about four people who, after their plane had crashed somewhere high in the snowcapped mountains of the Himalayas, found themselves led by an enigmatic Chinese man to the mythical wonderland of Shangri-la, a peaceful paradise in "the valley of the blue moon." Where was this Shangri-la? people wondered. Some said it was in Tibet, others in Sichuan Province, while still others claimed that Shangri-la is actually in Pakistan. Xuen Ke, the Naxi bandleader, believes Lijiang is the true Shangri-la. But the Chinese government said *No. You're all wrong.* Shangri-la can be found in Zhongdian, a town located on the finger of Yunnan that thrusts up into Tibet. Indeed, the government was so confident in its assertion that in 2001 they officially changed the name of Zhongdian to Shangri-la, leading some to point out that Shangri-la was always, in fact, a fictional place.

Nevertheless, the vaunted Shangri-la—a place of beauty and harmony—sets a very high bar as a choice destination for travelers who just happen to be wandering through China. So we resolved to visit this Shangri-la before Jack left to return to Hong Kong and then home, if only because we were so eager to get out of Qiaotou, a place, we discovered, notable for its barking dogs—dogs that barked through the night, relentlessly—bark, bark, bark, all night long.

The next day, we hopped into this minivan bound for Zhongdian. It was not at all like the spacious and comfortable minivans in the United States, but more like a toy minivan, made of tin, the tiny sort of vehicle that clowns would crowd into. The driver was a sane driver, possibly because the engine was no more powerful than a lawn mower's, and we chugged up the hills at a speed of approximately twenty-seven miles per hour, heading ever higher into the mountains, paying tolls at tollbooths staffed by soldiers, until finally, we emerged upon a vast, desolate plateau spotted with large open wooden farmhouses. And to my delight I saw that there were yaks, huge shaggy yaks. A yak is a ruminant's ruminant, the king of the bovine. We'd entered a region that was predominantly Tibetan in population, which explained the presence of yaks. With their immense horns and considerable size, they are intimidating, and yet in Tibet people not only use them to plow fields but they also race yaks. There is such a thing as yak racing.

Somewhere upon this plateau, we pulled into a dusty village, where we were joined by a gaggle of Tibetans: four, six, eight, nine. And soon there were twelve of us in a tiny bus designed to carry no more than four. We sat in laps. We stood. And we laughed, because it's funny to be in an overcrowded minivan made of tin. Our fellow passengers were very friendly in their colorful dress. Or, rather, their clothes would have been colorful if not so dirty. One by one, they broke into song, and as we rolled along, singing the Tibetan songs of yore, Jack and I doing our best to join in, all seemed good.

If there is a stranger place to call Shangri-la than Zhongdian, I cannot image it. It's a dirty frontier town, a place with a heavy military and Communist Party presence. And it sits near the edge of China, in a region largely populated by Tibetans, a place where the powers that be in Beijing seemed distant, and so to overcome this distance, Beijing manifests itself in Shangri-la with soldiers and ugly, boxy buildings of bureaucrats, functionaries, and Party officials. It was, of course, convenient to call Zhongdian Shangri-la. There was not a quicker way to turn a town near the Tibetan Autonomous Region into a Han Chinese city than by dangling the lure of money. And the name itself, with all its connotations of wonder and mystery and beauty, is nothing but a business opportunity.

But there was no wonder or mystery or beauty here. What had remained of the old village of Zhongdian had been swallowed by a scruffy Han city notable for its plethora of karaoke bars. Even the setting was uninspiring. I had expected that at

the very least, the bare minimum, Shangri-la would be surrounded by soaring mountains, towering eminences dusted
with snow. But this was not the case. There were merely a few
scrubby, barren hills. True, these were 11,000-foot hills, far
higher than most of the mountains in the Sierra Nevada. But
when viewed from our current elevation of 9,500 feet, they
looked scrubby, barren, and, well, decidedly small.

"So this is Shangri-la," Jack said once we'd adjusted to
the altitude. "It reminds me of Butte, Montana."

The most intriguing part of the city, when we finally
reached it, was the old town. This is because it was brand new.
In the center of the city, where there was once a typical Tibetan
village, we found hundreds of workers busy building a quaint
replica of a Tibetan village. And here, too, there were many
doors for sale, scuffed and dulled to make them look weathered
and old. In the shops, there was Tibetan this and Tibetan that,
knickknacks and leather cowboy hats like Jack's, most likely
made in a factory in Guangdong. We watched as, on cue,
ruddy-faced dancers arrived on the old town square and gathered the Chinese tourists, held hands with them, and showed
them how to dance Tibetan style. A small garbage truck drove
by, announcing its presence with music, just like an ice-cream
truck. Nearby, up a small hill and through an alley of shit—
human shit, mind you, left there by the workers constructing
the new Shangri-la—we made our way to a massive golden
prayer wheel, which was being turned by dozens of devotees.
They were Tibetan Buddhists, and we lingered for a while
watching them turn this wheel. It was but a glimpse of what lay
to the north. And it would be as close as Jack would get to
Tibet.

The next day, we found ourselves in the bus station in Shangri-la, surrounded by men who flashed covetous, cunning looks at our belongings. It was here that Jack and I would part ways.

"Just break the trip down into parts," I advised him. "A bus to Lijiang. You remember what Lijiang looked like, right? It's full of Naxis. Then a plane to Guangzhou, and from there a train to Hong Kong. And you'll have about forty-eight hours to do this if you want to catch your flight."

Jack stared at me blankly.

"Do you want me to go ahead and file the missing-persons report now, or should I wait a couple of days?" I asked him.

"I think you can go ahead and do it now."

When the bus arrived it was, as always, a scene of grim chaos as dozens of people scrambled for seats. Jack turned to me. "I don't envy you. I've got some serious China fatigue."

But I envied me. I was going to Tibet.

# 17

As everyone knows, *Tintin in Tibet* is far and away the best Tintin book ever conjured by the mind of Hergé, the Belgian writer and illustrator. As a young lad living next door in Holland, I did what all Dutch boys did: I wore wooden shoes, I put mayonnaise on my French fries, and I read Tintin. As I followed Tintin as he skipped from calamity to calamity around the world, these illustrated adventure books (do not even think of calling them comics) offered me my first glimpse of the world beyond the dikes. And *Tintin in Tibet* was the most outstanding book of them all. Oh sure, there are still some who claim that *The Blue Lotus* or even *Cigars of the Pharaoh* represent the apogee of Herge's work. But they are wrong.

*Tintin in Tibet* begins with a plane crash. So, too, did James Hilton's *Lost Horizon*. It makes you think. It made me think. It's so easy to crash an airplane into the Himalayas, that vast mountain range stretching from Pakistan to Sichuan

Province, a geological testament to the pushiness of the Indian subcontinent as it continues to slide into Asia. I'd once seen a T-shirt that said STOP CONTINENTAL DRIFT! But it cannot be stopped. Nothing can be done. The Indian subcontinent wants to be part of Asia. And we can only get out of the way. And it is all for the good—this long, interminable crashing and grinding of landmasses has given us some mighty fine mountains. Here, in the Himalayas, we have the highest mountains in the world. There is Everest, of course, coming in just a shade under 30,000 feet. But there are many, many other mountains in Tibet itself that reach up into the Death Zone, that breathless area surrounded by snow and rock where human beings are not meant to go.

I had decided to travel to Lhasa, the longtime abode of the Dalai Lama on the high Tibetan Plateau. Lhasa is the spiritual home of Tibetan Buddhism, though of course it is no longer the home of the Dalai Lama, who fled into exile when China crushed a rebellion among Tibetans in 1959. There are two ways to get to Lhasa from Zhongdian; there is the overland route that involves a 4 × 4 and a week of navigating perilous dirt roads over some of the highest mountain passes in the world. Or one can fly. I'd considered the overland route, but after the short drive from Tiger Leaping Gorge to Qiaotou, I'd abandoned the thought. The prospect simply combined too many fears I had in China involving driving and heights. And so I'd fly to Lhasa.

I waited at the Tibet Café for a ride to the airport. Technically, only foreigners in tour groups could get permits for Tibet. But there was a local fixer at the café who had helped me obtain a permit from the Office For Granting Permits For Tibet

To People Who Really Should Be Part Of A Tour Group But Aren't. Soon, I was joined by familiar faces.

"Look who's here. Where's the Republican?"

It was my cross to bear on the backpacker circuit, to be the guy traveling with the Republican, that oddity. I'd met the two Australian couples in Dali, where we'd shared a meal and beers and had all sorts of convivial fun.

"His politics are a little daft," said Lachlan. "But he's all right."

High praise indeed from an Australian.

It was a short flight to Lhasa, a short flight over the greatest mountain range on Earth. There were, however, snacks served on board. *Shalom,* said the package, which further informed me that I was eating a Hot Pickled Mustard Tuber and that it was a Ningbo Special Product. As I ate this Hot Pickled Mustard Tuber, I gazed out the window and was surprised to see that even though it was early October, all but the very highest mountains, the ones that stretched to tickle the fuselage, were barren of snow. Here and there I could see glaciers distinctly retreating, leaving huge barren half-pipes, a skate park for giants. This was not good, of course. Three of the world's great rivers begin in Tibet: the Mekong, Indus, and Yangtze Rivers all find their source here in its high mountains and glaciers. Those rivers are born of snow. But there was little snow now, and as I stared at the austere wilderness below, I couldn't help but feel that here, in the forbidding mountains of Tibet, was compelling evidence that the planet was changing, and I tried to squelch that gnawing feeling that we are on the cusp of unsettling times.

And yet, in barren valleys and clinging to precipitous

mountains, there were scattered villages. I could see terraced brown fields. I could see no evidence that anything actually grew in Tibet, but there were, in any event, terraced farm fields. Rarely, however, did I see anything resembling a road. The isolation of these Tibetan villages must be unforgiving. But that, presumably, is how the Tibetans prefer it.

But Lhasa is no longer quite so isolated. As we rode a bus from the airport over the lunar plains of central Tibet, a flat, rocky expanse surrounded by lifeless hillsides, I noticed that nearly every building, every home, was festooned with the Chinese flag. Subtlety, clearly, was not a strong suit for the Chinese government. But on the dusty hills there was Buddhist graffiti and thousands of prayer flags, little celebrations of color in this world of brown. And there was a sky so blue that you'd swear you were no longer on planet Earth, but elsewhere, far away, in a place with a different sky. But, alas, I was still technically in China, and it manifested itself in the outskirts of Lhasa with the bleak clutter of an ever expanding Han city of drab apart ment buildings, noodle shops, and karaoke bars. Surely, there was something more to this place. This was Lhasa! The fabled city on the rooftop of the world. Isolated for centuries. And yet there were car washes? Billboards?

At the bus station in the center of town, we were soon besieged by beggars—hunchbacked beggars, burned man beggars, monk beggars, women beggars, child beggars—but strangely, they were all jolly. I had not encountered happy beggars elsewhere in China. But here in Lhasa, the beggars couldn't have been more mirthful, even though the Australians were not particularly forthcoming with their *kuai*.

"Well, if they had puppies, maybe I'd give them something," Lachlan observed. He and his girlfriend had been traveling the world for a year. They'd become hardened by the road. And yet the beggars didn't begrudge them this. They smiled and waved and said a little prayer for us.

I made arrangements with the foursome to meet them later and took a pedicab to my guesthouse. I couldn't imagine a more grueling job up here at 12,000 feet than biking a heavy pedicab full of people. And not only was the driver shuttling me onward in the thin air of Lhasa, he smoked while cycling, a dazzling feat of lung power that left me awestruck. But I, too, was feeling fine with the altitude. Clearly, this was the upside to our brief stay in Shangri-la. A few days at 9,500 feet, and suddenly 12,000 feet just wasn't a problem.

At the guesthouse I was told that my room was on the fourth floor and that there wasn't an elevator, and so I huffed my pack onto my shoulders and made for the stairs, where soon, several flights up, I could be found with my arms on the wall, chest thumping, desperately gasping for air. My body had suddenly realized that circumstances are indeed different up here at 12,000 feet. There is, for instance, a lot less oxygen up here—40 percent less, as a matter of fact. But I've been acclimatizing you, I said, breathlessly, to my heart, which thumped alarmingly. Dali, Lijiang, Shangri-la—I've been slowly going higher just so we could avoid this unpleasantness. *Air!* said my heart. *More air!*

One should always listen to one's heart. So, it appeared, we would go slowly today.

Lhasa, as I had seen from the bus, is surrounded by drab, could-be-anywhere-in-China-except-I-can't-breathe suburbs, but in the old town around Barkhor Square, it is a different place. There are warrens of white, mud-brick houses and shops, and streets of monks—monks begging, monks giving, monks in swirling maroon robes and running shoes—and sidewalks covered with the carcasses of giant yaks. It is a town of pilgrims, and there were Tibetans from distant valleys who had spent weeks traversing the rugged paths to get here. In front of the Jokhang Temple, a monastery of mud bricks and gold that is the holiest sight in Tibet, I watched ruddy-faced pilgrims doing the Barkhor circuit, a clockwise perambulation around the temple that took them through a market maze and tables of prayer wheels. Dozens of people knelt and prostrated themselves before the temple's heavy wooden doors. Hundreds more were walking the circuit, spinning their own prayer wheels. Some had braided hair; others wore cowboy hats. And all had the distinctive ruddy red cheeks of the Tibetans. I thought of Jack. A little farther and he would have found his Other.

The late-afternoon light was ethereal, a darkening blue, but the mountains flared with sunlight. If Mars had been colonized by Buddhists, it would look like this. I felt awfully close to space here. I walked past bored-looking Chinese policemen playing cards at a table and headed across the square toward the Mandala restaurant. I had no expectation of finding good food, but they had a balcony that overlooked the colorful scene below. I climbed the staircase as if I were summiting Everest itself, a slow, arduous ascent with deep, labored breathing. Something told me to order vegetarian. This was a holy place, I thought, and perhaps I'd defile this holiness by eating flesh. I had no idea whether that was true, but it seemed like the right thing to do. California Buddhists eschew meat, ergo Tibetan Buddhists must avoid meat too. Also, the enormous yak carcasses strewn about the streets outside encouraged a vegetarian approach. I plucked at my noodles and vegetables and noticed two Tibetan teenage girls wildly out of control on a moped. They careened into another moped, sending everyone to the ground. I waited for the arguing, the screaming, the inevitable demands for compensation. I'd seen this show a hundred times in China. But no. They laughed. Everyone laughed. There was so much laughter. Oh, I thought. Oh, oh, oh. This is different. Laughter? After a crash? When there is damage? When there are dents? Scratches? When somebody has to pay for repairs? And they laugh about it in Lhasa?

Clearly, I'd entered a different world.

In the morning, when I awoke, the mountains were dusted with snow. But the air was very dry, dry enough to elicit the need for lip balm. I'd never felt the need for lip balm before. I am not a lip balm man. But here, up here, way up here, I had a need, and so I wandered into a Chinese pharmacy. The attendants were dressed all in white, as if this were a sanatorium, or possibly a lunatic asylum. I mimed what I needed and she understood completely. I was in need of skin-whitening cream for hands.

It's always interesting to see the enduring persistence of this fair skin nonsense. Presumably, once, not so long ago, fair skin was indicative of class. A mandarin, of course, certainly didn't work the fields under a blazing sun. One would think that the triumph of the proletariat would have dismissed the idea. But I liked my dark hands. It suggested the presence of sunlight, something urban Chinese rarely encounter. I again pointed to my lips, whereupon I was led to the lipstick display. Close, I thought as I set off to wander the aisles on my own, where soon I found a tube with a goo-like substance and decided that whatever this was, I was going to put it on my lips. This was because I was crackling apart in air that did not seem to possess even a hint of moisture.

And there was the sun. There is an awful lot of sun in Lhasa. You're so much closer to it, for one thing. I slid on my sunglasses and headed toward the Potala Palace. If there is but one image people have of Lhasa, it is of the imposing Potala Palace, this mount in the sky with the thousand rooms and two hundred thousand statues. It towers over the city, but it is not merely a majestic, looming presence. There is something whimsical about it as well. Let's paint this part white, I imagined the builders thinking. And over here, how about maroon? Maroon is good. And this part up here? Yellow. Yellow is perfect. The Dalai Lama adores yellow. And it's such a nice contrast to this blue, blue, sky.

As I stood before it, admiring its rambling contours, the way it seemed to encapsulate a people born of the mountains, I was joined by Tibetan women with veiled faces: Ninja curio sellers.

"You are very nice," one said, reaching for my face. "Like the yak."

I had grown a beard. It is, of course, de rigueur for Western men traveling to Tibet to grow beards. I have no explanation for this. But Sir Edmund Hillary had a beard when he climbed Everest. Brad Pitt had a beard in *Seven Years in Tibet*. The two Australian men I'd traveled with on the flight to Lhasa had beards (their girlfriends didn't, however). It is baffling;

Tibetan men don't typically have beards, so it's not as if we all collectively went native. And it's not merely Western men. I'd met two Japanese backpackers in my guesthouse. They both had beards too. All I can say is that if you are a foreign man considering a trip to Tibet, you will grow fur on your face. Resistance is futile.

Pleased though I was to have been favorably compared to a yak, I declined the women's offerings and returned my gaze to the palace. Built in the seventeenth century, the Potala Palace was originally the winter home of the Dali Lama. I could see why the current Dalai Lama wanted to come back. It's not a swanky palace. This was no Buckingham Palace, no Neuschwanstein, the fairy-tale castle built by Mad King Ludwig. It did not exude luxury. It was not a place for formal balls. Instead, there was a hominess to the palace, a sense that this was somehow the collective home of the Tibetan people. It was a mountain palace, built by devout people with their heads in the sky. It was not a home for kings or tyrants. It was the home of a living god, the Dalai Lama. But he couldn't go home, not now, not while the Communist Party was in charge. Indeed, to make the point that the Dalai Lama wasn't welcome—or at least a Dalai Lama that didn't kowtow to Beijing—the Party had razed the old town in front of the palace to put up an enormous Glory to the Communists monument.

They make things so awkward, these Communists. I was trying to lose myself in the moment—this Tibetan moment—and yet here, in the middle of Lhasa before the towering Potala Palace, I was obliged, simply by the mere presence of this monument, to acknowledge that I was standing in an occupied country. Tibet was an independent country when China invaded in 1950. And, as evidenced by the soldiers still present in Lhasa, the Chinese have no intention of leaving. Visiting the interior of the palace thus leads to very mixed emotions. On the one hand, you know you're not really supposed to be there. It is someone's house, after all, someone who's been called away for urgent business—that urgent business, of course, being the preservation of Tibetan independence. In the years after China "liberated" the Tibetans from themselves in the 1950s, more than a million Tibetans died. And it's not as if there's an excess of Tibetans around. Today, there are a little more than 2.5 million Tibetans occupying the land. Another 4 million find themselves living in neighboring provinces like Sichuan, Qinghai, Gansu, and Yunnan. When China invaded, countless monasteries were shelled into oblivion by the People's Liberation Army. The Dalai Lama, together with a 100,000 other Tibetans, fled.

But it's not merely political independence that's at stake, it's religious independence too. Just as the Chinese government appoints cardinals for the Catholic Church, so, too, it dictates who, precisely, can be incarnated as a lama, or teacher of Tibetan Buddhism. In China, Tibetan Buddhist lamas need a permission slip from the government in Beijing before they can be reincarnated. Indeed, when the Dalai Lama announced in 1995 that the eleventh reincarnation of the Panchen Lama, Tibet's second most revered lama after the Dalai Lama, had been found in Tibet, Beijing became so ticked off that it sent a Politburo member to Lhasa. In the Jokhang Temple, senior Communist leaders put the names of three boys in an urn and chose by lot the official Panchen Lama. The boy chosen by the Dalai Lama has since disappeared. So, too, has the monk who found him.

By buying a ticket to the Potala Palace, one is tacitly conceding that the palace belongs to the state. But what also makes it just a little more awkward is that the palace is one of the most important sites for Tibetan pilgrims. At first, after I'd entered, it felt like a dusty museum. There were even cats prowling in the hallways. And then, just as I was admiring a fine golden statue of someone in a blissful state of enlightenment, in came a family of braided pilgrims, dipping yak butter out of tin cans and placing it in candle holders. And then they would shower the room with fluttering notes of money. Every holy room was graced with hundreds of images of Mao.

But the monks inside seemed jovial enough. In one chapel, I found two monks, one chanting, the other poking at his cell phone. Then the pilgrims entered. The chanting monk gave the other a look that seemed to say, *Hey, put away the cell phone. It's showtime.* And indeed he did put it away, and he began to chant with a reverence reserved for visiting pilgrims, if not tourists.

In another chapel, an elderly Yoda-like monk approached me. "Where are you from?"

I told him and asked him about the pilgrims. They seemed different from pilgrims I'd seen elsewhere in China. They didn't seem to be praying for wealth, as they did on Tai Shan. Instead, they were distributing wealth inside the temples, sprinkling notes upon the golden statues as they shuffled from room to room.

"The pilgrims come from all over Tibet. They come not just once, but many times. This is a very important place, very important."

"Do you think the Dalai Lama will ever come back?"

"No. I don't think the Dalai Lama will ever come back. He left in 1959. It makes us very sad."

I spent several days in Lhasa, rarely leaving the tight confines of the old town. I could have remained for months, though it's possible I'd reconsider in January. Perhaps I could move my family here, I thought. Kindergarten in Tibet. That would be cool. And the air was clean up here. Of course, there wasn't much of it, so perhaps that would be a problem. Is it good parenting, taking kids up to 12,000 feet? Yes? No? I didn't know. But I could live here, I thought. The Tibetans were kind and affable. I'd expected to find a people crushed by Chinese oppression. The People's Liberation Army had been in Tibet for more than fifty years. They'd desecrated temples. They'd shot monks. But Tibetans are not crushed. Indeed, they are the jolliest people I'd encountered in China. I could live among these cheerful people. But the last thing Lhasa needed was another non-Tibetan to take up residence in their fair city. Lhasa was bursting at the seams with Chinese.

There are more Chinese in Lhasa than there are Tibetans. And with the new railway linking Lhasa to the frenzied cities of China, more and more Chinese are making their way up into the mountains, thousands of them, tens of thousands. Some are tourists. But many have come to settle in Lhasa, and quickly, so quickly now, Lhasa is becoming a Chinese city.

Except in the old town. I did not leave the old town except to take the bus to the Sera Monastery, a few miles outside Lhasa, where I settled myself in a courtyard beneath mountains dusted with snow and, as it melted in the afternoon glare, I watched the monks debate. I could not say what precisely they were debating. Perhaps it was the finer theological points separating the Red Hat sect of Tibetan Buddhism from the Yellow Hat sect. Or perhaps they were debating the lunch menu. It was unclear. Once there were 5,000 monks in the Sera Monastery, but then, of course, China invaded, soldiers plundered the grounds, and the monks were either killed or exiled. Today, the monastery has been restored and several hundred monks reside there, where they spend their days studying, meditating, and impassionedly debating whether to have the mutton on Tuesdays or on Fridays.

On most days, however, I joined the pilgrims walking the Barkhor circuit around the Jokhang Temple, Tibet's holiest sight. I liked the exoticism of it. It's as much a market carnival as a devotional pilgrimage. True, in front of the temple's doors, pilgrims with prayer mats and boards did their devotions in the dust. And some who did the circuit did so on their stomachs, genuflecting and prostrating themselves as they made their devotional perambulation. And many chanted ancient mantras. But elsewhere, through the twisting streets beside mud-brick walls, there was a lively market.

"Eighteen hundred," said the vendor when I stopped to consider a prayer wheel. "Look. Gold. Turquoise. Inside very old holy parchment." She opened it and pulled out a roll of paper with Tibetan writing. It had been browned and burned at the edges. "Very old. Very holy. How much?"

We bargained, until finally I had a change of heart, concluding that the prayer wheel was unlikely to be either very old or very holy.

"Four hundred," she said, and chased after me. I considered until a passing pilgrim shook his head no. Very helpful, these Tibetans.

Inside the Jokhang Temple, I encountered a Chinese man hawking and unleashing a huge glob of phlegm. "You see these Chinese," said the monk who took my ticket, laughing. "No respect for Tibetan culture."

And still he laughed. A Chinese invader had just unleashed a loogie inside the most revered sight in Tibet, and the monk chuckled. Imagine Santa Claus in a maroon robe. Abandon the paunch. Lose the beard. The hair too. Give him a tan. And you have this monk. Unflappable. Mirthful. Always looking at the bright side.

I asked him generally how things were.

"It's been very hard with the Chinese, though a little better recently. There's been lots of international attention."

The Jokhang Temple is more than 1,400 years old, filled with chapels and chambers and statues of Buddha. Nearly all the statues are new. After the invasion, Chinese soldiers ransacked the temple. And then, some years later, the Red Guards of the Cultural Revolution trashed it some more and placed a banner on its walls underneath a portrait of Chairman Mao— *Completely destroy the old world! We shall be the master of the new world!*

Today, the monks have returned to the temple. The Dalai Lama, however, has not. Inside, I found the Dalai Lama's big yellow cushion throne, disheveled and empty, and as I made my way up to the rooftop terrace overlooking old Lhasa, where I absorbed a vista of mountains, pilgrims, and palaces, I thought what a shame it truly is that the Dalai Lama and thousands of other Tibetans could not return to this wondrous city in the sky. Like them, I too hoped one day to return to Lhasa.

⌂

"Where are you going from here?" Cat, Lachlan's girl-friend, asked me. I'd met the Australians at a restaurant for lunch.

"I thought I'd head for the Gamden Monastery in eastern Tibet. It was destroyed by the Chinese, but I read that they're rebuilding it. What about you?"

Cat took a deep drag from her cigarette. "We're planning on biking to Everest Base Camp."

"Biking as on a bicycle."

She nodded. "Should be a bit of an adventure."

"Aren't some of the passes above 17,000 feet?"

They nodded absentmindedly. Yeah, I thought, that's going to end well.

When the proprietor came to take our order, Lachlan remarked with typical Australian bluntness, "I come here for the toilets, mate. You have the best toilets in Lhasa."

The owner beamed. "I clean them myself. And I do all the cooking. You must have the yak."

"What's not to like about Lhasa?" Cat observed.

Yak fatigue, for one thing. The Tibetans, I discovered, are not vegetarians. It is difficult to be a vegetarian at this altitude. There is a need for protein. And so the Tibetans eat yak. And it's good. I liked the yak. I'd gorged myself on yak. I had yak *momos,* simple dumplings filled with yak; I had yak filet; I even had Yak Bourgogne at a French-Tibetan fusion restaurant.

Such things exist in Lhasa. But I'd had my fill. I thought of the yak carcasses dumped onto the sidewalk. And I thought of the chef scrubbing his toilets until they became the pride of Lhasa. And then I thought of one thing that could mar my stay in this beautiful region.

"I'll have the vegetarian curry," I said.

Later, I ran into the Australians near the Barkhor Square. Lhasa, authentic Lhasa, is small and I often bumped into the same travelers again and again—many of whom I'd also met in Dali. Perhaps it was the promise of some kind of high that lured backpackers to both places.

"Did you guys get permits?" I asked them.

"No," Cat said.

"Neither did I."

It was the bane of traveling in Tibet. There is the Lhasa permit. Then there is the permit for the Tibet beyond Lhasa. And then there are the permits needed to travel on certain roads. And the rules were always changing. Sometimes permits could be had, sometimes not. The Chinese government is very particular about what foreigners are allowed to see in Tibet, and for inexplicable reasons, I hadn't been able to get a permit for the regions far beyond Lhasa. Perhaps something was happening elsewhere in Tibet. Of course, here we'd be the last to know; not since Hong Kong had I encountered a news source that hadn't been filtered by a government censor.

"We've decided to go anyway," Lachlan said. "What's the worst that could happen?"

Well, you'll soon find out, I thought. The odds of four smokers biking up to 17,000 feet on a heavily policed road in a region where, technically, their very presence was a violation of national security laws were, I guessed, not particularly high. I wished them the best of luck.

I, however, had changed my plans. Deprived of a permit for eastern Tibet, I would turn southward toward the monasteries in Gyantse and Shigatse. I had hired a driver, a friendly young man named Goba, who had an English vocabulary of about forty words, which he used to express less than enthusiastic opinions about the Chinese.

"Lhasa no good," he said as we sped past a billboard. *The Developing Zone Is Very Promising.* "In Lhasa, four Chinese. One Tibetan. No good."

To finish the thought, he took his hands off the steering wheel and made a grabbing gesture. "Chinese take. Take!"

We made our way through the blighted sprawl of outer Lhasa, underneath the twinkling gaze of an enormous portrait of Deng Xiaoping. Soon, we were passed by an SUV ferrying police.

"Chinese police. No good. Chinese no good. Shigatse. Two Chinese. One Tibetan. No good. Gyantse. Four Tibetan. One Chinese. Is okay."

We drove along a paved highway together with a few other trucks and SUVs. Soon, we had passed the last wispy trees and nearly all the traffic, and the landscape had become even more dry and ethereal, which I had not thought was possible. The mountains that surrounded us were more rugged and the highest among them had blinding snowpacks. The road itself was largely deserted except for the occasional solitary monk on pilgrimage. Up, hands to head. Pray. Hands to knees. Lie down. Up. Hands above head. Pray. Step forward. Repeat. It wasn't the fastest mode of transport, but I suspected that was probably the point. I had never been anyplace more devout than Tibet. I sensed that people here lived in a different universe from the one I inhabited; it would never occur to me that my spiritual well-being might be enhanced by prostrating myself on a highway in the middle of nowhere. The only other people I'd encountered with a propensity for lying down on roads were Pacific Islanders on payday Fridays. Of course, they were drunk, having found bliss through the bottle. But the Tibetans were sober, and yet still they lay down on roadways.

We followed the Yellow River, which flowed to our right in a blue, icy stream. Soon, Goba began to drive very fast, and I was beginning to regret stirring him up with the China talk. Then I considered. Hey, I'm paying for this. If we run over a monk doing his devotions, it's going to seriously mess up my karma. So I asked him to ease up.

He slowed to possibly twenty miles an hour. "Is okay?"

Leadfoot, of course, couldn't keep that up for long, and we flew along the highway until we stopped at a dusty roadstand, where Goba bought me a drink. It was a can of Red Bull, fuel of choice for drivers everywhere. We idled with some local truck drivers.

One pointed at my drink. "Yak piss. Ha ha ha."

I nodded. "I hear it's good for the heart."

Back in the car, Goba inserted a cassette into the tape deck. "Nepali-Tibetan. Okay?"

It was a groovy trance beat overlaid with what appeared to be Tibetan chanting. Together with the Red Bull, all that was missing were the Ecstasy tablets.

"Have you been to Nepal?" I asked him. After all, it was just across the border, albeit a very high border, and if the

Tibetans have an affinity for anyone, I figured, it would be the Nepalese. They are both mountain people and Buddhists. Indeed, in the seventh century, before the peace and love of Tibetan Buddhism had set in, the Tibetans had occupied Nepal.

"No passport," Goba said. "No Lhasa Tibetan with passport."

In the near distance was a snowcapped mountain that towered above 20,000 feet, and on its lower slopes rested a village with stony, terraced fields and fluttering prayer flags. They are everywhere in Tibet, long strings with colorful flags draped over mountainsides or hanging from masts like ships' pendants.

"Tibetan," Goba said, pointing to the village. "Very beautiful."

How, I wondered, did these people manage to live here? True, there was a haunting, austere beauty to the land. There was something elemental in Tibet that I had not experienced before. The sky disappeared into an endless blue-black void; the mountains were venerable, and the land hard. Perhaps it was the lack of oxygen, but in Tibet I felt near to something profound and powerful. It did not leave me with soft and fuzzy feelings. Instead, I felt something very like awe, a deep, primordial awe.

But few places could possibly be more inhospitable to human habitation than Tibet. There is, of course, the extreme altitude. But Tibetans have solved that problem by simply having stronger lungs than lowlanders. They've adapted and evolved, and now the average Tibetan has a far greater lung capacity than just about any other person on Earth. While I gasped at my first exposure to the altitude in Lhasa, my pedicab driver could merrily pedal and smoke without breaking a sweat. But still, there remained in Tibet a vast and challenging landscape that was ill-suited to human habitation. Little grows in such conditions. Tibet is essentially the final frontier of human civilization.

We had come to a fork in the road. We could continue following the paved road that would eventually wind up on the doorstep of Mount Everest. Or we could follow a dirt track that, from what I could see, led into a valley of desolation. We took the dirt trail.

Goba drove as if this was the Paris-Dakar road rally. But for once I didn't mind; there's something about off-road driving that brings out the inner twelve-year-old in every man. We passed through a small village of mud-brick houses and waving children, and then, over a small rise, we crossed the pass and entered a widening desert of stones. It was the strangest landscape, extraterrestrial. I'd been to a few remote corners of the world, but here, high up on the Tibetan Plateau, I felt like I'd taken leave of the planet. I was above 15,000 feet, higher than I'd ever been, but if there was one place on earth that I could compare it to, it would be one of the very lowest: Death Valley.

Soon, we found ourselves back on a paved road, passing Tibetan farmers on donkey carts laden with wheat, one of the few things to grow in Tibet. But, apparently, they could grow watermelons here too. We paused to buy one from a boy on the side of the road.

"Is good?" Goba inquired after he'd cut out a slice with his pocketknife.

"Is good," I replied. And also extremely small. I'd never beheld a watermelon the size of an orange. Considering the environment, however, it was a wonder that watermelons could be cultivated at all.

Finally, we pulled into the small town of Gyantse, where I was dropped off at the gate of the Pelkor Chode Monastery. Built in the fifteenth century, the complex is awash in whites and pinks, and is notable for housing monks from different sects within Tibetan Buddhism. I could only imagine what their debates must be like. Inside, monks in maroon robes were chanting. Others were at the gong. And one was both chanting and gonging. The incense smelled strangely like cannabis, and I watched pilgrims depositing their yak butter, which smelled like popcorn. Hey, I thought, cannabis and popcorn. Now, there was a combination worth traveling up to 15,000 feet for.

The monastery was renowned for its Kumbum *stupa,* a five-story octagonal pyramid with a golden dome containing 108 cavelike chapels with 10,000 painted images. It is the largest *stupa* in Tibet. I walked up and poked my head into the various chapels, which had all been decorated with Buddhist murals. From the top, there was an extraordinary view of the Dzong, a fourteenth-century fort that looms over the monastery, and the expansive, barren Nyang-chu Valley that stretched toward the mountains in the far distance. If you want to get away from it all, do a little meditating, Gyantse is a good place for it.

Back in the courtyard, there were dozens of listless dogs. Or perhaps they were just meditating. The flies, however, were quite active, and so, too, were the child beggars. In fact, I had never been besieged by so many child beggars, and I had been besieged by countless child beggars in China. Soon, I had run out of small money, and they followed me to the waiting car and surrounded it, whereupon Goba gave them his small money. But still, they persisted. I couldn't close the doors. And then Goba ran out, and yelled and threatened and made all sorts of scramlike motions.

Sadly, I wouldn't be staying in Gyantse. Despite the urchins, I found that in Gyantse it was possible to imagine the Tibet of yesteryear, its haunting austerity and those who regarded it as holy. On the road to Shigatse, Goba pointed to a mound of ruins on a hillside.

"Old monastery," he said. "Chinese. Boom, boom."

A few miles farther, there was another monastery that lay in ruins. "Boom, boom."

I counted three more monasteries that had gone boom boom. That was the grim reality of Tibet. True, there are more monasteries and monks today than even twenty years ago. But the sad fact remains that the Chinese have all but obliterated one of the world's most unique cultures. In the years following China's invasion of Tibet and continuing on into the Cultural Revolution, more than 6,000 monasteries were shelled into oblivion. All religious activity was banned. Land was confiscated. And China swallowed Tibet. And while a few monasteries have reopened, they operate under the strict control of the Communist Party. It is still illegal to carry even a photo of the Dalai Lama in Tibet. It is no wonder that, months later, Tibet would erupt as thousands of Tibetans took to the streets to protest Chinese rule, an act of defiance that, unsurprisingly, was crushed by Chinese troops.

As we drove on through the valley, we passed hardy farmers separating wheat from chaff and dozens of donkey carts; in turn, we were passed by a military convoy. And then, around a bend, we were flagged down by the police and told to line up with several other cars. Goba was not happy. He was told to get out of the car, and I followed. We were instructed to go to the police SUV, which was surrounded by a half-dozen other Tibetan drivers who had also been pulled over. We huddled around the window. Inside were four officious-looking policemen. Goba handed them 300 yuan.

"Why?" I asked back in the car.

"Say speeding. But no speeding."

True, Goba had been speeding everywhere else in central Tibet, but he had not been speeding here. Indeed, as we had curved around the bend, we could not have been going more than thirty miles an hour.

Goba gestured. "Police. Money." And he demonstrated how they put it into their pocket. "Chinese no good."

We passed a People's Liberation Army barracks on the outskirts of Shigatse, and as we entered the town itself, I was disheartened to find this home of the Panchen Lama and one of the great monasteries of Tibet had become just another unsightly urban sore in China. Shigatse is the second-largest town in Tibet after Lhasa and its traditional rival. And yet there was nothing here like the old town in Lhasa. It had been bulldozed in favor of a Han city of apartment blocks and electronics stores.

Goba dropped me off at a seedy hotel near the monastery. He would stay elsewhere for the evening, and I went to check in only to find that the hotel was run by the police. I dropped my backpack off in a vile room and walked through town, trying to find something to recommend it. But I couldn't. My opinion would rise—slightly—the following day, after I viewed the eighty-foot statue of Buddha inside the splendid Tashilumpo Monastery, but for now I was dismayed to find myself here. I'm in Tibet, I thought, the very distant rooftop of the world, and I've was in a fly-ridden Chinese restaurant pecking at a gloppy chop suey. But, I consoled myself, the restaurant did have yak milk. I took cautious sips of the bitter, buttery brew. Something this bad, I thought, could only be good for you.

## 18

*I curse you, Dan Brown!*

This was my thought as I awoke, bleary-eyed, early on a frosty morning in Lhasa. I'd gone to the book exchange at the guesthouse the night before and rummaged through its quirky offerings. I left behind an exceptionally boring book about Shanghai—a real drudgery, makes-you-think-of-homework kind of book—and picked up *Angels and Demons* by Dan Brown, because when confronted by a forty-eight-hour train trip to Chengdu it's good to have a fat, plot-intensive book. But it was just too tasty. Just one more chapter, I thought as the clock ticked past 2 A.M. It was only when the power failed at 3:30 in the morning and my room plunged into darkness that I finally set the book aside. But the damage had been done. I had little more than 100 pages left.

*Curses!*

"Do you need a taxi?" asked the Tibetan woman at the front desk.

"Yes."

"I will help you."

Very kind, these Tibetans, I thought.

"Forty yuan," she informed me as I hopped into a taxi. And then the driver began a long, haranguing monologue.

"Forty-two yuan," she updated me.

I agreed to the price, and soon I was barreling through the outskirts of Lhasa, crossing a bridge guarded by soldiers, speeding past a large military base where the People's Liberation Army could be heard going through their morning drills as the Potala Palace shimmered in the near distance. Outside of China, it's possible to believe that Tibet is simply a colorful province in a larger country. Inside Tibet, however, it can only be seen as a military occupation of a foreign land.

But not just a military occupation. The Lhasa train station, the ultimate terminus, is the means by which Tibet will finally become swallowed by China. *Lhasa, four Chinese, one Tibetan. Shigatse, two Chinese, one Tibetan,* Goba had observed. However, this is just the beginning. The new train to Lhasa, which began running in 2006, will enable hundreds of thousands more Chinese to come up high into the mountains of Tibet in pursuit of work opportunities. Clearly, the government really wanted this train. Indeed, they had spent more than $4 billion completing the project and more than 14,000 rail workers had been sent to the hospital with altitude sickness as they worked to lay the tracks. By the end of its very first year of operation, the Lhasa Express had already carried more than 1.5

million passengers into Tibet. The Chinese government regards this wonder of engineering as their gift to the Tibetans, as the train will bring opportunities, money, development, and economic progress to this poorest corner of China. They refer to themselves as a kindly benefactor generously helping the needy locals. Possibly, they even believe it. But the Tibetans don't want this train. They just want to be left alone.

Inside the new train station, it was the familiar bedlam as we boarded. *But we have assigned seats!* I thought. At least some of us did. I'd learned that hard-seat class operated on a first-come, first-served basis, and as I pondered the crowds battering one another to get on board, I reflected that I too would batter people for a seat on a forty-eight-hour train journey. Fortunately, I had paid a little more than a hundred dollars for soft sleeper class, and as I found my four-person sleeper cabin, it seemed positively deluxe compared to those of the other Chinese trains I'd been on—admittedly a low bar, but still. Each bed had its own flat-screen TV. And there were oxygen-supply units for every passenger, which was thoughtful. And necessary, of course, for those traveling from the other direction, coming from the flatlands below and rolling up to nearly 16,000 feet. Bodies don't like that. The head doesn't like it. Nor the heart. Nor the stomach. And thus the oxygen dispensers. It was a very tight fit for four, however, and I lived in hope that I'd have the compartment to myself. Meanwhile, through the window, two Tibetans in fur hats peered into my cabin. I waved. Nothing. Apparently, the glass was reflective. I put my nose to the window. I was an Eskimo kissing a Tibetan. But there was nothing.

"*Nihao.*"

Damn.

A couple entered. And then another man. We would be full up for this journey across the Tibetan Plateau, a trip that would take us up to the Tanggula Pass, the highest railway pass in the world at nearly 16,000 feet, before finally descending through the arid steppes of Qinghai Province and on into the Sichuan Basin and eventually Chengdu. As we departed Lhasa, a train attendant popped in to explain the usage and mysteries of the oxygen-supply units. Outside, I watched a farmer plow his field with yaks. The sky was a deep blue and there was a full moon. I'm on Mars, I thought for the umpteenth time. But Michael Jackson's "Heal the World" was wafting over the speakers. No, I realized, this was weirder than Mars. I searched for an off button. Surely, we, the four of us inside this small compartment, could agree that Michael Jackson's "Heal the World" was unacceptable music for a journey over the Tibetan Plateau. I finally found the off button and switched it off, raising my eyebrows, expecting to be praised for this quick communal resolution to an irritation.

The man across from me turned it back on.

Oh, my friend, I thought. We are going to have issues.

And so to the sound of "Beat It" we rumbled across Tibet.

The new railway joined Lhasa with Golmud, a grim mining town in Qinghai Province where China sends many of its exiles and prisoners. From here, the train connects to preexisting lines that link this remote region with the rest of China. Lhasa to Golmud, however, is not a natural place to put down train tracks. There is the rugged terrain, of course. There is the altitude. And then there is the permafrost. Half the track lies on permafrost, which is problematic, since it has a way of melting during the day and freezing again at night, causing land to move, and you don't want to lay tracks on land with wandering ways. Chinese engineers, however, had found a solution that involved gas and pipes and all sorts of other things that I didn't remotely understand, all in an effort to keep the permafrost permanently frozen. All I could think as we picked up speed was that I hoped it had worked and that the tracks hadn't suddenly lurched to someplace they were not meant to go.

I moved into the hallway and watched this world go by. The water, small ponds and streams, remained frozen under the sun of mid-fall, which boded well for the train tracks today. We passed a nomad's tent with a motorcycle parked outside, and beyond I saw herds of grazing yaks. Onward we climbed toward the Tanggula Pass, past Nam-Tso Lake and mighty Mount Nyenchen Tanglha. Outside, I saw a fox, the first real wildlife I'd seen in China. Now, if someone would please turn the fucking music off I'd be happy. For better or worse, we'd moved on through the *Thriller* years and were now being serenaded by the cloying, sentimental sounds of Chinese pop music.

The compartment next to mine was occupied by policemen. They're everywhere in Tibet, even on the train. They were smoking, of course, even though smoking was expressly forbidden, not only because smoking can be irritating to others, but because the train was equipped with pure, pressurized oxygen. And do you know what happens when a sufficient amount of oxygen meets an open flame? It blows up. Explodes. Boom. Really, the excitement never ends when traveling in China.

Just as I could resist the lure of Dan Brown no longer, we stopped at a train station a short distance from Nagqu, a town in the high grasslands of northern Tibet. I stepped outside. The air was crisp and so incredibly clean. We were at 15,000 feet and the sky here, its blueness, was stunning to behold. This was Tibetan Big Sky country. Hundreds of people who had neither the petty authority nor the colossal stupidity of the police, and thus had declined to smoke on the train, stepped out for a cigarette. I waited for the heart attacks.

It was, in fact, a very common occurrence on the way up. Lowlanders would suddenly find themselves in the thin air, light up a cigarette, and keel over dead. In the extreme altitudes of Tibet, it doesn't take much to push someone over the edge. A mere smoke can do it. Our stop, however, resulted in no such casualties, and we reboarded and continued on upward through a landscape that was becoming increasingly desolate and lifeless, and as I scanned these vast spaces and the white mountains in the distance, I was left amazed. I did not know Earth could look like this. On a small barren road in the middle of nowhere, truly the middle of nowhere, the ultimate nowhere, I saw a monk on pilgrimage, doing his devotions with each step. I did not know people lived like this either, I thought.

The train rumbled onward, and I made my way to the dining car for a meal of spicy beef and, inexplicably, Budweiser. As a darkening Tibet rolled by, I finished *Angels and Demons*. Come on, Dan Brown, I thought. I stayed with you through all that bad prose, through every preposterous turn of the plot, and you end it like this? You lost me with this ending. It's absurd. Not good absurd, but bad absurd. I was irritated. Fast-paced, plot-driven books depend on the resolution. Everything is in the resolution—all the buildup, all the tension. It works or fails by how it ends. I felt the same way I'd felt when I finished *The Da Vinci Code*: lightly soiled and snookered. And now I had another thirty-six hours to go and nothing to read. I returned to my compartment, hopped into my berth, and turned to go to sleep. My cabinmates were lying in the darkness, sucking down oxygen. Mere weekenders, I thought. Lowlanders. I'd become a mountain man myself. Well, not quite. But still, I did not need oxygen. I'd been in the high elevations of Tibet long enough to have adjusted to the thin air. I listened to them wheezing, and just as I dozed off, a cell phone jangled. "Wei!" said the Michael Jackson fan.

All right, I thought. Perhaps he forgot to turn it off. I watched as he had a long conversation. Then he fiddled with his phone contraption. I do not understand modern telecommunications. Once a telephone was simply a telephone; now it is invariably some sort of entertainment device. In the darkness, I listened as the grating sounds of Chinese pop music began emanating from his phone. Nice, I thought. Very considerate. *Prick.*

We are never more culturally primal than at breakfast. Instead of coffee, there was warm bean-curd milk. Instead of a bagel, it was braised cucumber. Instead of a bowl of cereal, there were shredded peppers with peanuts.

I had awoken to the sun on the shores of Lake Qinghai, the largest freshwater lake in China. What a vast country this was. The altitude monitor indicated that we remained above 9,000 feet, but the landscape was profoundly different from the unearthly sights of the Tibetan Plateau. It was like Vermont with Chinese characteristics: a hilly, wooded expanse with terraced fields and tall, thin poplar trees turning golden orange amid villages of stone farmhouses.

How idyllic, I thought. This was the land of the epic Chinese films, an old land of heroes and beauty, a place that was both majestic and humble. This was *nice*. True, a polluted haze had settled in the valleys, but if you ignored it—and you must ignore the blighted air if you are to feel anything but despair for China—this pristine landscape with the picturesque villages was like a pastoral antidote to urban China. I felt happy here, pleased to be traveling through such an alluring scene.

And then, inside the train, I looked into the bathroom. I was no longer happy. It was simply vile. Clearly, the people on this train car were not well. They were sick. Perhaps it was the altitude. Or possibly the spicy beef. It was the most repellent toilet I'd yet come across in China, and I cannot begin to express what an accomplishment that was. Public squat toilets in China are nasty, and here—on this most high-tech of trains, a train that had been written about in newspapers across the globe—I'd somehow managed to find the worst one yet.

Right, I thought. I would rather paralyze my bowels than use this toilet. And so that is what I did. I rifled through my bag and found my supply of just-in-case stuff and popped an Imodium. And so my happiness was restored. Medicated and numb, I had escaped from a perilous encounter with the most revolting squat toilet in China.

Feeling cheerful, I decided to share a peace offering with my nemesis, my traveling companion with the fondness for noise. I gave him an apple, which he gratefully accepted, and by lunch we were the best of friends. True, we didn't actually talk to each other, but still we were karmic friends. He had pulled out a can of warm Budweiser from his bag, offered it to me, together with some pickled meat he kept. *Xie xie.*

As we descended from the Tibetan plateau, China proper began to reassert itself. We continued to roll through rugged, forested hills shrouded in the haze of industrial pollution. We passed through Xining, an odious city, where every house seemed to come with a stack of coal in back.

I don't want to go back to this, I thought. Not yet. It had been weeks since I'd last set foot in urban China, and I was in no hurry to return. I liked western China. I wasn't ready to leave it yet. True, I'd read the stories about the foreigners who are forever disappearing there. But what's a little banditry? And so, as we rumbled into Lanzhou, a city hundreds of miles from Chengdu, my original destination, I bade farewell to my companions and jumped off the train.

It's a good feeling, hopping off a train in a city in the very middle of China. Actually, it's a good feeling hopping off any train you've been riding for thirty-six hours. And, as I breathed a thick whiff of coal, it was a good feeling knowing that I wasn't going to be spending a moment longer than I absolutely had to in Lanzhou.

I had decided to head for Dunhuang, a Silk Road outpost deep in the Gobi Desert. The thought of another thirty-six-hour train trip didn't much appeal to me, and so I resolved to fly. To that end, I had consulted my guidebook, which charmingly describes Lanzhou as "the most polluted city in the world." But there was a business hotel in town, and I thought I could buy a plane ticket there.

I picked up my pack and headed toward the taxi line. There were no foreigners here and everyone stared with undisguised curiosity. I put my bag inside the trunk of a taxi, whereupon the driver pulled out a 20-yuan note.

Bullshit, I thought. The hotel was less than a mile away, not more than a 10-yuan ride, maximum. And then I wondered what, precisely, had happened to me. It's not often that I take offense at the thought of paying $2.50 for a taxi. But China changes you. Simple commercial transactions are played like a zero-sum game.

I took my bag and walked away. I sensed that here, in a taxi line in front of the train station in Lanzhou, my presence was regarded in the same light as a hyena might regard the carcass of a lamb. A minibus driver offered to take me. He pulled out two tens. I walked on. A motorcycle driver pulled up. Not even if I were high on crack would I have gotten on a motorcycle in China.

I walked to the street and hailed a cab with the first honest face I saw. He put the meter on. It started at seven yuan. He made a couple of turns. He's running the meter, I thought. Instead, he smoothly took me to the hotel entrance. Seven yuan said the meter. I handed him a ten. He gave me back four. Surely, he had miscalculated. I pressed one yuan into his hands. No; he shook his head, and with his hands indicated that the correct fare was 6 yuan.

I decided I liked Lanzhou.

But not enough to stay.

I had chosen this hotel because I needed a few hours to book a flight, get some laundry done, and check e-mail, and a business hotel was the easiest way to accomplish all this. Still, I had become accustomed to guesthouse prices and was wholly unprepared for the budgetary mayhem that followed.

"How about 395?" I tried.

"I'm sorry, sir. It's 495."

I swallowed hard. Not since Shanghai had I spent that kind of money, about $60, for a hotel room. But hey, I thought, at least I'd saved a couple of bucks by not giving in to rapacious cabdrivers.

I got up to my room on the sixteenth floor and admired the view. Yes, Lanzhou is polluted, all right. I couldn't see beyond the neon Lenovo sign flashing outside my window. The pollution was literally breathtaking.

I took a quick shower, brushed my teeth with tap water—because I'm reckless that way—had my laundry taken care of, and went down to book a morning flight to Dunhuang.

"Big plane or small plane?" I asked the travel agent. These are the things that concerned me. She didn't understand, and so I used charades, imitating the sounds of a jet plane and a whirring prop plane, and succeeded only in frightening her. Who was this sputtering *laowai*? Nevertheless, I soon had a plane ticket, and with hours to spare before I actually needed to be anywhere, I decided to get a haircut at the hotel barbershop.

I had become decidedly hirsute in the previous weeks. That's the thing about beards—they keep growing. Some beards turn out to be Santa Claus beards. Or Tolstoy beards. Friendly beards. Some turn out to be Satan beards. Mine was such a beard. No wonder I frightened the woman at the travel desk, I reflected as I sat down in the barber's chair. With my beard, I looked like a crazed biker.

"Just a little off the top," I said. The barberess didn't speak a word of English, of course. She proceeded to put multiple layers of cloaks on me. What, I thought, is this going to involve X-rays? Wrapping one towel around my neck, she proceeded to keep it all together with streams of toilet paper. Nevertheless, she did a fine job.

Next to me, a man was being shaved with a switchblade. The barberess inquired whether I'd like a shave.

"Just a trim," I indicated.

I thought I'd keep the beard. True, it was approaching Grizzly Adams proportions and we didn't want that. I had a Jeremy Irons kind of beard in mind, the sort of beard that suggested, There goes a bad, bad man—yet he is also curiously intriguing. Like Satan.

With the first pass of the razor, however, I knew that wasn't going to happen. I stoically absorbed the assault upon my facial hair. When she finished, I regarded myself in the mirror. This was not the face of a bad, bad man. It was more like the face of George Michael. Indeed, with my fey George Michael beard, I looked like the sort of man who wears lots of cologne, and who lingers in nightclubs wondering where he's going to get the evening dose of cocaine. Perhaps, I considered, I looked like a terrorist. But no. I just looked preposterous.

When I left the barbershop, darkness had descended. Not that it mattered, of course. Lanzhou hadn't seen the sun in years. And then I noticed that the hotel restaurant was offering a Western buffet. I had been in China long enough to know that the words "Western buffet" should be regarded as a threat and one should flee to the nearest market. But I was in an upscale hotel in Lanzhou, and I thought, What the hell, embrace the escapism for an evening. Besides, in my brief glance of the city, Lanzhou struck me as an excellent place to get mugged. And so I entered, and loaded my plate with meat and potatoes, and a serving of frog legs done in the French manner. It was competently done, and incredibly bland. Even the frog legs, which do, in fact, taste like chicken. The flavors of China had fried my taste buds. I picked at my food, feeling clumsy and barbaric using a fork and knife again.

I looked about and was suddenly startled by the other customers. There was not a foreigner among them. Indeed, most of them were upscale Chinese parents teaching their kids how to use forks and knives and how to eat Western food.

"Ah, ah," tutted a father to his young son. "Only use English words."

"Do I have to eat this?" the boy pleaded.

Afterward, I marched up to the business center and sent an e-mail to my wife. *Start the boys on Mandarin lessons now. And have them use chopsticks.*

It's going to be a competitive world they inherit.

# 19

There are few words more evocative than *Silk Road*. Imagine a world inhabited by Sogdians, Gokturks, Ferghanians, Parthians, Bactrians, Nabataeans, Samanids, and other civilizations now lost to us, a world of traders and conquerors, missionaries and zealots, poets and muses, traversing the vast distances of Eurasia, trading the gold of Rome for the silk of Xi'an. There were hundreds of trails from the Mediterranean to China that would collectively become known as the Silk Road, lonesome paths over treacherous passes and barren deserts upon which civilizations rose and fell. One such path had skirted the vast desolation of the Taklamakan Desert in northern China and made its way to the town of Dunhuang, near the splendid Mogao Caves, where for centuries Buddhist monks had carved and painted scenes of wonder and devotion, a vast tomb of extraordinary artwork that for centuries lay lost and forgotten.

Flying in, I could see how this could happen, this losing of one of the great repositories of ancient art. The Mogao Caves lie at the very edge of the Taklamakan Desert, an enormous, expanding emptiness fringed by the soaring Kunlun Mountains. This desert is one of the world's largest sand deserts. And, of course, it can get a little dusty here as wind stirs the fine grains. Indeed, as I walked across the tarmac at the airport, I listened to the jet engines wheezing and sputtering from all the sand. I watched the mechanics on their bicycles, pedaling toward the plane to investigate this strange grinding and whirring of the engines, and I thought of Buddhism, its Zen variation, and once again noted that I should look into it, because I was not at all calm flying in China and I really needed to do something about it.

Fortunately, Dunhuang is a calm place. I checked into a hotel and walked outside in the late-afternoon light to have a gander. The architecture was utterly unremarkable, but there was a pleasant small-town vibe, a congenial unhurriedness. It was the first place I'd seen in China where drivers didn't sit on their horns. No one troubled me here. It was, dare I say it, laid-back. And nothing is laid-back in China. Dunhuang is also very mixed in its population. This is where China abuts into Central Asia. Though predominantly Han Chinese, there were also Uyghurs in Dunhuang, Muslims wearing their distinctive white hats. I made my way through a street that was setting up for the night market, past stalls selling books, ornaments, a little bit of everything, and settled at a table in front of a restaurant. Across the way there was a hairdresser's shop with heavily made-up hairdressers idling at the door, waving and beckoning me toward them as they stood and flitted in their tight-fitting, clingy clothes. *Messagee!* Even here? I wondered. In Dunhuang? This town, this little eensie-weenie teeny town on the edge of the desert? Jesus, I thought. It's startling the degree to which prostitution exists in China.

Before me, a friendly Muslim waiter set down a bowl of noodles with meat. I had pointed to it moments earlier and he'd cooked it up in a hotpot. It was good, a little gamey per-haps, and I opened up my guidebook since I didn't have any-thing else to read, and soon learned that the local specialty in Dunhuang is *luruo huang mian,* or donkey meat with noodles. Super, I thought. I'm eating an ass. That's all right, I reflected. For years, I'd been eating horse meat, a fact discerned only much, much later when Sylvia had accompanied me on a trip to Holland and, at my uncle and aunt's home in Brummen in rural Gelderland, she'd inquired what precisely was that curious-looking cold cut I'd just used to make a sandwich. *Horse,* she'd been told, whereupon I coughed and hacked and choked on my sandwich as my uncle explained that for dinner that evening we'd be having the hare he'd run over the previous day. They're good salt-of-the-earth people, my family in Holland, and I will not hear another word about how boring Dutch cuisine is. Indeed, it prepared me for China. If I could eat roadkill in Holland, I could certainly eat an ass here.

The Mogao Caves lie somewhere in the Hexi Corridor, once the only path between China and the West. Not far away is the Gilian Shan range, a solid wall of mountains that shoot out of the desert. Beginning in the fourth century and spanning more than a thousand years, worshipers of Buddhism filled the

492 grottoes of Mogao with art and thousands of ancient manuscripts. Once trade along the Silk Road collapsed along with
the Yuan Dynasty, however, the grottos and caves lay forgotten
until the early twentieth century, when Europeans began to
hear rumors of their existence and they hopped over to explore
and plunder, because that is what they did.

The Mogao Caves are not far from Dunhuang, and I
hailed a taxi with a driver babbling on his cell phone as he
drove me to a corner on the outskirts of town, where another
taxi idled along the curb. The driver indicated that I should
depart his taxi and hop in that one. Perplexed, I did as he
asked, whereupon the pockmarked driver began to yell into his
cell phone. They are not silent people, the Chinese, and I paid
no mind as we passed the last cotton fields and followed the
paved road through a barren desert of sand and stones.

Suddenly, the driver veered off the paved road to follow a
deeply rutted gully. And why are we doing this? I wondered.
Not for the first time, I wished I spoke Chinese. What's he saying on that cell phone?

*I have the foreigner. Now give me my money.*

I was beginning to grow concerned, because earlier I had
seen the turn-off to the Mogao Caves. And this wasn't it. We
went farther into the desert. We passed a dead dog rotting in
the sun. The driver continued to yell into his phone.

*I'm nearly there. Bring the gun.*

A surprising number of Westerners do get themselves
killed in China, victims of banditry. I was beginning to worry
here. This path could do some severe damage to a car. What
would the motive be for subjecting one's car to such risks? It
could only be something nefarious.

Suddenly, the driver veered back toward the paved road, and as we returned to it I felt true relief. What was that about? I wondered. I looked behind us. Of course. It was perfectly clear. We had taken a detour around the tollbooth.

I was let off before the entrance to the Mogao Caves, and the driver indicated that he was amenable to waiting for me until I'd finished. I explained, in that curious way one does when you can't speak the local language, that I might be a while. He shrugged and indicated that he didn't have anything better to do. It's a desert. Not a lot of passengers here. And he had a *laowai* here who thought he was very cunning with his bargaining, but really, it's like taking candy from a child. So he'd stay.

I paid the entrance fee and was pleased to find an English-speaking guide, who led me on a path through a small canyon. In its walls, hundreds of caves had been carved. They are known as the Thousand Buddha Caves, and inside the grottoes monks had painted vast murals and carved hundreds of stucco sculptures to encourage meditation and enlightenment. Many of the frescoes had been financed by Silk Road merchants. The Mogao Caves lie at the very edge of the Silk Road's most daunting challenge—the desert crossing—and travelers either expressed their gratitude for completing the journey or their hopes for making it across by paying for lavish testimonies to their devotion. For the sake of preservation, all the caves are now sealed and only a few are opened each day for visitors.

"This secret library cave," informed my guide, a young woman not entirely in command of the English language. "There were thousands very holy manuscripts. English people steal them."

"Is that right?"

"Yes. In 1900, they trick monk and steal manuscripts. And you see those Buddhas without faces? Muslim people deface the Buddhas in 1920."

There were more scratched-out faces in other caves. "It's a shame, isn't it?" I said. "Why can't we all just get along? Muslims and Buddhists, Christians and Jews. Live and let live, don't you think?"

"I know not what you say," she said perfunctorily. I got the feeling that she'd memorized a script and any deviation from it would prove troubling to her. Frankly, I understood little of what she said and just nodded thoughtfully as she explained the story behind the immense hundred-foot-tall Buddha in the largest cave in a language known only to herself. We passed an open grotto with a sign that declared that under no circumstances should one think of entering, so I entered to find men with brushes working on a faded mural of a divine bodhisattva. Was this restoration or re-creation? It can be so hard to tell in China, and I wanted to explore this point with my guide, who had yanked me back, but her answers were insensible to my ears. But here and there, as I followed her from cave to cave, I'd pick something up though the incomprehensible din.

"In 1924, Americans take the statue. Now at Hoffhod University."

"I'm sorry. Where?"

"Hoffhod University."

"Ah. Harvard University."

"Yes. Hoffhod."

I was completely sympathetic to the difficulties many Chinese have with that pesky *r*, as I could not fathom getting my mouth around the vast majority of Chinese sounds.

"Chinese people very angry. It is our cultural heritage. Many things stolen from Mogao Caves."

She did have a point. Throughout the nineteenth and early twentieth centuries, Western archaeologists had plundered the world, filling up the museums and libraries of Europe and America with international treasures. But, of course, China had had its own little Cultural Revolution—*Destroy Old Culture!*—so much of China's cultural legacy had been sadly destroyed by the Chinese themselves.

"Cultural Revolution finished now," my guide noted when I made the point.

Very true.

One of the appealing things about being in a small town like Dunhuang is that one can entertain the possibility of riding a bicycle without succumbing to mortal fear. After all this time in China, I had yet to avail myself of the preferred mode of local transport. Now seemed like a good time to do so.

"How about this one?" I asked at a café that offered bicycle rentals.

"No brakes."

"And this one?"

"Broken."

"So this one, then."

"Is good."

It was a bicycle meant for nine-year-old girls. Midget nine-year-old girls, I thought as I pedaled my way out of Dunhuang. And it's hard pedaling a bicycle for nine-year-old girls when you're not one. Without being able to extend my legs so that the thigh muscles could do the work, it was left to the kneecaps to do the pedaling. I rode like an oversized clown on a tricycle, grunting savagely as I made my way up a slight incline. Teenage boys overtook me on their big bicycles, laughing and jeering from their perches high above, and as they passed I hoped that one day soon they'd find themselves overcome by a debilitating bout of acne.

I was heading a few miles out of town toward the giant sand dunes that surrounded Crescent Moon Lake, which wasn't really a lake but a small pond with a pagoda, a classic oasis in the desert. The sand was alleged to sing atop these dunes, which stretched for miles into a barren wilderness. When I finally arrived, I uncoiled my legs and briefly contemplated stealing someone else's bike before hobbling though a gate, where I discovered to my delight that I was in the midst of a thousand camels, idling in the sun, waiting to ferry passengers up the golden Mountains of Shifting Sands, or Mingsha Shan. This thrilled me, because really, is there any better way to climb a sand dune than on the back of a camel—a creature so large yet so silly-looking, with its strange contours and perpetual countenance of dopey confusion, an expression I empathized with completely here in China. No, there is not, I concluded as I settled myself between two humps and with bewildered glee experienced the swift, staggered, doddering thrust of a camel rising. True, this was essentially the local equivalent of a pony ride, and I was led by a camel walker who guided the camels up the narrow, ever-shifting trail of sand. Lawrence of Arabia I was not. But it's a graceless ride that can only be embraced. So trust me here. If you're putting together a To Do list, include *Ride a camel up a sand dune.*

But hold on. Camels do not lightly set off their passengers. They collapse. First the front legs go, and just as you think you're about to hurtle front over end, the back legs go. It's a startling sensation. The camel doesn't so much sit down as fall down, and it's an interesting feeling—crumbling to the ground together with a 500-pound animal—and you feel lucky to have survived the experience. Still, we hadn't quite summited this mount of sand. There was farther to go, and I clambered up a steep wall of shifting grains.

At the top, it was alleged that this was where one could hear the sand sing. I did not hear the sand sing. I heard only the whoosh and demented cackling of someone hurtling down the sand on an inner tube. But it was not the only option for getting oneself down the other side; there was also something alleged to be sand surfing. Boys had carried the lids of wooden crates up to the peak, and the sand surfers were meant to sit on these lids of wooden crates and gently push themselves down the slope, which, frankly, looked like a really lame way to get down a sand dune. No, I thought. There's a right way and a wrong way to do this. So I went with the inner tube.

I settled myself inside the tube and gazed at the wonder of the scenery, the desert, the mountains in the distance. I considered going farther west into the emptiness, through Xinjiang, all the way to Kashgar, where China meets Pakistan. But what would I learn about China, Han China, that I had not learned in Tibet? There were Uyghurs out there, the poor Uyghurs, China's Turkic minority. Like the Tibetans, the Uyghurs, too, would prefer not to be a part of the People's Republic of China.

And so the government represses them with the same grim methods they use in Tibet. And while I had a pang of regret at missing the fabled market bazaar of Kashgar, it was time to turn my attention back to the east.

So I would go back to Han China. And as I pushed myself down and began the fast, oh so fast, descent down the swirling sands, I had one last thought in western China, a region I'd really come to enjoy. Perhaps, I thought as I hurtled perilously toward a herd of lumbering camels, I should have gone with the sand surfing after all.

# 20

I had come to Chengdu to see the pandas. I'm not sure why, exactly, I felt the need to see the pandas. I do not feel warm and fuzzy inside when in the presence of pandas. There are far more charismatic mega-fauna out there. But still, I was drawn to see them, if only because I'd been wondering whether the Chinese may have regretted giving two Giant Pandas to Richard Nixon in 1972, when he became the first president to visit the People's Republic of China. Since then, as any visit to a zoo that contains pandas will confirm, the public has responded with one long collective *aaaawwww*, assigning to them all sorts of anthropomorphic attributes. The pressure to ensure that Giant Pandas do not become extinct must be immense. And that's the last thing the Chinese government needs. More pressure.

But, as always in China, a visit to the Panda Breeding and Research Center was nothing if not interesting. I had expected to find it outside Chengdu, another urban megalopolis, somewhere in rural Sichuan Province. And once, that is where it was. But today, the lush grounds of the Panda Breeding and Research Center have been swallowed by Chengdu itself, and its bamboo-lined paths and frolicking inhabitants are now found in a light industrial zone on the outskirts of town. Inside its walls, there are, of course, Giant Pandas, dozing and munching on bamboo, and generally behaving like extremely contented animals. More interesting were the plaques and statues strewn throughout the grounds with quotes and testimonies attesting to the importance and value of the animal kingdom and that it is our responsibility as guardians of the planet to ensure their well-being. So said Gandhi and others. It's a lovely thought, of course, and as I recalled the peddlers of endangered animals in Guangzhou, I suspected that the sentiment wasn't universally shared in China.

There were other interesting sights inside the Panda Breeding and Research Center, including a baby panda nursery. For the panda lovers, this would be their nirvana moment, a large crib filled with a half-dozen baby pandas tottering about, ready for their calendar shoot. There were five little pandas, including two sets of twins, overseen by a man in doctor garb, complete with mask and paper hat, looking bored senseless as he sat next to a bucket full of soiled baby wipes. I began to wonder at the statistical likelihood of there being two sets of twins, born just days apart, in the Panda Breeding and Research Center. And then, as I read through the signs that out-lined the panda breeding process, I was informed that China practices the West Virginia model of panda breeding. This wasn't merely a kissing cousin situation. No, conjugal relations here were conducted in true hillbilly fashion. It makes them happy, the sign informed me. And if brothers and sisters fall in love, who are we to stop it? We want happy pandas. It's no wonder, then, that the first panda to be bred in the Panda Research and Breeding Center and released into the wild did not live long. It was a genetic mutant. This all made me think of the movie *Deliverance,* and I set off in search of a panda lounging in a tree, strumming his banjo.

Beyond mutant pandas, Chengdu pleased me in other ways. It has some scrumptious street food, which for someone like me, so easily flummoxed by Chinese restaurants, was a special treat indeed. The meat on a stick is lip-smacking good. I couldn't say for certain which animal in particular I was eating, but whatever it was it had a mighty fine spice rub. I wanted more.

And there were oranges, big, impossibly juicy, mouth-watering oranges. I had no idea where they might have grown. Chengdu, like every city in China, resided under a gray-brown haze of pollution. Indeed, surrounded by the high mountains of Sichuan, the pollution was particularly awful. But no matter. Someone somewhere in Sichuan Province had grown the most perfect oranges. And here they were.

Really, I was so happy I was nearly tittering. This is because not only was I in the possession of citrus, I also had in my hands a thick stack of magazines and newspapers—*Time, Newsweek, The Economist,* the *International Herald Tribune,* a full week's worth of news from the outside world.

How can this be? you wonder. Surely, it's not possible to buy unfiltered Western newsmagazines in a country so very,

very touchy about a free press. This is true. You can't. Not in Chengdu, in any case.

But you can steal them.

So steal them is precisely what I did. This was not a crime of opportunity even. This was planned. It had been weeks since I'd read a newspaper that wasn't a broadsheet of propaganda. Deep inside the Middle Kingdom, one could even doubt the existence of a world beyond the walls of China. True, the Chinese press was very diligent in reporting on the Deputy Minister for the State Economic and Trade Commission's successful meeting with counterparts in Tajikistan. And they did note that a Chinese firm had won a bid to build a road in Algeria. But this wasn't the news I was yearning for. Out there, beyond China, celebrities were falling apart in glorious splendor, politicians were soliciting sex in airport men's rooms, vice presidents were shooting people in the face, and the cost of housing in California was finally (finally!) coming down. Such were my informational concerns. And they had gone unmet in China.

And so I put on my cleanest clothes and did my best impersonation of someone who would pay $350 for a night at the Hilton, when you can get a very good room in a Chinese hotel for $35 (and it even comes with a brothel). "Good afternoon, sir," said the doorman as he opened the door, and I was delighted to discover that they speak English at the Hilton. Tempted as I was to stop and inquire about his life story, I marched in, busy-like, as if I had meetings or possibly an important conference call, and walked up to the business center. There arrayed ever so delicately lay my prize. A sign warned me to not even think about taking these magazines and newspapers outside the business center. But that was precisely my plan. I waited patiently, idly flipping though the *International Herald Tribune,* which informed me that while I was in Tibet, the Chinese army had shot two Tibetans on a mountain pass near the border with Nepal. Normally, of course, one wouldn't hear about the Chinese Army shooting Tibetans. But the incident had been captured on videotape by German mountain climbers on the Nepalese side of the border, and soon the tape, like all tapes today, had made its way to YouTube.

And then, when the attendant left to help someone with a fax, I rose from my plush chair and grabbed the newspapers and magazines. Not just one or two, but all of them. I stuffed them inside my backpack and fled.

So, as you can imagine, I was absolutely overflowing with glee. I found a backpackers' café on the Brocade River, ordered a Tsingtao, and flipped open my newspaper. Really, I couldn't have been more pleased with my world at that moment. It had been so very, very long since I'd beheld a newspaper beyond the peppy offerings of *China Daily.* It's astonishing, really, that in a country with 34 million bloggers and another 123 million Internet users, a number growing by leaps and bounds each day, that the government maintains such a tight grip on information. The media continues to serve the interest of the state, but online anything goes. True, there were thousands of Internet police officers lurking and trolling the Web. But they can only react once something has been posted. Meanwhile, information and opinion moves on to other sites.

But today I had newspapers. And I was connected to the outside world.

"Excuse me," said a very tall, thin *laowai* with a wispy mustache. "Can I buy you a beer?"

Well, okay, I thought. I have newspapers, magazines, and now complete strangers want to buy me beer. Good call, coming to Chengdu.

His name was Max. A Dutchman, he had on a uniform not unlike a chauffeur's. Gaunt and with a cadaverous pallor, he reminded me of a very young Vincent Price.

"So what brings you to Chengdu?" he asked as he settled at my table.

"Just traveling. You?"

"I live here," he said as our beers arrived. "Seven years now. I even married a local. And now I have a son. He is one month old. Everyone wants to look at him, this mixed-race child. They look at him like he's an alien."

The Chinese are nothing if not curious. I asked him what exactly he did in Chengdu.

"I'm a bodyguard."

"Really?" I had not in my lifetime actually ever encountered a bodyguard. The number of people willing to take a bullet for complete strangers is, presumably, small.

"You see, it says so here on my tag."

Indeed it did. *Bodyguard.*

With evident pride, Max showed me his gear: a walkie-talkie, a fold-out spring baton, and an electric shock zapper.

"I'm licensed for weapons here," he went on.

"Guns too?"

"No. But if you want a gun, I can get you a gun. Or cocaine, heroin—whatever you want I can get."

"I'm good with beer right now," I said, "but if I change my mind, I'll let you know." Though that seemed unlikely.

Thus far, I had maintained a firm Just Say No policy when it came to drugs in China. I was confused enough as it was.

"I don't do cocaine anymore," Max explained. "You never sleep when you do cocaine."

I'd already discerned that Max was unlikely to be helped by cocaine. He was a little bouncy, a little jittery, a little manic. His movements were sudden, jerky, as if he'd been seized by tics. I couldn't even begin to wonder what he might be like high on coke.

"You hungry?" he asked me.

"I am, actually."

"Do you want to get some hotpot?"

We finished our beers, hopped into a taxi, and sped through the glittering lights of the city. Although half the size of Shanghai, Chengdu is still an enormous city of 10 million. As the cost of doing business in Shanghai rises, ever more companies are moving westward to cities like Chengdu, another place where wrecking balls and cranes are transforming everything old into something new. It, too, is a city of vast buildings and construction, of crowded streets and honking cars, of beggars and entrepreneurs forging their way in the new China. As I watched the city unfold, Max turned to me.

"Just pretend you're my client, all right?"

"Um . . . okay."

Clearly, this was a man who loved his job. He got out of the taxi and opened the door for me. He began muttering into his walkie-talkie, his eyes darting through the crowd. He circled me closely, muttering away. The crowd stopped to stare. Well, I thought, we all know whom to shoot now.

As Max hovered protectively beside me, prattling into his walkie-talkie, I noticed a sign that informed us that we were on "a provincial-level model street without any fake product, striving to become a national level." We'll just bring the fakery with us, I thought as Max forged a path through the crowd for his pretend client.

Inside a restaurant, we dipped various meats and vegetables into a burbling vat of spicy flavored oil. This is really good, I thought. I was totally digging Sichuan cuisine. True, my eyes were watering, I was sweating, and my mouth was ablaze from the red Sichuan peppers that locals use to flavor everything, but this was some good food. Incendiary, but good.

"So who do you work for?" I asked Max as he scanned the restaurant for any patrons betraying malicious intent toward his pretend client.

"Businessmen. Mobsters," he said, momentarily relaxing. "It's the same thing here. They like to hire a foreigner as a bodyguard. It gives them prestige. I had a client yesterday, he asked me, 'Why aren't you wearing sunglasses?' He thinks foreign bodyguards should always have their sunglasses on."

"Is it just a prestige thing? Or do you actually have to defend clients now and then?"

It wasn't long before I regretted the question. Here inside the restaurant, Max proceeded to display his scars. There was the knife wound in his back, and the gash that had resulted from a steel pipe that had been smashed against his shins, and then there was the ice-pick incident with his forearm, and the crumpled knuckles. "It's always in the nightclubs," he said. "Once a week, something happens. My wife thinks I should find another job. But the money is good. And I like it. I'm one of the top bodyguards in Chengdu."

*Freak.*

We finished eating, and as we left the restaurant, he again circled me and whispered nonsense into his walkie-talkie to a phantom backup.

"So what do you say? You want to go to the nightclub?" he asked.

*With you?*

I have enough scars, I thought. This man seemed to act like a force of gravity for every weapon-wielding mobster in Chengdu. And with him muttering into his walkie-talkie, I'd convey the impression that I was somehow important, and I did not want the denizens of this city's nightclubs thinking I was important. Perhaps they'd think I was challenging them on their turf, sauntering into a nightclub with a bodyguard. Who does the *laowai* think he is? they'd grumble as they slammed back their Crowne Royale. Then there'd be trouble, and I did not want trouble. Plus, once I'd established that there were, in fact, nightclubs in China, the thought of lingering in the boom-boom environment of a Chinese nightclub was no linger interesting.

So I bade Max farewell, thanked him for the interesting evening, and returned to my hotel. Inside the elevator, I became curious as I noted an absence of a sign indicating what might be found on the second floor. The first floor was the lobby. The third floor was the restaurant. There was no fourth floor, of course, because the number 4 is considered unlucky since it sounds so much like the Chinese word for death. But on the fifth floor there was the mah-jongg room, karaoke bar, and spa, which was presumably the "spa." So why no sign for the second floor? I pressed the button for the second floor, and as the doors opened I saw that there was a bar. Well, why not, I thought. I'd read my magazines and have a nightcap.

I was escorted by an effusive host to a seat at a table. The bar was completely full. I ordered a beer. On a small stage there was big-screen video karaoke and young men were taking turns singing love ballads. I was beginning to sense something. Half the men were attired in short blue robes. I hadn't felt this since I'd arrived in China. Suddenly, I started to chuckle.

My gaydar was ringing.

I looked around. There was not one woman inside this bar. On the walls, there were huge black-and-white portraits of buff Chinese men. And all around, there were men chattering in short blue robes. And my presence had not gone unnoted. A table of young men with big spiky hair pointed at me. They started whispering.

"Check, please?"

I rose up. The host took me by the arm, looking concerned.

"Thank you. But I think I'll go to sleep now."

Misunderstandings could take so many forms in China. I could at least avoid this one.

In front of the elevator, there were more men lingering in the same blue robes. The bar was connected to a sauna. A short, rotund man of middle years in a little robe indicated he'd like to have a drink with me.

"*Xie xie*, but no," I said, making the universal gesture for sleep and pointing upstairs. He found this an agreeable answer and stood beside me waiting for the elevator, which would take us upstairs to "sleep," whereupon I gestured and explained that I meant sleep without quotation marks and that I thought I'd go ahead and do that alone.

Typical, I thought as I stepped into the elevator. Out of all the gin joints in China, I'd found the gay bar.

# 21

There are many fissures in Chinese society. There is the enormous gap between the rich and the poor. There is the simmering tension between the urban and the rural. There are multitudes of linguistic barriers. There is discord between those who are Communists and those who are not. And there is factionalism within the Communist Party itself. There is the Chinese Youth League faction under President Hu Jintao. And then there is the Shanghai faction that was aligned with Hu's predecessor, Jiang Zemin. The Shanghai faction is presently losing, though they cannot be counted out. They are very cunning, the Shanghai faction of the Chinese Communist Party, and not easily cowed.

But perhaps the greatest fissure in Chinese culture, I would soon discover, is the yawning chasm between the practitioners of waltzing and the devotees of karaoke. You must choose in China. Do you waltz or do you sing?

I'd found myself on a steel boat on the Yangtze River, a small cruise ship where the decks bounced as you walked over them and the boat staggered with a pronounced list that made sleep challenging. In my small cabin, I'd tried both ways. If I lay this way, as I was apparently intended to lie, the blood would drain into my head, but if I lay the other way, gravity pulled me down toward my feet. Was this troubling, this listing of the boat? I didn't know. It didn't pay to think like that in China. In for a penny, in for a pound, I say, and if listing boats were the norm on the Yangtze, far be it from me to worry. Besides, I had faith in the captain, a small, weathered-looking man resplendent in a red shirt emblazed with the steely visage of Tupac Shakur.

I had boarded the boat in Chongqing, a vast urban expanse of more than 30 million people. That sounded like hell to me. By now, I'd had my fill of Chinese mega-cities, thank you, and so I did not linger long in Chongqing. I had booked a cruise through the Three Gorges, emerald canyons that are said to offer some of the most enchanting scenery in China. All of the other passengers were Chinese tourists. They'd come from Fujian, Hunan, Hebei, Shaanxi, and Guangdong Provinces. Average age, possibly fifty-five. Socioeconomic class, middle class. Median height of the women, four feet. Disposition, variable. English proficiency, none. View of lone *laowai* on board: the ship's pet. During mealtime, my tablemates were very kind, and I sensed their admiration for my chopstick skills. As I poured tea into my neighbor's cup, I could hear the ladies twittering about my good manners. I'd been in China for some time now. I knew how not to be a barbarian. During our communal meals, I spun the glass wheel and attacked the food with the same gusto as my tablemates, because it was good food, very good food.

I'd joined them on the deck as we steamed our way to the Three Gorges, passing fishermen on the banks of the Yangtze sweeping giant nets in the brown, fast-moving water. There were other cruise ships and shallow container boats and truck ferries and coal barges plying this watery highway. It's an astonishing river, and for me, it had become inescapable. Whether I was in the far east in a city such as Nanjing, or in the distant western wilds of Yunnan, or near the very center of the country as in Chongqing, I was always tripping over the Yangtze River. As we headed downstream, I kept an eye out for the Baiji Yangtze River Dolphin. It had been years since anyone had seen this freshwater dolphin, and while I lived in hope, it seemed unlikely that this creature would escape extinction. There is the pollution, of course. The Yangtze is alleged to be a freshwater river, but it is a river of silt and mud. And there is the river traffic. Tens of thousands of boats ply the river, ferrying goods from the heartland of China to the ports on the coast. But it is also a fundamentally different river today.

A few years earlier, much of the Yangtze had been only a few feet deep and subject to fast currents and boiling rapids and all sorts of other challenging conditions that made navigating a boat difficult. Now, as the signs on the verdant limestone hills informed me, the Yangtze was more than 450 feet deep, and to ply down this river is to experience Noah's Ark–type sensations. The rising waterline had swallowed trees and villages, graves and temples, centuries of life and activity that now lay submerged below. This was because the Chinese government had decided to build a dam, a very big dam, fulfilling a long-standing ambition to plug up the Yangtze. Indeed, it was Sun Yat-sen who had first proposed the Three Gorges Dam in 1919. Mao, unsurprisingly, was also amenable. It would be the world's biggest dam, something every megalomaniac would like to claim as his own. Opponents of the idea were, naturally, disposed of in labor camps. Subsequent leaders, too, supported the dam, and so today the Yangtze has been flooded.

Fortunately, not every sight and diversion has yet been swallowed. Near the city of Fengdu, a little more than 100 miles downstream from our starting point of Chongqing, lies the Temple of Ghosts, and after we'd docked, I joined my cruisemates for a look at this famously haunted temple, perched on a hillside above the river. On the ramp, we encountered the usual plethora of map sellers and beggars and children whispering *hungry, money*. There was a chairlift to the summit, 600 feet up, but I'd been hankering for a walk, so I climbed the stone steps, listening to the strange Chinese pop music wafting though the speakers. I rejoined my cruisemates and tried to coax some English out of our tour guide.

"That's a new city," she said, pointing across the river to Fengdu. "Old city underneath walls."

It was just like Fuling, which we'd passed earlier, an old city consumed by a massive seawall with a new city built on top. It's an unsettling sight, seeing the effects of Beijing's whims, knowing that a Party official's ambitions could level hundreds of thousands of homes and displace millions, destroying the region's cultural heritage forever.

But at least we had our little Temple of Ghosts. The eminence upon which it stood was one of the traditional spiritual graveyards of Taoism. The earliest temples were built in the third century not long after two men who were said to have superpowers, Wang Fangping and Yin Changsheng, moved to the hillside and combined their family names to Yin Wang, which, apparently, means Ruler of Hell. There were a number of shrines and pagodas, as well as a few monks in saffron robes, but mostly this Temple of Ghosts existed as a maudlin tourist attraction. There were stone statues of a man beating a woman, another was holding his severed hand, and there was one depicting a woman breast-feeding a deer. And these were the tasteful statues.

"This the torture chamber," informed our guide. "Look, the playboy being ripped apart so all the women can have a part of him. There the playgirl turn into snake. That the bad husband being sawed in half."

And on and on it went inside the Temple of Ghosts. Frankly, I couldn't wait to leave. It had been a while since I'd been in the midst of something so very touristy, and as the ship set off, I was pleased to find myself back on the ship's deck, just idly watching the limestone cliffs pass by. After a convivial dinner, I made my way to the lounge, where I found half the passengers gliding under the disco ball, waltzing as if they were at a party in old Vienna. Waltzing, as it turns out, is very popular in China, and even President Hu Jintao himself was on the university waltzing team back in the day. I was unaware that waltzing was also a competitive sport, but in China the government, in an effort to overcome the rising rates of obesity that have occurred as more Chinese eat Western foods, has mandated that schoolkids will now be forced to waltz. Lucky for the Chinese, Hu Jintao was not a square dancer.

Then arrangements were made, compromises offered,

and the waltzers sat down and were replaced by the singers. The ship had a karaoke machine and soon the lyrics scrolled across the screen. I watched as a woman of middle years gleefully took to the stage and, to some exotic Arabic-sounding groove, began to sing before flubbing the intro and, after resetting the karaoke machine, started to sing again—and boy, I had to admit, she could really sing. They take their karaoke seriously in China. These aren't drunken Japanese salarymen here. No, no. They can sing. At least, the passengers on board this ship plying the nighttime waters of the Yangtze could. After a half hour of showstopping tunes, the waltzers returned to the floor, and I sat and watched them and, in a rare China moment, became all rosy-cheeked at the wholesomeness of it all.

"Do you speak Chinese?"

"I can say *nihao*, *xie xie*, and *bu yau*. That's about it, though I can count to ten with one hand. Do you want to see?"

Her name was Lu Hang, and she was leading a tour group from Xiamen, a prosperous city on the coast of Fujian Province. We stood on the ship's deck as we drifted through the jagged cliffs of Qutang Gorge, the first of the Three Gorges. It is a narrow chasm—not more than 500 feet in some places— and many regard this as the finest of the gorges. But perhaps I'd been spoiled by Tiger Leaping Gorge. Possibly, I expected too much. My expectations were too high. This, I thought as we passed through the stony escarpments, was *nice*, not awesome, just nice. But it was not without its finer sights. Much of the cultural heritage of the gorges—ancient temples, stone pathways, calligraphy, not to mention thousands of homes—now lies underwater. But high above were wooden coffins, some nearly 2,000 years old, which had been placed in small crevices and caves, most likely during the Han Dynasty. Before the dam, these coffins would have been more than a thousand feet above the river, and to this day no one is certain how exactly those caskets were brought to such lofty heights. As we glided below, Lu Hang translated what the onboard guide, our very own Julie McCoy, was saying through her loudspeaker.

"She is describing what each hill looks like. This one looks like an eagle, and that one looks like a cat."

This was amusing to me. I thought I'd been missing out. I thought she'd been talking about the caves I'd seen. I thought, perhaps, there had been commentary on all the villages that had to be relocated, or a discussion about the impact of the rising waters of the Yangtze and the mud slides that have killed dozens as the earth shifts to accommodate the surging river. But no. An eagle. A cat. Sometime around the age of nineteen, I had lost the poetic impulse. I did not see eagles and cats. I saw a big hill. Okay, a nice big hill.

"It's very beautiful," I said. Okay, a nice big, beautiful hill.

"I think it is very boring," Lu Hang informed me.

"Really?"

"Yes. It was much more beautiful before the dam."

"Do most Chinese people think the Three Gorges Dam was a good idea?"

"No," she said. "People think it was a bad idea. They say it has ruined the beautiful scenery."

"That's true, but at least it provides electricity."

"Only for Hubei Province. People in China think the dam only benefits Hubei."

Lu Hang was friendly and inquisitive, and she asked me about my travels.

"You must join my tour," she said. "After the cruise, we are going to Wuhan."

"Maybe I will. Does your tour come with hats? I can't join a tour group unless it comes with hats."

"I will get you a hat," she said.

"Can it be orange?"

"I will get you an orange hat."

We glided onward to the Little Three Gorges, a canyon that meandered away from the Yangtze following a tributary called the Shennong River.

"In a minute you will see acrobats," Lu Hang informed me. *Say wha?*

What was this about acrobats? What were acrobats doing here at the confluence of the Three Gorges and the Little Three Gorges? Who would be doing acrobatic endeavors amid the gorges of Hubei Province? *Vroom.* This could not be real. My eyes were deceiving me. But there, way up there, 200 feet up there, on a thin strand of wire stretched above the river, a motorcycle roared overhead, followed by an acrobat spinning and jumping and not only defying death, but taunting it. And then they waved. We slid farther up the Shennong River, past more hanging coffins, wooden caskets perched in impossible locations. Death happens—always has, always will—and one would think, surrounded by these coffins, that the acrobats would understand restraint. But they do not. And so they twirled on a wire high above the river.

We'd entered the land of the Tujia, one of China's distinct minorities. Once they had been trackers, using thick ropes to pull river traffic through the shallow rapids of the Yangtze. Famously, the Tujia men were always naked as they heaved the boats over the shoals. Chafing, apparently, was an issue. But, of course, today the river is deep and there is no need for the Tujia boatmen, and so instead they make their living from us, the tourists, pulling sampans, little flat-bottomed wooden boats, up shallow rapids. And, as I was gratified to learn, they keep their clothes on now. Lu Hang left to attend to her tour group, and soon we had all hopped off our little cruise ship in Badong, another new city of apartment blocks built far above the remains of the old town, which lay submerged. Next to us was an enormous cruise ship. *Ikea Components Kick Off,* said the sign draped over the side. We boarded another, smaller boat, which would take us to the even smaller sampans.

"This is a new village," said our guide, pointing. She was a young woman of the Tujia tribe with a golden laugh, the sort of rare, perfect laugh like a baby's that you want to box up and take out from time to time because it makes you feel all warm and fuzzy inside. "See, all new houses, very nice. You like wine? They don't drink beer here, only corn wine."

Above us was a village of new cinder-block houses, con-structed for the farmers who had lost their homes to the deluge caused by the Three Gorges Dam. Maybe they were better off. Probably not, I thought. Hundreds of thousands of people were claiming that they hadn't been compensated fairly. Every-one displaced by the rising waters had to start anew. New vil-lages, new apartments, new land, new work, new relationships. Everything was new, and not everyone likes new.

"What do you think of the dam?" I asked the guide.

"It is safe," she said neutrally.

Let's hope so.

We were let off next to a small stream where we could board the sampans.

"They are called peapods," my guide informed me as we stepped in and six men began to pull us up the stream using bamboo rope. They sang and they raced against the other boatmen pulling tourists. They wore shoes made of rope as well.

"Fifteen years ago, the boatmen were naked," the guide informed me. "Their clothes were rough and hurt the skin when wet. When hot they drink the river water, and when cold they drink spirits. Before the dam was built, they pulled the river traffic. Now they pull tourists."

It all seemed kind of pointless to me. I listened to the singing and scanned the canopy of trees looking for monkeys. The government had reintroduced macaques to the region and, very thoughtfully, was training them how to ask for food from tourists. Ideally, they should do a performance. It's endless, really, the lengths to which the government will go to ensure that visitors have a good time in China. I, however, did not see any macaques, and so I reflected on the trackers pulling this sampan of tourists. It seemed like an inane endeavor. But, I thought, the dam had put the Tujia boatmen out of business. And pulling sampans filled with frolicking tourists has got to beat pulling barges of coal. And they seemed to be enjoying themselves, and that's a good thing, this enjoyment of work.

My guide began to sing a soft, piercingly haunting song, and when she finished I asked her about its meaning.

"We sing this song when we get married. When girls get married, it is the custom to cry for fifteen days."

But there would be no tears today, not for her, she of the golden laugh. I spent the remainder of my journey up the Shennong River, pulled by the no-longer-naked Tuija boatmen, doing everything I could to elicit this laugh because it was so splendid.

Normally on board this cruise ship on the Yangtze, we woke to the strains of *Doctor Zhivago* softly wafting through the intercom system. On this morning, however, we arose to the bleating of fog horns, and as I looked out the window I could see why. We were enshrouded by a wet cloud, a billowing fog that reduced visibility to less than fifty yards. This would be my last morning on board. We'd celebrated the end of the Yangtze Cruise the night before with a crew fashion show followed by karaoke and waltzing. The boat could go no farther on account of the dam, and so after breakfast we'd clambered into a bus to go see the Three Gorges Dam itself.

Sadly, we could barely see it, this very large dam that should not be hard to see. It's more than a mile long and 610 feet high, but so thick was the fog that little could be seen beyond the locks that carried ships above it. There was a sound system near the viewing platform and it informed us that "when the dam is completed it will have the attention of the world." This seemed very important to China, to be noticed, to be paid attention to.

And they could already see that the world was watching. The Three Gorges Dam generates 22,500 megawatts of power, which sounds like a lot but comprises a mere 3 percent of China's energy generation. The Three Gorges Dam seemed like a lot of trouble and destruction for a 3-percent bump in the power supply. It does little to alleviate the burden from China's 21,000 coal mines. And nuclear energy still produced only a little more than 2 percent of electricity in China.

And only now is the dam's environmental impact becoming evident. According to Xinhua, the state-run news agency, the lack of water flow in the Yangtze is preventing the river from flushing out the pollution, and needless to say, there is a lot of pollution floating in the Yangtze River. Increasing levels of sedimentation have become problematic, and today the Yangtze is an extraordinarily brown river. And now there are algae blooms too. The eroding banks along the reservoir have caused landslides and waves that, incredibly, have reached 150 feet high. And these are the problems that the government admits to. Who knows what's really going on.

"So will you join my tour to Wuhan?" Lu Hang asked me as we walked around the visitors' center. "I will get you a hat."

"I am very tempted because of the hat."

But there are 10 million people in Wuhan, and those were 10 million very good reasons not to go there (no offense, good people of Wuhan). Instead I made my way to Yichang, a modest city on the banks of the Yangtze, where I walked around trying to figure out why there were so many coffee shops. And as I walked around some more, I came to the inescapable conclusion that there were so many coffee shops because Yichang itself is such a sedative. True, there were people waltzing in a riverside square. And there was a strange plethora of bridal boutiques. But this small city lacked the mad vibe I'd come to expect in a Chinese city. It was strangely quiet. I walked into the Old Street Café Bar, which was doing a very good imitation of a Hungarian café, with its high ceiling and gold inlay and wall paintings done in the style of Titian, ordered a coffee, and wrote postcards featuring giant earthmoving equipment and cranes for my sons. There are quite likely only two groups of people who think that building the world's largest dam might be a really cool thing to do—Communists and the Bob the Builder set.

# 22

Xi'an reminded me of Dusseldorf. This was the peculiar thought I had as I wandered around the Bell Tower, a gray stone eminence from the Qing Dynasty that marked the center of the city. How can this be? you wonder. Isn't Xi'an the fabled terminus of the Silk Road? Yes, it is. Isn't Dusseldorf in Germany? Yes. And isn't Xi'an in China? Yep. And aren't Germany and China, you know, *different*? Truer words have never been spoken. So how can Xi'an be like Dusseldorf?

I know. It's weird. Here I was in an ancient capital that had presided over the rise and collapse of eleven dynasties, and I was thinking of Dusseldorf. Perhaps it was the rain. Whenever I'm in Dusseldorf, the weather is dreary. And it was dreary in Xi'an too. I'd haggled for what I estimated, by this point, was my twenty-eighth umbrella in China. I did not have twenty-eight umbrellas in my possession, of course. The world is divided between those who lose umbrellas and those who don't. I lose them. But it wasn't merely the damp spittle that conjured up a city in the Ruhr Valley. From the Bell Tower, I could see a sign informing me that Starbucks would be brewing soon. There were two McDonald's within my line of vision. The streets that fanned out from the Bell Tower were all lined with bourgeois retailers. Before me, there was an enormous new shopping plaza. It seemed so comfortably prosperous. Like Dusseldorf.

Even the beggars in Xi'an were fat. In front of the Bell Tower Hotel, two obese teenage girls glided by on pullies in the rain, showing their curled feet and bent toes to any and all. The idea being, apparently, that they had suffered cruelly from bound feet. Surely, the upscale tourists who stayed at the Bell Tower Hotel would greet these girls with hoots of derision. Binding feet had ended generations ago. There wasn't a woman alive in China whose feet had been bound. And then I watched a couple in their North Face parkas drop 50 *kuai* into their fat hands, and suddenly I was filled with admiration for these enterprising youngsters. The tourists would go home with tales of the poor young women disfigured by bound feet in Xi'an, and the girls would go to McDonald's. And then I came across a man on the sidewalk who was missing a third of his head, as if it had been sliced off by a blade, a blade that had also taken both arms, and who stood painting calligraphy on the sidewalk before taking a microphone between his stumps and belting out a few tunes. Okay, I thought, so maybe Xi'an isn't like Dusseldorf after all.

Nevertheless, I was struck by the prosperity evident in the streets spilling out from the Bell Tower. I even found a bookstore with an English-language section, and as I perused their eclectic selection of titles I wondered how the censors had missed *Penthouse Letters*. I bought a book about Harry Truman, and as I went to pay for it I noticed the bestseller list hanging on the wall. And who might we find at the summit of the Chinese bestseller list? *The Da Vinci Code* by the nefarious Dan Brown.

I had more to shop for, however. When I'd left months ago, I'd packed for spring in Beijing and summer in tropical Hong Kong. I was no longer in tropical Hong Kong. It was November. Indeed, before my journey's end I had plans to go up to Harbin in the far north of China, where the newspaper confidently informed me that it was presently well below freezing, suggesting the need for a warm coat. I did not have a warm coat. To rectify this deficiency, I wandered around downtown Xi'an popping into stores and trying on coats of various styles and shapes. I, frankly, often wished that men's fashion had remained frozen in 1940 so that every day I'd know to wear a gabardine suit and a fedora and I wouldn't have to spend any time choosing what to wear and wondering what my sartorial choices might reflect about me. I didn't care about clothes. But I also didn't care to look like a dweeb. So, I suppose, I did care. But I didn't want to. I wanted to reach into my closet and grab my gabardine suit and my fedora without another moment's thought. It's a complicated mind, that of the male animal.

So I walked around Xi'an trying on coats, where it soon became clear that I was getting ahead of myself wondering about style issues, because as I tried coat after coat, it became evident that Chinese men, apparently, did not have shoulders. I couldn't find anything that fit. I walked into a high-end mall, and ambled past a woman playing a grand piano, and loped among stores selling Polo, Versace, Hugo Boss, and other upscale brands, and wondered who in China spends $5,000 on a coat. And was there some essential *Chineseness* being lost as the Chinese started to buy cars and condos and lattes and $5,000 coats? And was this good or bad? Will we all be united in consumerism? And then I realized there wasn't a soul buying anything in this upscale mall. There rarely is. The Chinese are frugal. They do not waste. So I guess that's that, I thought, and then I figured since I'm here I might as well try to find a clean toilet, but a sign informed me that it was Restricted To Four Star Patrons Only. And this I know about myself: I am not a Four Star Patron.

And so I set forth for the Muslim Quarter. There are Muslims in Xi'an. Lots of Muslims. Sixty thousand Muslims. True, it's all relative in China. There are 10 million people in Xi'an, give or take, and 99 percent are Han Chinese, non-Muslim. Unlike the Uyghurs, the Muslims in Xi'an are Hui, another of China's diverse minorities, and they'd settled in the sprawling warren of alleys and streets beneath fluttering, colorful streamers near Xi'an's Great Mosque. I walked in what I presumed was the general direction of the mosque surrounded by men in white hats and women in headscarves and more than a few Arabs and Africans. I could hear the call to prayer emanating from loudspeakers. Every second shop in the Muslim Quarter appeared to be a butcher's shop, and inside these shops dangled the carcasses of cows and goats and sheep. There were hunks of flesh everywhere, much of it spilling onto the ground. Meat is rarely refrigerated in China, and as I walked among all this flesh and bone, I contemplated a permanent conversion to the vegetarian cause, until I came across two women selling delectable-looking meatballs, the ultimate comfort food, and I reflected on the art of cooking, and that's why we cook food—right?—to kill the germs, and so it was perhaps okay to eat meatballs amid this scene of bloody carnage.

I approached these two women in headscarves and indicated that I'd like to give them money for their meatballs, and that I was amenable to being overcharged. In response, they stared at me with contempt. What? I thought. Is it the beard? Was it unwise to wander around China with facial hair? Chinese men are not creative in this way, and since my barber experience in Lanzhou, I'd again let things slide. But this was the Muslim Quarter. Isn't there something in the Koran about beards and that men, ideally, should have one? All of our most famous Muslims today have beards. So that probably wasn't it. Was it an infidel thing? Iraq? That wasn't my idea, you know, and I was tempted to blame George Bush for this denial of cooked and delectable-looking food. But this was hardly the first time such a thing had happened, and as I had long since learned, for many people in China, *laowais* are like an alien species. What does one do when confronted by an alien species? Some are curious, wanting to know what it's like on Planet Laowai. Others see an opportunity to take advantage; the alien does not know the ways of Planet China and is easily snookered. Some regard the *laowai* as a harmless freak and they mock him or want to have their picture taken beside him. And some simply have contempt for the Other.

So I moseyed on and bought a hot bun with a vegetable filling from a Muslim man who was only too happy to feed me, and he took a moment to point me in the direction of the Great Mosque, because as always, I was lost here on Planet China.

Non-Muslims cannot go inside the Prayer Hall itself, which is a shame really, because it is said to be wondrous and can accommodate upward of a thousand worshipers. Like the Catholic church in Dali, the mosque has a distinctly Chinese architecture, with sloping tile roofs and stone archways. Originally built during the Tang Dynasty in the year A.D. 742, the Great Mosque of Xi'an has four courtyards where visitors can admire the arches and halls and the photos of Muhammad Ali visiting the mosque. It's a contemplative place, and as I watched art students sketching and men with hats and dangling prayer beads wandering among them, I was reminded yet again that once I'd been so wrong about China. I'd assumed it was a monolithic place. But it is not a monolithic place. Planet China is as varied and diverse as Planet Earth.

The Terracotta Warriors are in Xi'an. Actually, they're a ways outside Xi'an, surrounded by fields of pomegranates. With reluctance, I had joined a tour group to see these Terracotta Warriors, and as I settled myself among the Western tourists on a tour bus, I felt more than a little *ugh* about the whole endeavor. Had I become a travel snoot? I'd been traveling on my own for some time now, and if I did touristic-type excursions it was in the company of Chinese tourists, and while I couldn't actually understand what anyone was talking about, I still absorbed things. I could not speak the language, but I could still learn. I learned through osmosis. And now I was in the midst of people speaking my language. It was discombobulating, like going to the aquarium instead of donning snorkeling gear and heading out for the reef.

Our first stop would be the Big Wild Goose Pagoda. Built during the Tang Dynasty, it was seven stories tall, and was named the Big Wild Goose Pagoda because one day, right in this very spot, some monks got hungry, whereupon a big wild goose fell out of the sky. This seemed auspicious, demonstrative of a benevolent deity, and so they built a pagoda to commemorate this big wild goose that fell from the heavens. But by now I'd been in China for months and had seen and experienced approximately 742 pagodas. And so I had pagoda fatigue. I climbed it for the exercise and at the top peeked out of the window to see a couple waltzing below. I couldn't see anything else, of course, because this was China and China lives in a cloud of smog.

Back down at the base, some tour group members, who had found the Big Goose Pagoda about as enthralling as I did, were asking our young and friendly guide Polly about Mao and his legacy.

"I think he was mostly good except when he got old," she said. "I don't think he was right in the head. There was the Cultural Revolution from 1966 to 1976," she went on. "My parents suffered. They were sent to the countryside. My mother could not go to school beyond primary school."

And yet, as with so many of the Chinese people I had encountered, Mao was still mostly good in her world. This remained both fascinating and perplexing to me. He was a bad, bad man, Chairman Mao, and yet he was still regarded as mostly a good man among the people who had to endure his colossal badness. It's a complicated country, China, full of complicated people.

We hopped back on the bus and continued with our tour. I'd hoped that we'd go directly to the Terracotta Warriors, the thousands of fearsome stone statues that Emperor Qin Shi Huang had constructed in the third century B.C. so that he'd have an army to rule the underworld. The Chinese refer to the warriors as the Eighth Wonder of the World. Clearly, this was something to see. It was grand. It was important. It was the *Eighth Wonder of the World!* So we should get going. Move on. Enough with the dawdling.

So we went to the souvenir factory.

*See how the ancients made the Terracotta Warriors,* said the sign as we hopped off the bus. It should have read, *See how the moderns make cheap trinkets to sell to tourists.* Here you could buy little warriors, big warriors, warriors on chariots, archer warriors, really, any kind of warrior. It was a warrior mill. But I was not yet so jaded as to resist bargaining for a box of mini warriors for my kids.

"Two hundred yuan," said the saleswoman.

"How about thirty *kuai*," I offered.

We settled at 160, not a strong performance on my part. I'd been schooled by this saleswoman, and I trudged back to the bus. Soon we went onward, not to the Terracotta Warriors but to the Huaqing Hot Springs, where we could see where Emperor Xuenzong cavorted with his favorite concubine during the Tang Dynasty. All right, I thought as I wandered the grounds. I'm bored senseless. So, I thought, perhaps I had indeed become that most insufferable of persons, a travel snoot. Onward to lunch, past the Eight Wonders of the World theme park, where along with the seven original wonders of the world the park had included replicas of the Terracotta Warriors. The Chinese will no longer be ignored. They will be heard. This failure to include the Terracotta Warriors as one of the wonders of the ancient world was clearly an oversight on the part of Herodotus, the ancient Greek historian who compiled the first Top Seven list. It must be rectified.

Meanwhile, we found our restaurant and began to graze through the buffet line.

"This is so good. Isn't Chinese cuisine marvelous?" commented Janet, a kindly woman from Albuquerque.

"Yes," I said. "It's good."

Actually, it was awful. It was the kind of food you'd find at the Lucky Dragon lunchtime buffet in Boise, Idaho. Reflecting on this, I concluded that I had also become a food snoot, the second most insufferable of persons.

At our table, we discussed leather goods. Normally, leather goods do not figure very prominently in my conversations, but Janet was a professional purveyor of leather goods and she'd come to China to do business-type endeavors with her manufacturers.

"About eighty percent of the manufacturing is done in China now," she noted. More than ever, it seemed as if eighty percent of everything was manufactured in China. "So what are you doing here?" she asked.

"I'm just kind of wandering around," I said.

"And where have you wandered?"

I told her, and as I mentioned taking the train from Lhasa to Lanzhou, the other tablemates interjected.

"You took the train from Tibet!"

I had encountered English train buffs.

"What kind of engine was it?" asked an older man with a white mustache. "Diesel? Electric?"

I didn't know. If he wanted information on the condition of the train's squat toilets, I could have offered a few observations. But locomotive engines? No. I was busy reading about nefarious doings in the Vatican. If he wanted to know what it's like to listen to "Billie Jean" at 15,000 feet as the train rumbled past a Tibetan nomad's tent, I could have offered some insight. Or what it's like to lie in the darkness inside a small compartment next to the noisiest man in China. Or the odd sensation of finding yourself in the most remote, inhospitable corner of Earth as you guzzle a can of Budweiser, a beer that you're calling breakfast. These are things I could have helped him with, not train engines. Still, I tried to be helpful.

"Um . . ." I said. "I think it was electric."

"Really. Are you sure? If it was electric, they'd need to construct a mainframe with about fifteen gigawatts of torque. Wouldn't you say, Lester?"

"Provided, of course, they used an A-frame design. Did you happen to look?"

"Er . . . perhaps it was a diesel."

"Yes. Quite likely. Now, I heard they blasted a tunnel through an ice mountain to build that railway. Did you see it?"

I don't know. I was busy rummaging around trying to find the Imodium.

"Well, I slept through the highest parts of the journey," I explained. Sensing the inadequacy of my answer, I hastened to explain. "It was dark. You know, nighttime. But I have a distinct memory of being awoken by a strange noise. We were in a tunnel. And the noise? It was different than a regular old train tunnel. It didn't go clickety-clack. There was something other-worldly about it. Something . . . *icy*."

"Marvelous, marvelous."

Finally, it was time to see the warriors. We'd been told that we might have the opportunity to meet the farmer who'd found them one day in 1974 as he dug for a water well. He'd be in the visitors' center signing books. Of course, it's not always the same farmer who greets visitors, but China aims to please, and if visitors wanted to meet the farmer who'd found the Terracotta Warriors, then they'd meet the farmer who'd found the Terracotta Warriors.

The sight of this farmer's findings is essentially an ancient mausoleum. It is near the tomb of Emperor Qin Shi Huang, who ruled during the Qin Dynasty. The emperor had found ruling the known world such an agreeable experience that he set off to rule the unknown world as well. And thus the Terracotta Warriors. Hundreds of thousands of workers had labored for years to give the emperor a life-size fighting force of thousands of stone statues to help him conquer that world he'd encounter upon death. Clearly, this was a man who thought ahead. Fortunately for us, the warriors remained in this world and we can only hope that Emperor Qin Shi Huang isn't lonely there on the Other Side.

And I could see why he might miss them. The Terracotta Warriors are extraordinary, an entire army of archers and cavalry, generals and foot soldiers, horses and chariots, and each statue is unique. True, Emperor Qin Shi Huang was the Henry Ford of his time, constructing assembly lines where workers fashioned the torso and limbs of each warrior. But every face is individualized, and to gaze upon these statues is to glare into the past. And there were thousands of them. More than 8,000 had been found thus far, but many more are believed to remain unearthed. More than 700,000 workers were needed to construct the warriors and the enormous mausoleum, and it took them nearly forty years to finish.

The warriors are contained in three pits. Pit one was the first to be excavated, and many statues had been reconstructed and repositioned to provide a semblance of what they must have looked like when they'd first been sent forth to the Other Side. The remaining statues that had been unearthed were still broken and severed, victim of a warlord's looting just five years after they'd been interned. Polly informed us that they weren't excavating any further until the technology was there to preserve what they'd found. The statues had been brightly painted when they were first unearthed, but the colorful artistry had disappeared due to sunlight and pollution. Nevertheless, they are an astounding sight. Earlier, I'd read an account of a tourist who had disguised himself as a Terracotta Warrior and who had hidden among these statues, standing rigidly at attention. I could understand the compulsion. Actually, no. Clearly this was someone off his meds.

On the way out, I discovered that the little figurines I'd bought before lunch could now be had for 10 yuan. And suddenly I no longer felt like a travel snoot. I felt like a chump.

# 23

It's cold in Harbin. It should be cold. It would be unsettling if it were not cold. Harbin is north of Vladivostok, home of the Russian Pacific fleet. So it's cold. This was not the tropics. Harbin is in the far north of China. So the coldness should be expected. But *man*, it's cold in Harbin.

I'd felt this coldness, this very intense nostril-freezing coldness, the moment the flight attendant opened the door. We'd been crowding the aisles waiting to disembark the plane since, well, I don't know, probably an hour before we landed. *Please remain seated until we reach the gate.* As if. This is China. We do not remain seated in China. And I further endured this bitter coldness in front of my hotel when I'd had to deal with the usual let's-rip-off-the-dumb-*laowai* routine of the airport taxi drivers. It no longer even fazed me. It was normal, just part of the experience.

"Four hundred and fifty *kuai*, do you say? Well, yes,

that sounds reasonable. But let me ask the doorman what he thinks."

So I got the doorman and I got the guy at the check-in counter and I'd asked passing pedestrians in fur hats what they thought of this 450-*kuai* fare, and soon the cabdriver was surrounded by dozens of people heckling and jeering him because everyone's been ripped off in China, everyone's been cheated, tricked into overpaying, and no one liked it one bit, and now they had one of these cheaters on their hands and they shamed him and told me not to pay one yuan and to report him to the police. But this I did not do. I asked the crowd what is the standard taxi fare from the airport to downtown Harbin and that is what I magnanimously paid the driver, who slinked off into the night like a chastened fox.

I continued to experience this coldness as I waddled up the cobblestones of Zhongyang Dajie wearing seven layers of clothes, everything in my possession. My quest for a warm coat, abandoned in Xi'an, had suddenly become more urgent. Style? Who cares. A good fit? Immaterial. And soon I became the owner of an enormous parka, a coat that would eventually make its way to a member of the Beijing Choral Society, because I have no need for an enormous parka. Except in Harbin. Because it's cold.

But I liked the cold. There's something about freezing together that brings the warmth out of people. Extreme heat tends to make people irritable. But in the cold, particularly when you have a heavy coat and a fur hat, mirth ensues. *Brrr, it's cold,* you say. *I know,* says your friend. *Let's get some hot chocolate.* Happy times.

But in Harbin it wouldn't be hot chocolate. It would be

tea, hot tea, served in the Russian style. This is because it feels like Russia in Harbin, the capital of Heilongjiang, the northernmost province in China. It is surrounded by Russia. To the north, there is Russia. To the east, there is Russia. If you don't like Russia, you can go to the west and find yourself in Mongolia. But still, Harbin seemed like a Russian city. Sure, the city is surrounded by the grim factories common to every city in China nowadays, and the downtown is rife with glitzy new high-rises, and the Songhua River is hideously polluted because of an explosion upstream at a benzene plant, but nevertheless in the Daoliqu District in Harbin, it feels like Russia. There is, for instance, Stalin Park. Yes, it's true. A pretty riverside park full of inline skaters and waltzers is named after Joseph Stalin. Nobody names anything after Joseph Stalin anymore. Except in Harbin, apparently. And to complete this little tableau of yesteryear, there are also bread lines. I'd found a bakery selling bread, which was odd because the Chinese don't eat bread, except apparently in Harbin. Odder still was the long line of customers waiting outside to purchase this bread. Normally, the Chinese are pretty good at matching supply with demand. But here there were bread lines.

And there were onion domes. Russians had moved into Harbin early in the nineteenth century when men such as Rasputin, Lenin, and Tsar Nicholas II began their fateful dance, making life just far too interesting for many Russians, and some found their way to Harbin, deep in Manchuria, where they built Orthodox churches and charming cafés that remain to this day, serving blintzes and borscht and sausages and demitasses of vodka. But I had not come to Harbin to eat blintzes and borscht washed down with a clarifying shot of vodka, though I did do that and it was good. Nor had I come to Harbin to meander among cobblestone lanes while humming the theme from Dr. Zhivago, nor had I come here because I thought I might like this city of 4 million, which I did. I actually liked it very much and hoped one day to return for the Ice Lantern Festival, when ice sculptures are shaped into fantastic, whimsical creations such as the Forbidden City itself.

No, I had come to Harbin to explore China's peculiar relationship with the animal kingdom beyond the endangered-species markets of Guangzhou. Take the Yangtze Sturgeon, for instance. When I was in Chengdu, I'd seen an engrossing program about the Yangtze Sturgeon on CCTV's nature show. Yangtze Sturgeons are, unsurprisingly, not particularly happy at present. It's a migratory fish that lives in the Yangtze but returns to the ocean to do other fish-type business. It goes back and forth, freshwater to saltwater, doing fishy things, following a cycle that has lasted millennia. But now with the Three Gorges Dam the sturgeons could no longer go back and forth from river to ocean. So this is a problem. But the Chinese, naturally, have a solution: They're going to train the Yangtze Sturgeon to remain content in the river, to give up its wandering ways, and to forgo its need to do business in the ocean. To that end, they'd captured a couple of Yangtze Sturgeons and put them in a tank where they would be trained to dispense with millions of years of evolutionary adaptations and learn how to live happily in this all-freshwater-all-the-time environment. Training consisted of, as far as I could tell, placing many divers in the tanks to pet these large Yangtze Sturgeons, to pull at their tails—in fun, surely—and to hold on to their fins so that they could catch a ride. Alas, the announcer informed me, despite all this love the Yangtze Sturgeons refused to feed. Typically, they feed in the ocean. But this wasn't the problem. The problem was that the sturgeons were depressed. And that's why they were listless and wasting away. Fish depression. That's what they were working on now, a treatment for fish depression, and so the show ended on a hopeful note.

I found this an interesting approach to wildlife, and to learn more I headed toward the Siberian Tiger Park a short distance outside Harbin. There are only about 500 Siberian Tigers remaining in the wild, roaming across a vast terrain in Russia and northern China. To boost these numbers, China has a breeding program where tigers born on the grounds of the Siberian Tiger Park would eventually be released into the wild, free to live out their lives as nature intended. I'd bought a ticket at the park's entrance and joined a handful of convivial Chinese tourists inside a minibus and spent the next ten minutes having my picture taken next to them. Soon, we set forth. We made our way through a fenced enclosure, meandered past a frozen pond and acres of high brown grass and scrubby trees, and I took note of mysterious piles of chicken feathers and— good Lord, those tigers are big. I did not know this, but the Siberian Tiger is immense. There were six of them, the largest nearly ten feet long. I had not seen ten-foot cats before. I'd always assumed lions, king of the jungle and all, to be the largest feline. But in comparison to a Siberian Tiger, a lion is a mere house cat. There was one, no two, three now, up on their hind legs, huge paws on our windows, their striped faces and teeth just inches away—

This was a minivan we were in. No cages. No bumpers. No reinforced glass. Nothing.

And I remembered that two people had already been killed by these tigers inside the Siberian Tiger Park, and when I'd read this, I'd wondered how this could happen, what circumstances had prevailed when these two people were killed, and suddenly a white, caged SUV shot past us.

The tigers went nuts. They leapt toward this SUV, which had skidded to a stop, sending dust billowing into the wind. And suddenly, quickly, so quickly, a door was opened, a hand was exposed, and it was clutching chickens, live chickens, and very quickly, desperately, these chickens were tossed into the air and the tigers, these enormous creatures, pounced. They surged upon the SUV. They leapt upon its roof and the chickens—the chickens were no more. Four times this happened. The SUV driver lurched here and there, sending forth plumes of dust, and the hand of a crazy man would emerge with live chickens, and the tigers, nearly as big as the SUV, growled and snarled and pounced and gobbled.

So today was chicken day. But it's a varied diet that the tigers here at the Siberian Tiger Park receive. Sometimes live ox are deposited inside the park. At other times, it's live cows. Sometimes pigs. They take care of the tigers here. Okay, true, they had developed a taste for farm animals, had come to associate human beings and SUVs with feeding time, and were thus forever doomed in the wild. They would gravitate toward people and they would kill people and they would be shot and their paws would end up in the market in Guangzhou. But the important thing here is that we were having fun. My fellow passengers oohed and aahed and snapped pictures. It was party time on the minibus. Never more so than when we retreated through the automatic gate and a tiger cleverly followed us out.

A Siberian Tiger was loose here on the outskirts of Harbin. What would be the solution here, I wondered, to the problem of Siberian Tigers wandering outside the confines of the Siberian Tiger Park?

A demolition derby.

That is what we did. Our minibus charged at this Siberian Tiger. The horn blared. A moment later, the SUV returned, and together we charged at this tiger, backward, forward, we lurched at this tiger. We played chicken with him. The gate was reopened. The other tigers stood by impassively watching. They weren't leaving; they knew where their meals were coming from. And soon we'd succeeded in haranguing this enormous animal back into its enclosure. The passengers on this minibus were thrilled. Such excitement.

But there would be more. We drove by cages of lions, leopards, cheetahs, jaguars, and baby tigers, all gathered around another cage with a bird inside, a stork, a very nervous stork, and then we were taken to a concrete walkway, where we could walk just above an enclosure of tigers. We ambled past a baby tiger, lethargic and sleepy as it dozed upon a tiger skin. For an extra 30 *kuai* we could pet it. On the walkway sat a woman in a uniform with a crate of live chickens before her. One of my fellow tourists approached her with some money. The woman dipped her hand inside this crate of chickens and took one out, tying it by its feet and attaching it to a four-foot stick, before handing it to him. The man took the fishing pole with the dangling chicken, squawking and ill-disposed, and lowered it out over the tigers, taunting them. He dipped it a little lower. A tiger leapt up and shredded a wing. The chicken wailed. Oh, the fun we have in China. He lowered the chicken again. A tiger shredded a leg. The chicken screamed. Everyone laughed. Because this is funny in China. Slowly, painfully, piece by piece, the chicken was shredded into oblivion. Finally, I approached this woman in the uniform and bought a chicken myself. She attached it to the fishing pole and I was ready now to fish for tigers. I took this shrieking chicken, flung it over the side, and reached down and watched a tiger quickly shred it to pieces.

And why, one may reasonably ask, did I do that?

I did it for the chicken.

# 21

The lunatic paced up and own the aisle, screaming. There was a crazy man on board this train to Dandong, walking up and down the aisles of the hard-seat car, yelling at all the devils around him. There were only a handful of people on this train to the last stop in China before North Korea. And there were devils. What would he make of the foreigner, the *laowai*?

I had boarded this train in Shenyang, a grim industrial city south of Harbin in Liaoning Province, a city notable for having one of the finest statues of Mao I'd yet seen, a monument that reflected the very apogee of Socialist Realism. But I had not lingered in Shenyang. Nothing about Shenyang encouraged lingering, and I'd boarded the slow train to Dandong. It had been a full train in Shenyang, and I sat in hard-seat class next to two workers who kindly shared an orange with me. It was moments like that, gestures of unexpected graciousness, that offered the yin to the yang of traveling in China, which is often difficult and exasperating, the yang of Chinese travel that was now manifesting itself as a deranged maniac stomping about the train. I sat and peeled my orange, marveling that there were, in fact, oranges way up here in northern China in December, and tried to ignore the man's ranting. The train rumbled through the brown hills, stopping at every hamlet on the way, discharging passengers until only a handful remained. I had spent so very much of my time in China traveling—finding tickets, queuing among people who did not queue, flying on planes piloted by teenagers, rumbling on crowded buses, my guard ever up as I passed through train and bus stations where one moment of absentmindedness would lead to robbery or worse. It was nearly over, this trip of mine. I would go to Dandong, and then a night train to Beijing, and I would fly home and see my family, my wife, my boys, these boys who were probably men now. It had been a long trip. There is so very much to see in China. There is so very much that must be seen. I had traveled thousands and thousands of miles across this vast country. And I'd still seen little, all things considered. What is here cannot all be seen by one man. Not in a lifetime. And what you saw yesterday is always different today, and it will be different again tomorrow. *Everything is changing so fast.* Yes it is, in China.

Meanwhile, there was a lunatic on board this slow, far too slow, train to Dandong. The landscape here in the vicinity of North Korea reminded me of the opening credits to the show *M\*A\*S\*H*, and this pleased me because, of course, *M\*A\*S\*H* is the very best show ever made. As the lunatic rambled and screamed beside me, I thought of Hawkeye, and what Hawkeye would do in this situation with the dangerous-looking madman. He'd probably tell him to shut up, I thought. So scratch that. Hawkeye could not help me here. I wanted to be invisible to this lunatic, the invisible *laowai*.

It was nighttime when we finally arrived in Dandong, and I bounced happily off the train, pleased to put some distance between myself and the crazy man. I'd splurged and found a room in a hotel overlooking the Yalu River and, across the way, North Korea. I stepped into the hotel, handed over my passport, checked in, dropped off my backpack, and stepped back out again and walked through an underpass beneath the Friendship Bridge, which spanned the distance between China and North Korea. It's a strange, lively bridge with a laser show of green lights and strobe lights, a bridge that dances, that gets down, but only halfway—and then it dies at the halfway mark. And then there is darkness, nothing but a black void. That would be North Korea, lit only by the headlights of trucks streaming across the bridge.

I walked along a riverside park, Yalujiang Park, where groups of middle-aged people were playing hacky-sack with a feathered ball. Even though it was dark, they were able to play because there is so much light coming from the Friendship Bridge. It is a bridge in the style of Las Vegas, and the light that cascades from it illuminates everything—including people of middle years playing hacky-sack in Yalujiang Park. I stared at the enigmatic emptiness across the river. What is over there? I wondered. Where are those trucks on the bridge going? What are they bringing into North Korea? Are there not sanctions against North Korea? The little monster, Kim Jong-il, had been playing with his bombs recently. It should be quiet on this bridge, no?

I stepped into a restaurant for some Korean barbecue. There were Koreans in this restaurant. They were legal, I presumed; Chinese-Koreans, or perhaps South Koreans who had come to look at North Korea from the other side. They were most certainly not North Koreans. North Koreans who manage to cross the border hide. They stay in the darkness. And they stay hidden. Or they try to find a way to South Korea. But they do not eat in restaurants near the neon glare of the Friendship Bridge. This is because China sends them back, these escapees from North Korea, and then bad things happen to them. Bad things happen to their families. And this is because Kim Jong-il is a monster.

I returned to my hotel, this hotel overlooking the Yalu River and the Friendship Bridge and beyond that the darkness of North Korea. A Britney Spears tune was playing in the lobby. Inside the elevator, a dapperly dressed Chinese man turned to address me.

"Good evening," he said in English.

"Good evening."

"And you are from California, yes?"

"Uh . . . yeah."

Nothing about my being suggests California, with the possible exception of a fondness for flip-flops. But this was the North Korean border in December. I was not wearing flip-flops. So this was eerie. The dapperly dressed man got off the elevator before I could inquire how he might know that I lived in California, and I was left alone to ponder this spookiness.

In my room, I sat at the window and watched the trucks rumbling over the Friendship Bridge toward North Korea. One certainly wouldn't know there were sanctions against the regime. Not here, I thought as I viewed the proceedings from my perch above the border crossing. This was the perfect spy room. I could count trucks. I could take pictures. There was all sorts of information that I could discern from my place at the window of this hotel. Yes, I thought, there is not a finer spy room than this one. Then it occurred to me.

It's probably bugged.

It has to be bugged. Things were afoot in North Korea. Spies would stay in this room. And this is China. There are no legal hassles here to prevent the government from bugging hotel rooms. So this room was most certainly bugged.

I resisted the temptation to speak to the lamps.

Should I speak to the lamps? What would happen if I spoke to them? No, I shouldn't speak to the lamps. And then I spoke to them anyway.

I turned to the lamp shade. "Alpha, Charlie, Delta. This is Renegade One. Repeat. Renegade One. The package has left the building. Repeat. The package has left the building."

And I spent the rest of the night waiting for my door to be kicked in.

---

I had come to Dandong because it seemed like an interesting place to ponder choices. Here was a vivid display of roads taken and not taken, of destinies forged by choices and the consequences of those choices. Once China and North Korea had been brothers. I saw vivid examples of this brotherhood in Dandong inside the Museum to Commemorate U.S. Aggression. They are not subtle, the Chinese, when it comes to naming museums. We call it the Korean War, while the Chinese call it The War To Resist America and Assist Korea, which is interesting, to see this war where the United States is portrayed as the bad guy, the imperialist thug, because one gets used to seeing America as the one wearing the white hat. In 1950, there was a civil war on the Korean peninsula. The Americans took one side and the Chinese the other, and when China saw General MacArthur marching up toward the Yalu River and the Chinese border, Mao sent his People's Liberation Army into the fray. And then they did that war thing, and after three years of doing it, they called it a tie and everyone went home. China and North Korea pledged to be Best Friends Forever, and for several decades they were, happily being evil Communists together behind their walls.

But then China started to take down those walls, and today there is light and laser shows and dancing and money and films and energy, so much energy, in China. There is everything in China. Not everyone can have everything in China, not yet, but every day there are more who do. If you ignore the environment—and you can't because the damage is utterly overwhelming—the future looks sunny for China—okay, smoggy—and I suspected that China would find a way to manage all its fissures and problems and perhaps Chinese society would indeed become harmonious—barring a complete societal collapse as the environmental degradation undergoes devastating feedback loops. It's a complex country, not easily summed up. It could still go in so many directions.

But once, not so long ago, China had been like that place across the river. When the sun came up, to my great surprise, I found myself facing the city of Sinuiju, a Potemkin village complete with a Ferris wheel. Of course, the Ferris wheel wasn't turning; there is no electricity in Sinuiju. That is why I couldn't see this city at night. There are only the rusting carcasses of old boats on the shores. And there were people.

There are, in fact, two bridges across the Yalu River. Or rather, one and a half. The Americans shot one up during the war, and today it extends only as far as midriver, since the North Koreans have dismantled the remainder. I wanted to get a little closer to North Korea, and so after breakfast I walked along this blasted bridge past a few lonely vendors selling North Korean trinkets, which I strongly suspected were made in China.

It's a dreary-looking city, Sinuiji, and if this is the best the North Koreans could do in terms of its face to the outside world, it must be bleak indeed. I came back to the Chinese side and walked along the river path, where soon a man offered to take me in his little speedboat for a closer look at North Korea. Cool, I thought. I didn't hesitate a minute and soon I was speeding across the murky waters of the Yalu River. We careened around the remains of the old bridge and suddenly we were in North Korean waters. Well, okay, I thought. I'm in North Korea. I am technically in North Korea. Holy shit. And we sped closer to the North Korean shore. Behind us a rusty and decrepit trawler bearing the North Korean flag chugged along. Okay, Jesus, we're deep in North Korean waters now. Ha! And we went farther. We went to the very shoreline. He slowed the boat and we cruised six feet from the actual land. I could hear a megaphone, a rally. I'm in North Korea. I am in fucking North Korea! There were people behind these wrecked ships. Soldiers. I was giddy. I waved. They did not wave back.

They looked upon me with stony faces. I waved some more, but they did not wave. I was the imperialist dog. *Yoo-hoo. Hello. Give up your bombs and we'll send your leader a hairstylist. Some new platform shoes too.* But they did not laugh, these North Koreans. The soldiers eyed me. I'm in North Korea. I'm in fucking North Korea. Ha!

And the engine died.

What is this? Are you shitting me? Here, six feet from the North Korean shore, the fucking engine dies. You have got to be fucking kidding me. Whatever happens, I thought, do not get out of the boat. That is what I told myself. Jesus. All I had was a California driver's license. That'll go over real well with the North Korean authorities. The soldiers were alert. They were watching me. They were watching us drift, drifting closer to shore, ever closer. Jesus. Could you get that fucking engine started? It coughed. It hacked. The engine did not start. Fuck. Come on, start. Goddamn it, start. But the engine would not start, and we drifted closer and I looked across the river to China, to soaring China, to those brand-new buildings and glittering lights, and I yearned for China. I wanted to embrace China. I love you, China. Please, China, take me back.

# Acknowledgments

The author would like to acknowledge that he is a bad man. As evidence, he offers this e-mail from his editor's husband: *This is Ann's husband. She is in labor at the hospital now. I have printed out the Chengdu chapter for her at her request.*

The author doesn't know what to say. He is mortified by this. He had, of course, known that his editor, Ann Campbell, was with child. It was not a surprise. Indeed, his book deadline had been some months before her due date. The author, however, is very bad with deadlines—we needn't go into this; deadlines are not interesting—but here, at least, was a very firm date. He could not tweak and tinker and revise beyond the due date. The book *had* to be done. The author is a parent himself. He knows newborns and they are unforgiving. He has stood in the delivery room himself. He knows, if only as an observer, what childbirth is like. And yet, because he is a very bad man, his editor, in between contractions, with pencil in hand, was compelled to focus on a gay bar in Chengdu.

The author wishes to acknowledge this. His editor had been—as if she didn't have enough to deal with—forced to grapple with a book that wanted to become a 500-page monster, and she'd tamed it into something manageable *during labor.* He cannot thank her enough. He also cannot apologize enough, so he has decided to flog himself here, out here, on the stage.

He would also like to acknowledge all the other people at Broadway Books whose lives he's made challenging—Clare Swanson, Laura Lee Mattingly, Anne Watters, and Rachel Rokicki. He'd long believed that for a July publication, May, possibly even June, might be a good time to submit a manuscript. He has since been disabused of the notion. He would also like to thank his agent, B. J. Robbins, whose good humor and optimism coaxed him through.

Regarding China, the author received invaluable assistance from Dan Friedman, Greg Adler, and Huaping-Lu Adler. *Xie xie* very much. Also, to the farmer who offered him an orange on the train from Shenyang to Dandong, he would like to say thank you. Just as he was succumbing to China fatigue, Jack St. Martin came out to travel with the author for a couple of weeks. And they got drunk. Several times. The author is grateful.

Finally, the author would like to acknowledge his family. His boys, Lukas and Samuel, no longer remember the long absence as he wandered around China. But the author does. He will not miss out again. And to his wife, Sylvia, thank you. And yes, once again, he owes her big-time.

# Further Reading

Among the books I consulted, several proved particularly useful. Surely *Mao: The Unknown Story* by Jung Chang and Jon Halliday is now the definitive word on the Great Helmsman. Jonathan Spence's *The Search for Modern China* offers a sweeping and elegantly written overview of modern China. Iris Chang's *The Rape of Nanking* ensures that one of the great crimes of World War II is not forgotten. And finally, if there is a funnier and more harrowing account of what it's like to do business in China than Tim Clissold's *Mr. China,* I have yet to find it.

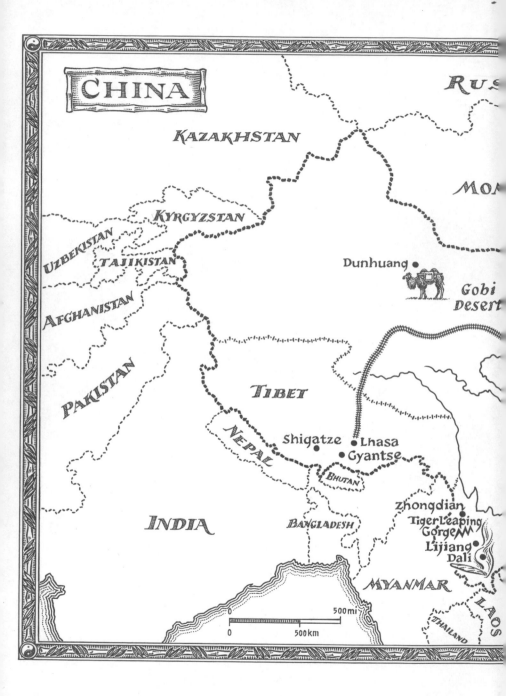